Ethics for Managers

This book examines issues relating to ethical decision-making. It is intended to help managers reflect on the impacts of their decisions and to help them in making such decisions ethically. In the first part of the book, the author explores the meaning of ethics and, in the second part, its application to the task of management. While there are chapters on ethics in general and on three different approaches to ethics, these are intended for managers who do not have a background in philosophy.

Joseph Gilbert is an Associate Professor of Management at the University of Nevada, Las Vegas. He co-teaches a required MBA course in Law, Regulation and Ethics. He earned a doctorate in Business Administration from the University of Southern California with a concentration in Business Strategy.

Ethics for Managers

Philosophical Foundations and Business Realities

JOSEPH GILBERT

Routledge
Taylor & Francis Group
NEW YORK AND LONDON

First published 2012
by Routledge
711 Third Avenue, New York, NY 10017

Simultaneously published in the UK
by Routledge
2 Park Square, Milton Park, Abingdon, Oxon OX14 4RN

Routledge is an imprint of the Taylor & Francis Group, an informa business

Library of Congress Cataloging in Publication Data
Gilbert, Joseph, 1941–
Ethics for managers: philosophical foundations and business realities/Joseph
Gilbert.
   p. cm.
   Includes bibliographical references and index.
   1. Business ethics. 2. Management–Moral and ethical aspects. 3. Business
   enterprises–Moral and ethical aspects. I. Title.
   HF5387.G552 2012
   174'.4–dc23   2012003055

ISBN: 978-0-415-80708-1 (hbk)
ISBN: 978-0-415-80709-8 (pbk)
ISBN: 978-0-203-15365-9 (ebk)

Typeset in Garamond
by Wearset Ltd, Boldon, Tyne and Wear

SFI Certified Sourcing
www.sfiprogram.org
SFI-00453

Printed and bound in the United States of America
by Edwards Brothers, Inc.

To John, who manages managers, and to Jeff, who manages
  programmers.
To Pamela, who manages second-graders, and to Samuel, who
  manages grandparents.
And most of all, to Emily, who manages me, and does it very well.

Contents

one
Introduction

Managers are people who are paid to oversee the work of others.[1] In this role, they often make decisions that impact other people. This book is intended to help managers reflect on the impacts of their decisions and to help them in making such decisions ethically. In this book, I broadly define a manager as anyone who is responsible for work done by others, whether that person is a supervisor of bank tellers or an executive vice president who is responsible for overseeing several vice presidents.

The word "ethics" is often used loosely, and it is not hard to find discussions of medical ethics (cloning), business ethics (predatory lending), legal ethics (tort reform), professional ethics (accounting) and various other kinds of ethics. Actually, ethics has been recognized as a branch of philosophy for many centuries. The earliest writings on ethics that we still have available to us in the Western tradition of philosophy come from Plato and Aristotle, and are nearly 2,500 years old. Ethical issues have concerned thinkers and writers ever since, and we will briefly examine some of the answers they have provided and have argued about in their efforts to understand the good life for humans. In Part I of this book, we will explore the meaning of ethics and, in Part II, its application to the task of management.

There have been managers for thousands of years, but not nearly as many as there are now. In the Western world, the only large organizations until the eighteenth century were churches and armies.[2] For most of human history, people have worked at home, for themselves or their families, and essentially without bosses or managers. This is still true of a significant number of all humans alive today. Our concern in this book, however, is with those who work in organizations with structured authority. If you visit your local bookstore and go to the section covering business, you will find shelves full of books on leadership. You will find books telling you how to be a good manager in one minute or how to learn what MBAs know in a matter of hours. You will find books on investing, and on selling, and on starting new businesses. One area of management on which you will find almost nothing is on how to be an ethical manager.

Goals of This Book

Ethics, as we will see, has to do with interpersonal or social values and the rules of conduct that derive from them. By the time an individual becomes a manager, he or she has a sense of moral right and wrong. (In this book, the terms "ethical" and "moral" are used interchangeably.)[3] We will examine the sources of this sense, and how it is shaped and changed by various influences. Nonetheless, the point of this book is not to instill a previously missing sense of ethics or to critique an individual's existing sense of ethics with an eye to making it right where it is now wrong. Only two tasks will be attempted in this book. The first is to make clear the ethical implications of actions taken by managers. The second is to provide some time-tested ways of thinking about ethical issues when they arise, and especially when it is not clear to the individual manager what the "ethically right" answer is.[4]

This book is intended for managers and managers-to-be who want to do what is morally right and who are open to thinking about such issues. It might also prove useful to others who have input into, or are affected by, the decisions of managers.[5] If I were to say to a CEO, "Look, you have two choices. You can report your annual results honestly and show that your company had a loss, or you can cook the books, tell big fat felonious lies, and show a profit—which will it be?" and the CEO were to reply, "Can I have a minute to think about it?", this book is not for that CEO. Such a CEO will almost certainly not be deterred by ethical considerations.

However, if a manager came to me and said, "I have to lay off ten people who work for my division, and I feel terrible about it. It makes me feel guilty. Am I doing the right thing?", then this book can help.[6] This manager recognizes that the act of laying off employees has ethical implications, but is having a hard time sorting out the morality of the action. In the chapters that follow, we will consider three basic approaches to ethics. These are utilitarianism, rights and duties, and fairness and justice. They are based on the writings of philosophers who have thought long and hard about the moral implications of our interactions with others. Hopefully, these three approaches to ethics can help the manager to think more clearly about the issues involved in layoffs, and in particular about the issues involved in the actions that he is about to take.

This book is not for readers who want an introduction to business ethics in general. There are many such books available.[7] In these books, there is often a minimal discussion of philosophy and of ethics, as such, and extensive discussion of topics relevant to managerial ethics, as well as more general topics in business ethics. Among the topics often included in business ethics textbooks are the morality of Western capitalism as a system, the role of the corporation in society and corporate governance. While these topics are important and interesting to many managers, the scope of this book is narrower. Its purpose is to assist managers to make thoughtful, ethical decisions in their work lives.

The Tasks of Managers

Managers are people who have a certain role to play at work. They also play other roles in life. They are parents, spouses, friends, volunteers, dreamers, doers, and much more. Most people, in whatever position or role they find themselves, want to do what is right and to succeed. They want to feel good about themselves, to take pride in their accomplishments, to work or play well with others. They want people to think well of them, especially people they know well and whose opinions they value. Managers bring with them to their work experience, values, attitudes and desires.

Many employees think of managers or bosses with suspicion and distrust. "They" are out to get "us." Griping about bosses is a time-honored tradition. People join labor unions and pay dues to them not because they are pleased with and confident in their managers, but because they view managers with fear and distrust. When a company does well, there is a tendency to praise management. During the 1990s, there was a cult of the CEO-hero. Jack Welch at General Electric and Louis Gerstner at IBM were widely described as almost mythical superheroes. Unfortunately, Dennis Kozlowski at Tyco, Kenneth Lay at Enron and Bernie Ebbers at WorldCom were similarly described. Early in the next decade, when things went bad at some of these companies, management was blamed and vilified in ways normally reserved for mass murderers. More recently, executives of large financial institutions have been described in very unflattering terms in books, articles, and Congressional hearings and reports.[8]

MBA programs train people to be masters in the administration of business. This often, but not always, means that these programs train people to be managers. I have taught MBA students for the last twenty years, and I like to think that I have been doing a good and honorable thing, not creating monsters. Enrollment in MBA programs and Executive MBA programs has grown substantially during the last two decades. In addition to rapid growth in U.S. enrollment, there have been numerous programs initiated in

Western European countries, and some increase in programs in other parts of the world. Clearly, many individuals are willing to spend substantial resources, in time and in money, to become managers or to improve their skills as managers. Other business people carry out the duties of managers without the benefit of formal training for their jobs. There are also many people who play the role of manager in the public sector. Governors and mayors, police chiefs and fire chiefs, school principals and hospital administrators all are paid to oversee the work of others. Like their counterparts in the private sector, these people also play multiple roles in life, and want to do well and be thought well of.

In the following chapters, the discussion of managerial ethics pertains to all those individuals whose primary job is overseeing the work of others, whether in the private or the public sector. This includes supervisors who directly oversee workers, mid-level managers who oversee lower-level managers, and top executives who (among other tasks) oversee the work of lower-ranking executives or managers. There are managers of accounting, and of marketing, and of production, and of customer service. There are managers in manufacturing firms, and in service firms, and in public agencies. What they all have in common is the task of overseeing and directing the work of others.

Among the tasks that all managers have in common are selection of employees, training of newly assigned employees, motivating employees, assessing, reporting and rewarding the performance of employees, assignment and distribution of tasks among subordinates, budgeting and monitoring expenditures, and reporting and coordinating results with other managers at various levels. In carrying out these tasks, managers make decisions that have direct and indirect impacts on employees, other managers, customers and investors. In some circumstances, managers are limited in making decisions. For instance, managers whose employees belong to a union and are covered by a negotiated labor-management agreement are limited in the way they can reward employees by the terms of the contract.

This book examines issues relating to ethical decision-making for managers. Decisions also have other components, which we will consider peripherally if at all. A manager's decision can be technically correct, meaning that it involves the optimal application of technology to the matter at hand. It can be economically correct, meaning that it achieves desired financial results. It can be socially correct, meaning that it meets the approval of society at large or of some interest group or groups within society. It can be legally correct, meaning that it conforms to current applicable laws and regulations. We will examine in the following chapters what it means for a decision to be ethically correct. This is the main focus of the book.

Outline of Book: Part I—Ethical Theory

In the first part of this book, philosophy and ethics are explored. Many books on business ethics devote only a brief introductory chapter to philosophy, then proceed to analysis of particular issues and cases. The whole first part of this book, consisting of five chapters, covers philosophy in general and ethics in particular. Since this book does not assume any background in philosophy, it is important to provide enough depth to help the reader understand what philosophy is, and how ethics fits as one branch within the larger discipline of philosophy. Three different approaches to ethics will be explained, since the history of philosophy contains a number of different theories of ethics that cannot simply be reduced to one common theory. The second part of the book then takes up the application of ethical theory to specific topic areas of interest and relevance to managers.

The second chapter of the book discusses the nature of philosophy, which is a discipline or field of study like physics or sociology or history. It has its assumptions, its rules, its common topics and areas of disagreement. The discussion in the first part of this book does not assume that the reader has had any previous course work in philosophy. Many college students take a philosophy course as undergraduates. This is frequently either a survey course that skims lightly across the surface of deep waters, or a course in logic, which some would argue is only marginally within the realm of philosophy (while others, particularly some twentieth-century philosophers, would argue that it is the totality of philosophy). The approach taken here is to recognize that, while all thinking adults sometimes philosophize, they are often unaware that they are doing so, and will find it useful to consider the major rules and topics of philosophy. The next step is to situate ethics within the broader realm of philosophy, of which it is a part. This chapter includes a discussion of the relations between philosophy and religion.

The third chapter takes up the specific discussion of ethics. As part of this discussion, the relation between ethics and law will be addressed in some detail. Many business people tend instinctively to equate law with ethics (our actions were fully justified; we did not break any laws). As we will see, there are close ties between law and ethics, but there are sound reasons for maintaining that they are not and cannot be identical.

The remainder of the first part will be taken up with somewhat detailed discussions of three basic approaches to ethics. Different authors cite different schools of ethics, but certainly three of the most common are utilitarianism, rights and duties, and fairness and justice. A chapter is dedicated to each of these approaches, with brief discussions of the major philosophical figures most identified with each of the three approaches. While there are some common elements among them, each has a different emphasis and asks different questions in trying to determine whether an act is ethical. When all three approaches reach the same conclusion, the degree of ethical certainty about that conclusion is high. When the three approaches do not lead to the same conclusion, there is obviously less certainty. The detailed discussion of each approach will suggest which might trump the others in a case of disagreement. However, philosophy is not like physics in the sense that there is not always (or even often) one right answer. Life is much more complicated than textbooks, and thinking people who are trying hard to do the right thing can honestly differ as to what that right thing is. As stated above, the purpose of this book is to identify the moral implications of actions and to provide some tools for thinking through difficult moral questions. It is not to provide the one right answer.

This last statement often troubles managers.[9] They are in the business of making decisions, of finding answers. They try to find the right answer, or at least the best available one. Further, managers sometimes expect that ethics or morality, whether it is based in religion or in philosophy, should tell them what to do and what not to do. As we will see at several points in the course of this book, it is easy enough to get agreement on general principles (e.g., treat others with respect) but much harder to get agreements on specific applications (e.g., listen calmly and courteously to this employee who is telling you that you do not know what you are doing).

Outline of Book: Part II—Applied Business Ethics

The second part of the book takes up specific areas of application in business where moral questions often arise and shows how analysis using each of the three approaches to ethics helps to sort out relevant issues and arrive at conclusions about the morality of actions. The areas of application discussed in these chapters have been chosen because they present issues and questions that managers must deal with in the course of their jobs. These issues include employment, performance appraisal and compensation, privacy, terminations and financial reporting. The list of topics is certainly not all-inclusive; rather it is illustrative of the kinds of moral questions that managers face and how the three approaches to ethics can be helpful in thinking through specific situations.

Chapter 7 deals with employment situations which involve a number of issues that most managers deal with on a somewhat regular basis. To the extent that a manager, at whatever level, influences or makes the decision about who gets a job and who does not, that manager is exercising control over a valuable resource that each applicant wants to obtain (the job). The outcome of the decision has real consequences both for the applicant who gets the job and for those who do not. The outcome of the decision also has consequences for the manager and for the new employee's fellow workers.

Laws and regulations, company policies or civil service rules, and the manager's personal preferences all play a part in shaping the employment decision. In this chapter, we also examine the relations between law and ethics with regard to issues of affirmative action. Another issue that arises under employment situations involves promotions. While this involves similar considerations to those in the employment decision, there are some additional considerations when a promotion of a current employee is involved.

The evaluation and compensation of current employees is one of the duties of managers. In Chapter 8, we will consider the rights and duties of managers when they evaluate the work of their subordinates. We will also discuss the importance and moral basis for truth-telling in performance appraisals, even (and sometimes especially) when this makes for difficult and contentious interviews with the employee being evaluated. Managers usually work within a compensation system in determining raises and bonuses for their employees. We discuss both the moral implications involved in designing such systems and the ethical aspects of individual managers' decisions in recommending compensation increases for their individual employees.

Termination decisions also involve moral implications. In Chapter 9, we consider the legal notion of employment at will, the issue of layoffs or downsizing, and the issue of employment contracts, including those negotiated by unions in labor-management bargaining. A job is much more than an assigned task in an organization or a source of income. It is also for many people a part of their self-identity, a source of social connections, a source of important financial benefits such as health insurance and retirement income, and more. Managerial actions that terminate an individual's employment have major repercussions for that individual. Further, the tasks performed by the terminated individual can seldom be completely eliminated, so the termination of an individual has immediate consequences for co-workers, customers and perhaps others. There are costs for a company involved in recruitment, selection and training of replacement employees. At least in the United States and many European countries, there are increasing risks of litigation or inquiry and action by regulatory agencies when an employee is terminated. Thus the decision to terminate can have far-reaching repercussions, whether these are considered at the time the decision is made or not.

Privacy and computer technology are closely intertwined. Issues discussed in Chapter 10 include an individual's right to privacy in a corporate setting, and possible uses and abuses of advanced technology by management to oversee workers. Included in this discussion are drug testing, electronic monitoring and management's knowledge of and decisions about workers' off-the-job activities.

Financial reporting is an area of management responsibility that has received a great deal of publicity in the recent past due to various scandals that have been widely reported. Not every manager is involved in financial reporting, but many managers do have budgeting, expense reporting and other aspects of financial reporting as part of their responsibilities. In Chapter 11, we will examine the moral issues involved in setting up and maintaining accounting systems.

Finally, Chapter 12 discusses some general themes that emerge from the individual chapters in the second part of the book. In this chapter, we will consider what it means to say that a company is ethical or unethical. We will consider company codes of ethics and their impact on managers and employees. We will review the notion of ethical climate or culture and how the prevailing moral views in a company enhance or constrain the efforts of individual managers within the company to be ethical in their decisions and their actions.

These chapters do not by any means cover all of the issues that managers face in their working lives. They cover topics selected both because they are relatively common issues for managers to deal with and because they give, in total, a fairly wide perspective of examples of ethical issues. These chapters provide specific examples of decisions where the ethical implications might not be readily apparent, and yet they are significant. They also give examples of how analysis using each of the three major approaches to ethics can help managers to decide on an ethical course of action. In some obvious situations, it is immediately clear what course of action the ethical manager will take. In other more complex situations, it may not be clear even after a thoughtful analysis what the most ethical course of action is. However, for the manager who has considered the philosophical bases for ethical reasoning and made an honest effort to do such reasoning, the likelihood of choosing the ethical action is considerably increased.

This book can be usefully read, in its entirety, by managers who want to think seriously about ethics in business and the morality of their own decisions and actions. Even if a manager is interested in solving a particular problem, it will be best to read Part I of the book before reading the chapters on application. These first chapters lay the foundation for thinking through the ethical implications of a particular issue or situation. The manager might then turn to the chapter in Part II of the book that covers the topic of particular interest.

Notes have been included for each chapter to serve two rather different purposes. The first is the standard one of identifying the source of quotations or ideas taken from the works of others. The second is to provide the reader with suggestions for further reading in an area that might be of particular interest, or to provide more general sources for ideas when they do not come from one identifiable source. These notes are included separately in order to avoid burdening the text with too many digressions and with material that some readers might not find of interest to them. In general, this book is written in a conversational style. Hopefully this makes it easier for the busy manager to grasp the ideas without having to spend a lot of time deciphering technically complex or academically dry language. Particularly in the first part of the book, there are times when the discussion necessarily becomes somewhat dry and abstract. Plato's dialogues, perhaps the most readable serious work by a major philosopher, have the same problem, and I can scarcely hope to put things more clearly than Plato! In summary, this book is for the reader who wants to learn something both theoretical and practical. If it serves that need, it will have succeeded.

Part I
Ethical Theory

two
What is Philosophy?

Philosophy as a Field of Knowledge

What makes a human different from other living things? Are we really free to choose different actions? What is the good life for humans? These are philosophical questions. One can try to answer them using facts known from biology, or psychology, or literature, but the attempts to answer them usually involve philosophy. Isaiah Berlin has described philosophy as dealing with those questions for which there is no clear agreement on where to look for answers. We know how to determine whether a certain drug cures a certain medical condition, or how far it is from Los Angeles to New York, or who won the World Series in 2005. We do not have clear agreement on how to decide whether universities should prepare good workers or informed citizens, or when a cause is worth dying for, or how much freedom individuals should have while living in society.

Philosophy is sometimes described as a discipline or a science or a field of knowledge. The Greek origins of the term involve two words meaning friend of or love of wisdom. In the Western intellectual tradition, we have fragments of philosophical writing that date back more than 2,500 years. The first complete writings (as opposed to fragments) that we have are from Plato and Aristotle, Greek philosophers who lived in Athens in the fourth century B.C.[1]

At least in a limited way, at one time or another, we all do a little philosophy. The manager who makes numerous decisions each day at his desk may stand out under the stars at night and think philosophical thoughts about how small he is under the night sky. He may sit at his desk and ponder whether his son who is a marine and who has just shipped out for a combat zone will make it back, and if not, why not, and what all this means relative to decisions about capital spending and budget over-runs. He may ponder what to do about a long-time colleague, a steady solid performer, whose alcohol addiction or child custody battle has reduced work effective-ness below the minimum acceptable level. He may wonder fleetingly whether there is any connection between his long work weeks and frequent travel and his teenage daughter's experiments with drugs. He may be decid-ing how to deal with a troublesome whistle-blower, or a possible product defect. Now and then, we all do a little philosophy.

As long as we are going to do a little philosophy, it might be good to learn a little about philosophy. Some very insightful individuals have pon-dered these same questions, and others like them, and have produced answers that have been studied by others for hundreds or even thousands of years. Writings that survive that long, and are read and discussed by many genera-tions of people with questions, might just be worth a look. The purpose of this book is not to produce philosophers or to provide definitive answers to life's toughest questions. It is to help managers to think about issues and reach ethical decisions in their work lives. By the end of the book, I hope it will be clear why philosophy, and especially that branch of philosophy known as ethics, is not really foreign to the objectives either of an MBA program or of a manager.

As with any field of knowledge, philosophy has limits to the topics or issues it considers. One key point that sets philosophy apart from the phys-ical or social sciences is that philosophy deals with very general questions that underlie the foundations of the other sciences. For example, the branch of philosophy called metaphysics deals with basic questions of existence—what does it mean to say that something exists or does not exist? The branch known as epistemology deals with basic questions of what we know and how we know it. If you and I are talking face to face, there is not much question in the mind of either of us that the other exists and is speaking words that communicate meaning. Do sub-atomic particles, or the human soul, or justice exist, and if so, how do we know, and what can we know about them?

Issues of existence and knowledge are critical for each of the physical and social sciences as well as for applied disciplines such as business. To some extent, they are addressed by each science, but the issues raised and the tools used are really those of philosophy. The same is true for our uses of language. It is one thing to say that my love is like a red, red rose, but quite another to say that she is prickly and requires periodic applications of insecticide and fertilizer. Philosophy allows for and can explain the use of both poetry and scientific language. Without such distinctions, explanations of lightning as an expression of anger by the gods or as an electrical discharge would have to compete on equal terms. Since the recent financial crisis and recession, there has been a good deal of discussion of "the market." It is important to be clear on just who or what constitutes the market, and philosophical concepts can be critically important in addressing this issue.

The physical sciences, such as biology, physics and chemistry, rely on experiments as a way to establish and verify the truth of claims. To varying degrees, the social sciences, such as sociology, political science and organization theory, also rely on experiments. Philosophy, while it uses the findings of both the physical and the social sciences as input, does not rely on experiments to establish the truth of claims. However, most philosophers accept the facts established through scientific experiments as grist for their theoretical mills.

Philosophy and Religion

Philosophy, like any discipline or field of study, has its rules and procedures. Some of these are accepted by almost all philosophers; others are the subject of considerable debate. Some philosophers have been deeply religious individuals (e.g., St. Thomas Aquinas) and others have been non-believers (e.g., Bertrand Russell). Philosophy deals with many questions that are also the subject of religion, but the two are not the same. One of the most commonly accepted rules or assumptions of philosophy is that religion or divine inspiration cannot be used to answer philosophical questions. This troubles many individuals, because their religion is central to their understanding of life and its most important issues. Because philosophy deals with a number of fundamental issues that are also the objects of religious consideration, it is important to be clear about the relationship of philosophy and religion.[2]

If one asks what is the right way for a human to live, or what are the principal goals of human life, or whether individual humans have a continued existence after their physical death, religion provides answers to these questions. Different religions provide different answers, but each religion accepts the fact that God says so, or God's inspired book (the Bible, Quran, Torah) says so, or God's designated spokesman says so, and this constitutes a valid reason for accepting an answer to these very basic and very important questions. Philosophy does not say that such answers are right or wrong; it simply says that when doing philosophy, they are inadmissible. Other sources must be found to justify or validate answers given by philosophy.

A religious person might well ask why, if religion provides clear and authoritative answers to life's most important questions, philosophy is needed at all. One practical answer is this. In the contemporary world, at least in Western countries, one deals with people who believe in a variety of different religions, and some who deny all religion. If people of varying religious beliefs and no religious belief are to hold serious conversations about how to live and act, some commonly accepted basis for discussion will have to be found.[3] Philosophy can provide such a common basis for discussion. A second important answer in terms of business practice is that most religions do not have a developed body of doctrine, in their sacred writings or in the works of their religious leaders and theologians, about business practices. The sacred books of most religions were written hundreds or thousands of years before the development of the large corporation or of modern business practices.[4] Thus these sacred books have very little to say directly about the morality of business practices. Even believers in the same religion might find themselves with very different answers to practical business issues based on the teachings of their religion.

Philosophy, then, provides a way for thoughtful people to discuss important issues of values and behavior with one another without reference to religion. It thus provides at least the possibility of common understanding and agreement on issues of business morality in a pluralistic society where individual religious beliefs (or lack of such beliefs) might otherwise preclude any hope of a common basis for discussion, much less of agreed-upon conclusions. Philosophy also provides a way to link specific issues of business practice with larger issues, such as what makes a good life, the role of business in society and ways to deal with conflicts of value in specific situations.

Clear Thinking and Proper Naming

One branch of philosophy, logic, deals specifically with rules for reasoning. In an important sense, logic underlies all of the other sciences. An example of the fundamental importance of logic in reasoning involves what Aristotle called the principle of non-contradiction. This principle states that a thing cannot be and not-be in the same way at the same time. We rarely think about such fundamental principles, but they underlie all of our reasoning. A thing cannot be both alive and dead at once. Either it is raining at a given location, or it is not. A chemical element has a certain atomic weight, but at the same time it cannot have a different atomic weight. In a criminal trial, an individual is found either guilty or not guilty of a given charge, but not both. In its pure, logical form, this principle seems innocuous enough. However, as we shall see later in the book, when a CEO or CFO is required to certify that a given financial statement gives a true picture of the firm's financial condition, the issue of true and not-true becomes a good bit more cloudy.

One basic premise on which philosophers generally agree is the importance of clear thinking. In order to think clearly and accurately about something, it is important to take care in naming things. If we are going to argue that something causes something else (a reduction in the capital gains tax will cause the economy to improve), we need to be clear about what is the cause, what is the effect, and whether we are in fact observing causation or correlation.

Clear thinking and proper naming of things are characteristic of philosophy. They are not unique to philosophy by any means, but they do distinguish philosophical analysis from more common kinds of talk and from a good deal of popular writing and journalism. As one reads the works of the great philosophers, it is striking to note that, even though they may take very different positions on the same issue, the care to name things correctly and to be clear and precise in thought processes is a common concern. The physical sciences share this concern for careful naming and step-by-step reasoning. The social sciences tend to be less precise in these areas. Terms like amoeba and velocity have very precise meanings in biology and physics; culture and emotion have less precise meanings in sociology and psychology.

Clear thinking and precise naming are also important in business disciplines. One of the most basic rules in accounting is that revenues should be matched with expenses. One of the most difficult problems in accounting is the same: what constitutes revenue or expense, and when should each be recognized in a given situation? Much of micro-economic theory revolves around the decisions of rational makers of goods and of the rational utility maximizers who purchase those goods. One of the more difficult problems in micro-economics concerns the degree to which either makers or buyers act rationally.[5] Marketing likewise has issues of clarity. If I sell you a car for $20,000 and immediately send you a rebate of $2,000, is this any different from selling you a car for $18,000 and not sending you a rebate?[6]

One particular topic on which philosophical analysis tends to be especially careful is that of causation. Anyone who has taken an introductory course in statistics knows that causation is not the same as correlation. There may be a snowstorm in New York City on the same day that a major company in Texas declares bankruptcy, but it does not take a detailed study to determine that the snowstorm did not cause the bankruptcy, nor did the bankruptcy cause the snowstorm. Much of science is dedicated to identifying and confirming causes. Philosophy also deals extensively with causation and uses the findings of science in explaining it. Thus philosophy as a discipline is not, as it is sometimes portrayed, highly abstract and far removed from the concerns of the real world.

Again, there are numerous parallels in the world of business. Do price reductions cause retail sales to increase in the week before Christmas or are last-minute shoppers driven by some other force? If I urge employees to put in a full day's work each day, and tomorrow they hear about impending layoffs, do they work harder because of my eloquence or their fear of losing their job? The famous Hawthorne studies of the 1930s concluded that productivity of a group of factory workers improved when lighting was increased and also when it was decreased. Ultimately, those doing the studies concluded that productivity improved because someone was paying attention to the workers![7]

Induction and Deduction: The Methods of Philosophy

If philosophy does not accept religion as a source of answers and does not rely on experiments, how does it reach any conclusions? There are two basic approaches that we take when we try to find answers, whether as philosophers, as scientists or as ordinary thinking humans. One is called induction, the other deduction. In its broadest sense, induction means that we reason from specific examples to a general rule. If I drop an object from a given height and measure the time it takes to fall a certain distance, I know one particular fact. If I drop other objects from different heights, carefully measure the time it takes each to fall a certain distance, and compare the results, I might conclude that there is a pattern or a rule about the rate at which some objects fall. As I further test the rule and find that additional examples also conform to the rule, I become more confident that the pattern or rule I have reached from my specific examples is valid or true. Note that I do not yet know why various objects fall at the rate they do. I can predict or affirm regularity without understanding causality.

The second basic approach to finding answers is called deduction. This approach starts with a general rule, applies that rule to a specific situation and argues that the results in the specific situation will be such-and-such because this is an example of the general rule, and that rule will apply to this particular occurrence. While we do not always realize that we are using deduction, this is a common method for making business decisions. If a CEO decides to aim for 15 percent growth in profits next year, he may be relying on an unspoken general rule that, in our industry, companies that attain 15 percent profit growth are favored and their stock goes up. He may also be relying on the fact that his company attained 12 percent profit growth last year, and the expectation of his directors and shareholders is that profit growth will increase by more than 12 percent next year. Note that the general rule is not questioned in deduction; the question at issue is whether this particular case is in fact an example of the general rule.

Philosophy by itself is a fairly abstract endeavor. It is concerned with general rules (either finding them or applying them). It is even more general than the physical and social sciences because it deals with questions and methods of reasoning that underlie all of these sciences. Yet, philosophy involves a good deal of practical knowledge of the real world in which scientists and managers operate. Induction as a method of reasoning tries to find general rules, but it relies on specific examples to attain these rules, and it then tries to confirm and extend these rules by testing other specific examples. Deduction starts with general rules, but its purpose is to explain specific examples as illustrations or examples of these general rules. In both cases, specific examples come from the practical world in which we live and conduct business. While philosophy is sometimes accused of being irrelevant to real-world concerns, the fact is that if we understand what philosophy is really about and what philosophers really deal with, its necessary links to the everyday world are evident.

The Branches of Philosophy

Some branches or divisions of philosophy are more abstract than others.[8] Earlier in this chapter, we noted that metaphysics is the branch of philosophy that concerns itself with questions of existence. This is perhaps the most abstract of all the branches of philosophy. Epistemology concerns itself with what we know and how we know it. Many philosophers have wrestled with the problem that our senses, which seem to be the primary sources for our knowledge, can deceive us. They then seek to show how we can know anything for certain. Another central question in epistemology is how we can know abstract things like numbers or dimensions. Plato, one of the greatest of the Greek philosophers, maintained that we know individual things in a shadowy way, but anything that we humans know is only a faint replica of the perfect thing that exists apart from us and our knowledge. While this might seem esoteric in the extreme, the practical implications of this question will arise in the next chapter when we discuss such issues as rights and duties, and fairness and justice.

Logic, as mentioned above, is the branch of philosophy that deals with rules for analyzing and establishing truths, as well as for naming and classifying things. Some philosophers have maintained that logic is all of philosophy—that we cannot know or say anything meaningful except to talk about our own statements. While this rather extreme approach is hard to understand by those who struggle daily in the real world, this approach did occupy much of the attention of European and some American philosophers during most of the last century. Logic underlies mathematics, science and many of the practical tools we use in our daily lives. Computers would be impossible without the extensive application of logic in programming.

Rational psychology, or the philosophy of man, is the branch of philosophy that deals with what it means to be human. While this branch relies heavily on both biology and psychology, it addresses questions about such topics as reasoning and emotions from a more integrated perspective than any one of the physical sciences. The same Greeks who spent much of their lives discussing, arguing about and writing about philosophy were also great admirers of poetry and theater. Indeed, some of the greatest plays ever written were produced during the height of the philosophical period in Athens, and such key philosophers as Plato, Aristotle and Socrates regularly quoted from plays and from poetry. The philosophical attempts to understand what it is to be human drew widely and unapologetically from personal experience and from literature, as well as from science.

Aesthetics is the branch of philosophy that deals with beauty. What does it mean to say that a painting or a symphony or a sunset is beautiful? Why do standards of beauty change over time? Why do some people find beauty in rap music, while others find it in jazz or in classical symphonies? Are there any objective standards of beauty, or is it entirely a matter of personal preference? What should we teach our children in school about art or music? These and other such questions are the province of aesthetics. The answers over the centuries from philosophers have been many and varied, but the questions persist.

Political philosophy considers the nature of government and the relations of the individual and the state. Both Aristotle and Plato saw this as a part of ethics, or the branch of philosophy that deals with human interaction. This view no longer prevails. Philosophers have written extensively about the reasons why people form governments and what sort of government makes the most sense for humans. The limits of government and the relation between governmental laws and human liberty have been a topic of philosophy from the ancient philosophers to the present day.[9]

Finally, ethics is the branch of philosophy that deals with how humans should act in relations with one another. Ethics is about relationships. It can be defined as the study of social or interpersonal values and the rules for behavior that follow from these values.[10] If you were alone on a desert island, and no one needed you back, you could not really be ethical or unethical. Some philosophers maintain that an important part of ethics is an individual's relation to the environment, or at least to other living things. This area of concern is, for the most part, beyond the scope of this book. Ethics is also about actions as well as thoughts. In later chapters, we will see that one view of ethics defines good actions by their results and another view defines them by the intentions of the actor.

While the primary concern of this book is with ethics, and particularly with ethics as it applies to those people who are paid to manage the work of others, the above descriptions make it clear that the branches of philosophy intertwine. As we will see in the next chapter, one of the classic statements of the subject matter of ethics is Aristotle's question, "What is the good for humans?" Another way of asking this question is to inquire, "How should a human live?" In order even to begin to answer these questions, we must have some concept of what it is to be a human. Are humans free to choose among alternatives or are our actions pre-determined by genetics, upbringing or fate?[11] Does being human necessarily involve concern for other people, so that any guidance as to the good human life must include how we treat other humans? Is there a ranking of values that applies to all humans, so that when I try to decide what course of action to choose, I must value some actions or results more than others?

Philosophy and Business

These topics, and others like them, are quite different from the things that occupy managers in their day-to-day work life. In an MBA program, courses tend to be directed toward specific skills (finding new customers, calculating the cost and benefits of a proposed project, keeping the books correctly) or toward somewhat broader but still business-related themes (economics, strategy). Thinking about what makes a good life may be fine for people in church, or for poets, or maybe even for professors, but not for practical, down-to-earth, hard-headed executives and managers. Or perhaps there is more to this than meets the eye.

Business ethics is a topic of major concern, primarily because so much news about business in the recent past has highlighted some rather spectacular lapses in ethics leading up to the housing crisis and the recent recession. Previously, similar concerns about business ethics were raised in the early 2000s with the collapse of Enron and the revelation of major ethical lapses at companies like Tyco, HealthSouth and WorldCom. It was also a topic of concern in the late 1980s after the trials and convictions of people like Michael Milken, Ivan Boesky, Dennis Levine and others. About a century ago, some American CEOs became known as the "robber barons." Undoubtedly, we have not seen the last cycle of such behavior and subsequent concern for business ethics. However, many of my students who are managers do not really feel that they are criminals or robber barons, and they sometimes wonder why a program designed to teach mastery of business administration includes a segment on ethics.

Questions of ethics necessarily involve questions of metaphysics (existence and causation) and of epistemology (knowing). A number of years ago, managers at United Airlines chose to pay their workers more than managers at other airlines paid their workers. Presumably the managers at United thought that higher pay would result in some good (working faster, or smarter, or staying with the company longer, or not going out on strike) that could not be attained at a lower rate of pay. In other words, a higher pay scale would cause workers to do good things they would not otherwise do. Events proved the managers at United wrong. The company's costs (at least partly driven by higher labor costs) outran its revenues and it declared bankruptcy. How did they, or could they, know what results would be caused by their decision to pay higher wages and benefits? How were they mistaken in their conclusions? Did the managers at United do anything ethically wrong in managing the airline into bankruptcy, or were they just unlucky? In other words, should they have known what would and would not result from their decisions about wages and benefits? What about the executives at General Motors or at Chrysler? Both companies reduced wages in bankruptcy after agreeing over many years to a series of increases in wages and benefits that proved not to be sustainable.

Managers do not need to know a great deal about philosophy to do their jobs well, and there are many successful managers at various levels who have never studied philosophy at all. So why bother? The two purposes of this book are to make managers aware of the ethical implications of their actions and to provide them with tools for thinking through ethical problems that they face in the course of their work. The first of these goals, ethical aware-ness, does not require any knowledge of philosophy. However, the second goal does. In the next chapter, we will see that various approaches to think-ing about ethical dilemmas involve such notions as rights and duties, and fairness and justice. These are philosophical concepts, and to think clearly about them requires some basic understanding of philosophy.

For example, a manager might know intuitively or from reflecting on her experience that fairness is a desirable trait in management decisions and that it will promote better results than unfairness. But she still must ask whether fairness means treating everyone equally or assuring that, regardless of process, results are equal for everyone, or treating everyone in ways that are proportional to their skills and knowledge or their time on the job. Is it fair to pay all workers in a given job class the same wage, or to pay those who perform better a higher wage, or to pay those who have been on the job the longest the highest wage, or to pay those whose need is greatest the highest wage? Such questions cannot be answered thoughtfully without some analy-sis which is, at root, philosophical. Managers who make such decisions and do such analysis may not know that they are doing philosophy, but they are. One of the aims of this book is to help managers reflect on their decision-making processes in situations involving ethics and to improve the clarity with which they make such decisions.

Managers are not the only ones who might benefit from a bit of philo-sophy. Workers who do not have managerial responsibilities also make or have input into workplace decisions that have ethical implications. Profes-sionals who advise management on compensation systems, administrative policies, legal or accounting matters, and mergers and acquisitions all have a role in decisions that have major ethical implications.[12] Other workers may not have input into such decisions but are affected by such managerial decisions and may be quite concerned about these decisions. Investors con-sidering the purchase or sale of a company's stock or bonds have an interest in the accuracy and truthfulness of the company's financial reporting. Residents who live near a company's plant have concerns about emissions and pollution. Government officials concerned about terrorism have concerns about the sale of certain chemicals, computer systems or fighter planes. Journalists who criticize the actions of an individual company or of business in general might benefit from more perceptive analysis of the factors affecting management decisions.

Employees and voters also have impacts on how business is conducted and determine to some extent the range within which managers can make decisions. If employees, through their unions, demand compensation that is beyond the ability of management to deliver, constraints are put on the decisions of managers. If individual executives demand contracts guaranteeing them large amounts of severance pay, regardless of their performance, companies end up making payments that most rational people would, and do, question. If voters demand laws that extend paid vacations and leave to a significant portion of the working days available, as has happened in some Western European countries, and unions demand high wages and unproductive work rules, the ability of managers to price their products or services competitively can be seriously constrained.

While there are many individuals and groups that have some impact on the performance of organizations, in this book we will be mainly concerned with the decisions and actions of managers. Although they are often constrained, to a greater or less degree, by the actions and inactions of others, managers do still have the freedom to make choices in meaningful ways that affect and often determine the performance of the organizations for which they work. To some degree, organizations can and do influence the thoughts and actions of their stakeholders. Legislators are lobbied, unions are sometimes shown the financial details of a company's books, efforts are made to inform and persuade journalists. In the last analysis, managers must make specific decisions, and it is the use of ethical analysis in such decision-making that we will next consider.

three
What is Ethics?

In the previous chapter, we saw that philosophy is a discipline or field of knowledge with a number of sub-disciplines, one of which is ethics. In this chapter, we will explore the sources of ethics, similarities and differences between ethics and religion-based morality, and the rather complex relations between ethics and law. The following three chapters will explore three different major approaches to ethical reasoning that have been dominant in philosophy, and that are widely cited in courses and writings on business ethics.

There is no clear, agreed-upon definition of ethics, so description will be attempted rather than definition. Ethics is a branch of philosophy. In its most general sense, it deals with the question of how humans should live. Socrates was quoted by Plato as saying that the unexamined life is not worth living.[1] Ethics is about that examination. Aristotle asked, "What is the good for humans?"[2] Ethics is generally considered to deal with relations of humans to each other. Some mostly contemporary philosophers also see ethics as concerned with how humans deal with other living things and with their environment in general.

One way to describe the field of ethics is that it deals with those actions affecting other people that make us feel good or bad about ourselves. While this description points to important elements of ethics, most philosophers agree that ethics is not just, or not even primarily, about how we feel. Ethics is part of philosophy, and philosophy is a rational discipline. Ethics, then, is also a rational approach to human interactions. Feelings of guilt or pride or shame might well be an indicator that we are dealing in the area of ethics, but almost all philosophers would agree that there is more to ethics than a simple formula stating that human interactions that make us feel good are ethical and those that make us feel bad are not.[3]

Ethics is the study of interpersonal or social values and the rules of conduct that derive from these values. It is about right and wrong actions or intentions in our dealings with others. However, there are other ways to judge actions or intentions as right or wrong that are quite distinct from ethics or morality. We can act in ways that are right in terms of efficiency. This means that we act in ways that will produce the most output for the least input. We can act in ways that are legally right, meaning that we have conformed to existing law. As we will see later in this chapter, law and ethics often agree, but also sometimes disagree. We can act in ways that are politically right, meaning that most voters agree with our actions. We can act in ways that make us feel good, even though a rational analysis might decide that our actions were ethically wrong.

Ethics, then, is one way among many to make judgments about our actions and intentions. In the following chapters, we will examine more closely three definitions of what constitutes the ethical or moral act.[4] The first of these is that the moral act is the act which provides the greatest good for the greatest number of people. This approach is called utilitarianism. The second approach says that the moral act is the act which recognizes the rights of others and observes the duties that these rights impose on the actor. This approach is named variously by different authors: we shall simply call it rights and duties. The third approach says that the moral act is the act which treats similarly situated people in similar ways with regard to both process and outcome, and maintains a sense of proportion in results. We will call this approach fairness and justice.

There is a fourth approach to ethics which is cited fairly widely in current writings on the subject. It says that the moral act is the one which a virtuous person would perform in a given circumstance. This approach, which has its origins in the writings of Aristotle, is usually called virtue ethics.[5] We will not consider this approach extensively because of some major problems with applying it to real-life situations. Even the proponents of this approach recognize the difficulty of translating it from a theory of moral behavior to a practical means of judging individual actions.

The field of ethics is usually divided into descriptive and normative ethics.[6] Descriptive ethics simply describes what people say and do. It considers what actions people take that have ethical implications and what they say about these actions. Normative ethics prescribes what people should do. Various lists of "thou shalts" and "thou shalt nots" come within the area of normative ethics. Something as simple as the Golden Rule (do unto others as you would have them do unto you) can also be considered as normative ethics. Many books on business ethics take as their main goal normative ethics. Many managers do not like to be told what to do, particularly in the realm of moral right and wrong. The primary aim of this book, as stated in the introductory chapter, is not to tell managers what to do, but to help them recognize when their actions will have ethical implications, and to provide tools for thinking through difficult ethical situations that arise in the course of their work as managers.

Sources of Ethics

All humans have a basic sense of right and wrong, which develops quite early in life and is often modified with maturity and experience. The only exception to this statement seems to be a rather small number of individuals who appear to be without concern for the impact of their actions on other humans. Psychologists label such people as sociopaths. James Q. Wilson has written an interesting and wide-ranging book titled *The Moral Sense*.[7] In it, he argues from a wide array of data and conclusions that humans do have a moral sense, that it shares common elements but shows wide divergence in terms of applications, and that some elements of it seem to be independent of upbringing or schooling. Wilson cites results from several different disciplines, including psychology, criminology, sociology and educational theory, to support his conclusions.

Wilson's discussion in his book summarizes some of the arguments that have gone on for generations as to whether babies are born with some knowledge or inclinations, or whether a newborn baby is a blank slate, with all knowledge and inclinations provided by experience. This is a complex issue, sometimes referred to as the "nature vs. nurture" debate, and has been the subject of a great deal of study and experimentation. The present evidence seems to suggest that, in some ways, newborns are not all alike.[8] In layman's terms, infants are born with personalities or pre-dispositions. All share certain physical instincts, but such traits as excitability or placidity seem to be present in varying degrees from birth. However, a baby's upbringing from its earliest days also has significant influence on how it reacts to the world around it. There is enough evidence to conclude, at least tentatively, that children brought up in secure and nurturing environments show a strong tendency to view the world differently than children raised in less secure and more hostile environments.

David Brooks, in his book *The Social Animal*, summarizes a good deal of research into the ways that infants learn and how early life experiences shape individuals.[9] In his book titled *Moral Minds: The Nature of Right and Wrong*,[10] Marc Hauser reviews available information from several scientific fields and finds evidence for a universal moral sense or instinct in humans. He proposes an evolutionary explanation for this instinct. While all of this research establishes how patterns of decision-making and concepts of right and wrong emerge from early life experiences, it is important to note that influence is not the same as determination. Unless individuals, in at least some instances, make truly free choices, the concept of ethics makes no sense. It is a principle of both philosophy and law that no one is obliged to do what they cannot do.

Such discussion may seem far removed from the topic of managerial ethics, but the sources of an individual manager's sense of moral right and wrong lie to some extent in their personality, and this is impacted by early childhood experience.[11] Parents are clearly one major influence on the sense of ethics that adults bring to their work. Consider the statement, "She has a good work ethic." It is a common way of saying that someone has certain beliefs and attitudes that influence their performance at work. If this can be said of someone in her first job, then the good work ethic must have been formed before they became an employee. For most people, this means that it was formed at home as they were growing up. Here the parents are one obvious influence. Even adults who no longer agree intellectually with their parents' teaching about right and wrong behavior often acknowledge that teaching as influencing their thoughts and actions. Hence parents are one source of the sense of ethics that managers bring to their work.[12]

Other widely acknowledged sources of an individual's sense of morality include peers, teachers, culture and religion. It is important to recognize the reasons why we think and judge as we do, and why others might think and judge quite differently about matters of morality. Most of our ethical judgments are instinctive. That is to say that we do not stop and reason things through, but instead we apply rules and decision-making models that we have come to accept in the past and that seem to fit the present situation. We may not know just why we accept or apply the rule that we do, but our decisions are shaped by the sense of ethics that we bring to a particular situation. Usually, it is only when someone questions our judgment or when results that we find unacceptable cause us to question our own judgment that we engage in conscious review of the sources of our decision-making.

Peers can be siblings, schoolmates, college roommates, fellow workers or members of a club, team or social group to which an individual belongs. One example of the influence of peers on an individual's sense of ethics is the often-noted tendency of teenagers to define themselves by their group of friends. Adults also have their views shaped, at least to some degree, by their peers. It is said that police officers often have a more negative view of humanity than those in some other professions because they spend so much of their time dealing with criminals. Two books about the internal operations at Enron in the last years before its bankruptcy make it clear that employees who went along with the questionable financial dealings were made to feel like successful performers and members of the team, while those who questioned some of the transactions were made to feel like outsiders.[13] In his detailed study of the U.S. government's decision-making before and during the Vietnam War, David Halberstam provides example after example of the powerful influence of peers in various parts of government on individual thinking and decision-making.[14] Several books about the recent financial crisis make it clear that peer influence played a major role at mortgage lenders, investment banks and other institutions involved in the reckless securitization and sale of subprime mortgages.[15] The influence of organizational peers is examined more closely in the last chapter of this book.

Peers can also be members of the same profession. Accountants, attorneys, medical doctors and members of other professions undergo extensive schooling. They learn not only how to minimize taxes or diagnose diabetes, but also how members of their profession act and think. Professional education involves socialization as well as information transmission. As more and more students obtain MBA degrees, this socialization also becomes more common for managers. Obviously, not all accountants or attorneys think alike. However, an argument can be made that members of a given profession think more alike than non-members of that profession. Another factor involving peer influence in the professions is the existence of professional codes of conduct. These are not perfect, and they do not influence all members of a profession equally. However, they do provide a starting point for making some kinds of ethical judgments, and they are more or less widely known within a profession.[16]

Teachers are another source of an individual's sense of morality. Whether it is the simple but often-repeated rules of grammar school or the more involved exposition that occurs in college classes, teachers as authority figures do communicate in ways that influence the reasoning and judgment of at least some of their students.[17] For a case in point, almost all teachers communicate, subtly or overtly, that cheating is wrong. They say this, they write this in syllabi and on exam instructions, and they act on this when they detect cheating. While most schools do not go this far, the U.S. military academies and a few other schools have honor codes that require the expulsion not only of cheaters but of those who know of cheating and fail to report it. Teachers also often communicate the value of doing assignments, or thinking clearly, or doing one's part in group projects. The cumulative impact of teachers does have an influence on the formation of an individual's sense of ethics.

Culture also influences an individual's moral sense. Culture can be defined as the unspoken rules and assumptions about how we do things around here.[18] When considered in this way, culture is subtle because it is unspoken.[19] Most organizations do not have explicit rules that dictate who shall be called by their first name and who shall be addressed more formally. They do not have explicit rules about the use of profanity at work, or the degree to which client information is kept confidential, or the kind of jokes that are acceptable or unacceptable in the workplace. Although none of these things is formalized, there often are unspoken rules. An observer of the behavior of workers at a construction site and at a law firm would notice immediate and profound differences in individual behavior and methods of conducting business. The two have different cultures.

The history of racial discrimination or of sexual harassment in some industries makes it clear that a behavior which is in accord with existing cultural norms is not necessarily morally acceptable.[20] However, an individual's sense of ethics is shaped by the culture or cultures in which he operates. One of the goals of this book is to help the reader to be aware of the ethical implications of managerial actions. Sometimes this awareness requires an examination of accepted cultural norms. Countries have cultures as well as companies. In fact, one of the more interesting issues in managerial ethics concerns the degree to which behavior such as bribery, which is accepted and commonplace in one culture, can or should be accepted in a different culture or by members of a different culture.[21] Another interesting issue concerning culture and ethics is the personal integration of ethical standards in an individual's different roles. Can a person follow one set of standards with her family, a second set with co-workers and a third set with customers or regulators? We will address such issues in subsequent chapters.

Still another significant influence on an individual's sense of ethics, and for some people by far the most important, is religion. People who were raised in a religion, even if they no longer believe or practice it, often have the teachings of that religion as part of their sense of ethics. People who do believe in and practice religion typically find the moral rules or dictates of their religion the most meaningful way to answer questions about right and wrong behavior. What does philosophy have to say about that? As we noted in the last chapter, philosophy does not accept religious teachings, either from sacred books or from individuals with religious authority, as the basis of answers when doing philosophy. Some noted philosophers have been deeply religious people. Obviously, then, the two can co-exist.

Another point worth noting is that truly awful things have sometimes been done in the name of religion. Most religious people would agree that it is not a good thing to tie someone to a stake, surround them with wood and set them on fire in order to encourage them to share one's religious beliefs. Nor is it a good thing to commandeer passenger airplanes and fly them and their passengers into buildings in order to avenge one's god or to send a religious message. Most religious people would agree that doing such things in the name of religion is to misunderstand or misinterpret religion. If religion and philosophy can be compatible, then perhaps in extreme kinds of behavior, philosophy can provide one tool for thinking about when actions are not compatible with a religion.

It is also worth considering that many of the finest things done by humans have been done in the name of religion. Artists and artisans have created cathedrals, statues, paintings and music that are widely acclaimed, and done so in the name of religion. People have taught students, cared for the sick and provided for the homeless with almost no personal financial reward, and done so in the name of religion. When we think about morally good and bad acts by individuals, we cannot do otherwise than acknowledge the impact of religion in shaping many people's sense of ethics.[22]

The forces discussed above are not the only ones that shape an individual's sense of ethics, but they are among the most common and most important. Because each individual brings his or her sense of ethics to the start of any discussion of this topic, it is important to know what has shaped that sense. Often an individual's intuitive sense of ethics is based on past experiences or reflections on those experiences. Unless we are consciously aware of why we accept the assumptions and rules that we do in the area of morality, it is not really possible to reflect on them and decide whether they are appropriate to situations that arise from the task of management. It is often uncomfortable to question our own assumptions, particularly in areas that matter to us. Yet, without knowing what our own individual assumptions are on which we base our own sense of morality, analysis of managerial ethics is reduced to criticism of any theory different from our own, and we do not really have a thoughtful base from which to conduct such criticism.

Since each individual brings his or her own sense of morality to the discussion, and since this individual sense is based to varying degrees on parental and peer influence, past and present religious beliefs and various cultural assumptions, is there any hope of a rational, thoughtful discussion of normative ethics—what a person should or should not do in a given situation? In fact, there is. Take, for example, the issue of rights and duties. Individuals have a sense of their own rights. National cultures vary considerably in their assumptions about rights, but these cultures do shape individual assumptions.[23] On the question of individual rights versus group rights, a person who has grown up in the United States will most probably put more emphasis on individual rights, while a person who has grown up in Japan will probably put more emphasis on group rights. When we translate this general question to the specific application of a manager's right to monitor an employee's email, the first instinctive response of the American will probably differ from the first instinctive response of the Japanese.

As we will examine in more detail later in the book, the issue of privacy in the workplace does have moral implications for managers and for employees. Once this fact is established, we can begin to discuss what rights an employee has to privacy in workplace email communication and what duties, if any, those rights impose on managers. While it is unlikely that such discussion will result in universal rules that all managers everywhere are morally obliged to do or not to do something in this area, our understanding of the issues and awareness of what others think about these same issues can go a long way in determining what constitutes a moral action in a given circumstance.

Ethics and the Law

One other influence that shapes many people's sense of morality is the law. In fact, business people often seem to equate the two. It is remarkable how many of the comments made in their own defense by executives at Enron, Arthur Andersen, Countrywide and other companies involved in scandals said, in effect, "What we did was not wrong because it complied with the law, or with Generally Accepted Accounting Principles." In other words, many people, at least some of the time, do not make a distinction between what is legal and what is moral.

Ethics, as we have seen, is a branch of philosophy. Law is seen as a quite distinct field.[24] Legal systems, or groups of laws, have existed for thousands of years.[25] Law is a function of government, in that laws are made, changed and enforced by governments. Laws apply in specific places and have their standing from the government of countries, states or other political entities or groups of entities (there is some international law). In the case of monarchies, the monarch makes, interprets and enforces the law. There may be elaborate governmental structures for carrying out these tasks, but the ultimate authority rests with the monarch. In the case of democracies, government officials chosen by the people (or, in rare cases, the people meeting as a whole) make, interpret and enforce laws. There are several ways in which legislators and those who enforce the laws are chosen, but the source of authority in legal matters comes from the people and not from a single individual, such as in a monarchy. Typically in a democracy, the Constitution or other foundational document provides rules for how laws are to be made and changed.[26] In the United States, laws can be passed by federal legislators for the entire country. In matters over which the national Constitution does not specify federal control, laws can be made by elected officials at the levels of state, county and municipality. The laws of a given jurisdiction can be changed by legislators of that jurisdiction, according to rules specified in the jurisdiction's Constitution or charter.

Regulations have the force of law, but are generally more specific and are written and approved by regulatory agencies within the framework of the elected government. Regulators are generally appointed rather than elected. Regulations are intended to provide detail specifying how broader laws apply to specific cases and examples. Most businesses are subject to several regulatory agencies and must comply with detailed regulations in such matters as taxation, financial disclosure and product safety. All businesses are also subject to a variety of laws and regulations in matters relating to employment.

In law, unlike philosophy, all in a jurisdiction are subject to the same laws. Two people can disagree about many things in philosophy, and there may be absolutely no practical consequences. If the laws of my state provide for residents to pay income taxes to the state, and the laws in your state do not, you and I can agree or disagree philosophically about the value or appropriateness of state income taxes. However, whatever my philosophical position, I am legally bound to pay income taxes to my state as provided by its laws and will be subject to legal consequences if I fail to do so. You can rejoice in your state's wisdom in not having an income tax, but you still must pay federal income tax if you are a citizen of the United States.

A variety of criminal and civil laws and regulations apply to managers in their role as managers. While it is rare in the United States for managers to be charged or tried for criminal violations, it does happen. Recent changes in federal law, most prominently in the Sarbanes–Oxley Act passed in 2002, make it likely that such criminal charges will become somewhat more common in the future. Involvement in civil litigation is a common fact of life for companies and managers in many industries. Managers are not personally charged nearly as often as companies are, but in many industries most companies have a variety of civil legal proceedings under way at any given point in time. Companies are more often defendants than plaintiffs in such cases, but in some industries, companies regularly pursue legal charges against others to protect patents or licenses or to recover loans or other damages under various contracts.

One consequence of the frequency of business litigation in the United States is that some actions that might be seen as ethical are discouraged because of their possible legal consequences. If a company does something that it later considers wrong, the CEO or other spokesperson might feel that he or she is morally obliged to accept responsibility, and say what was wrong and what the company plans to do about it. If there is a chance that the company or the executive will be sued for the actions in question, the legal advice will almost certainly be to avoid any statement which could subsequently be used as evidence in litigation. Thus, accountability is sometimes in conflict with the prevention of adverse legal consequences.

Ethics and Law Not the Same

While ethics and law deal with many of the same issues, and often come to the same conclusions, there are several reasons why it is not valid to equate one with the other. One consideration is this: law-makers are often not noted for their refined moral sensibility. In fact, in a number of classes when I have asked students whether they would be satisfied to have either national or local legislators make up their moral code, the response has been a rather spirited negative. This should not be surprising, for in a democracy, candidates for office generally do not claim to be the most virtuous or the most morally sensitive individuals in the country. If they did make such claims, one suspects that they would be met with no little skepticism. It seems to be a general rule that saints do not make good politicians, and vice versa. In addition to legislation, much of the legal burden imposed in a democracy is designed by regulators. These are typically non-elected bureaucrats and, like legislators, are not selected for high ethical sensitivity. This is not to say that most politicians and regulators are liars and thieves. It is merely to say that they are not chosen and kept in office because of their moral sensitivity.

Another reason why it is dangerous to equate the legal with the moral is that laws change, while many people expect at least the basics of morality to be unchanging.[27] In the State of Nevada, prostitution is legal in all but two counties. While the legal status of the act can change from county to county, it is difficult to argue that prostitution is moral in one county and immoral in the next. Early in the twentieth century, the eighteenth amendment to the United States Constitution made production and sale of alcoholic beverages illegal. The twenty-first amendment reversed this position. Morality should stand on firmer ground.

Some actions, such as adultery, are considered by many people to be immoral, yet in many parts of the United States there is no legal prohibition against adultery. Many parents teach their children that it is immoral for the children to lie to their parents, yet there is no legal prohibition against such lies. The absence of a law against an action does not necessarily constitute grounds for deciding that the action is ethical. Is the opposite true?

General Premise: It is Ethical to Follow the Law

All of the major systems of ethics include an assumption in favor of obeying the law.[28] Note that this is an assumption, not an absolute mandate. Each of the major systems of ethics at some point critiques laws and provides a basis for analyzing whether or not a given law is ethical. However, this is different from an approach that makes no presumption either in favor of or against observing the law. Since we must live and work in the real world, it does not make sense to start from an assumption that it is unethical to follow the law. The remaining two possibilities are an assumption that it is ethical to follow the law or a neutral stance that assumes that each individual law or even each individual circumstance must be analyzed to determine whether it is ethical to follow the law. Notice that we have proceeded so far simply by applying logic (that is, by doing philosophy!). It is both impractical and unreasonable to analyze each law or each application of the law, so we will start with the assumption that it is ethical to follow the law.

There is another way of reaching this same conclusion. Laws are made to reflect and protect the values of a society, at least in a democracy. If they do not reflect society's values, new law-makers are elected by the people. While this view is somewhat oversimplified, it is basically descriptive of what happens in democracies over a period of time. Ethics is also about values. If a society values the individual's right to speak his or her mind, its laws will tend to protect free speech, and most censorship will be considered illegal. If a society values the common good above individual rights, it might reflect these values in its tax laws and welfare structure. Wealthy people will also be seen as having a moral duty to contribute in some way to the support of the poor. Thus the values expressed in a democratic society's laws will also be reflected in its sense of morality. Not every law will be considered moral by every citizen, but an assumption that it is ethical to follow the law will fit comfortably in the large scheme of things within that society. In the United States at the present time, it is neither illegal nor generally thought to be immoral for an executive to make a good deal of money.[29] However, it is illegal, and is generally considered to be immoral, for that same executive to fail to pay legally imposed income taxes.

When and how do we test whether a law or its application is moral, given our starting assumption that it is moral to follow the law, but our unwillingness to simply equate legality with morality? There are two kinds of situations in which one might question the link between morality and obedience to a given law. One is a matter of degree, and the other involves the basic values expressed in a law. A driver who is exceeding the speed limit by one mile per hour is technically in violation of the law. However, neither the driver nor the policeman behind her is likely to consider that she is doing anything wrong, in the moral or even the legal sense. We can and do argue about how much over the speed limit and under what conditions fast driving becomes a violation of law and/or ethics, but at the very margin, we do not generally maintain that the tiniest infraction of a law constitutes an immoral action.

In marketing, claims for a product or a service that just slightly stretch the truth are almost expected. Many consumers consciously or unconsciously scale down the claims made in advertising when forming their own expectations. However, outright material lies about a product are not considered acceptable, either legally or morally.[30] Such matters of degree trouble some individuals more than others. Individuals differ in their tolerance for ambiguity. Some prefer rules, whether they are laws or ethical prescriptions, to be simple and clear. Others feel that life as we live it is not simple, so ambiguity must be allowed for and expected in the rules by which we live our lives. Anyone who fulfills the role of manager for any length of time will find that, in the real world of organizations, ambiguity abounds. Further, simple clearcut cases seldom are presented to managers; they are resolved by subordinates. Individuals with high needs for clarity and simplicity in their decision-making often have trouble succeeding in the role of manager because of the inherent ambiguities in the task of managing.

The second and more unusual kind of situation when the link between following the law and being ethical must be tested involves laws which express or enforce values that are not consistent with an individual's or society's sense of morality. There is much that can be said about the role of ethics in evaluating laws that is beyond the scope of this book.[31] However, the issue does sometimes arise in various business settings, and some thoughts on it may prove helpful. Under the law, neither ignorance nor disagreement is a valid excuse for violating a law. A moment's thought will show that it could not be otherwise. If laws did not apply to those who were not familiar with them, anyone could plead innocent to anything, and in order to apply the law and its sanctions, the knowledge of the offender would become the key turning point in legal proceedings. Proving what someone knows or does not know is a very difficult thing to do. If laws only applied to individuals who agreed with them, anyone could plead innocent to any offense by simply stating their disagreement with the law in question. Clearly a society could not operate on such a basis. Business people cannot know all of the laws and regulations that apply to them in detail, yet they are not excused from compliance by ignorance of a given law or regulation. They are expected to be generally knowledgeable about laws and regulations applying to their business. They are also expected to have access to and make use of specialists (generally speaking, but not always, these specialists are attorneys) who can identify and interpret applicable laws and regulations.

Business people, like other citizens, can and sometimes do disagree with a given law or regulation and can work to change it. The *Wall Street Journal* has for many years been the most widely read newspaper of business. On its editorial pages, the *Journal* often criticizes current laws and regulations and argues why and how they should be changed.[32] However, the *Journal* does not advocate that its readers, who include a good many managers, should ignore or fail to comply with laws or regulations that it disagrees with. Companies hire lobbyists, make political donations and engage in other forms of political activity with the intention of shaping laws and regulations in ways that favor their business. They often advocate changing present laws or regulations. Yet, they generally acknowledge the need to comply with those laws or regulations until such time as they are changed.

The decision that a law is unethical or immoral, and that an individual is compelled by his sense of morality to disobey that law, is relatively rare. This is a quite different thing than deciding that one thinks that a given law is based on bad reasoning, or supports the wrong values, or cannot be fairly and reasonably enforced. Going so far as to say that an individual's sense of morality requires him to disobey the law carries consequences. In the case of civil disobedience, such as that practiced by civil rights leaders of the 1960s in the United States, some individuals did decide that they were morally required to disobey laws that denied ethnic minorities certain rights. These individuals for the most part knew what they were doing and accepted the consequences. When they were jailed or fined for disobeying the law, they accepted the punishment. They did not judge it morally right, but they did acknowledge the existence of the law and its consequences.

Historically, few if any business people have concluded that a business law is immoral and that they are obliged by their personal sense of morality to disobey the law and accept the consequences. Many business people have disagreed strongly with some law or regulation, and have worked to change it, but this is a large step short of concluding that they are morally obliged to disobey the law and accept the consequences. It appears that, in the case of scandals involving Enron, Adelphia, HealthSouth and other major firms, individuals broke laws. They obviously did not feel that observing the laws was the best thing to do. However, it appears that their judgment was instrumental rather than moral. In other words, they concluded that their company could make more profit or attain other corporate goals more effectively if they broke a law. They did not do this, apparently, because of their views about the immorality of the law or their ethical obligation to break the law and accept the consequences.

Earlier in this chapter, we showed that there are several reasons for not simply equating ethics and the law. Reference was made there to the frequent defense against charges of corporate wrong-doing that whatever action is being challenged complied with existing laws or regulations. The point was made that an action is not automatically moral because it is legal. Are managers, then, sometimes morally obliged to go beyond the letter of the law? The short answer is yes. However, since this seems to many managers (and their attorneys) to be naïve, unrealistic, and soft and squishy in a world where the prescribed managerial reading includes *The Art of War*,[33] *Jack: Straight from the Gut*,[34] Machiavelli's *The Prince*[35] and other non-naïve, realistic titles, we need to discuss the issue a bit further.

Ethics and Managers

Most textbooks on Business Ethics or Business and Society include a chapter on the role of the corporation in modern society. Since corporate decisions are made by managers, this topic can be seen as the role of the manager in modern society. The chapter in question almost inevitably includes reference to and quotations from a very famous piece written by Milton Friedman for the *New York Times Magazine* in 1970 entitled "The social responsibility of business is to increase its profits." In this piece, Friedman, a Nobel

Prize-winning economist, argued that the role of the manager is to act as the agent of the owners of the business that he or she manages, namely, the stockholders.

Friedman says that the manager as agent of the owners:

> ...has direct responsibility to his employers. That responsibility is to conduct the business in accordance with their desires, which generally will be to make as much money as possible while conforming to the basic rules of society, both those embodied in law and those embodied in ethical customs.[36]

If this is not the strongest statement of a manager's responsibility being not to himself but to his stockholders, it is certainly the most quoted. Even in Friedman's statement, there is explicit reference to ethical customs as well as to the law. In reaction to the sentiments expressed in Friedman's article, a good deal of discussion has ensued around the notion that corporations and their managers have responsibilities to stakeholders. R. Edward Freeman, a professor, has written extensively on the notion of stakeholders. He gives a narrow definition of the term stakeholder as describing "those groups who are vital to the survival and success of the corporation."[37] He also gives a wide definition which "includes any group or individual who can affect or is affected by the corporation."[38]

Earlier, we defined ethics as the discipline that studies interpersonal or social values and the rules of conduct that derive from these values. Certainly the decisions of managers do affect other people, including their subordinates, others within their organizations and various people beyond the organization, including but not limited to the stockholders or owners. Managerial ethics, then, must of necessity examine the impacts of the actions of managers. This examination cannot be limited to the compliance or noncompliance of those actions with laws and regulations.

A somewhat different way of looking at this is to ask what the individual manager, as a person, considers important and valuable. When I was a manager, I felt better about myself and my job at the end of some days than others. I cannot remember ever looking back on a day with satisfaction and saying to myself or anyone else, "I had a really good day today—I complied with the law!" When one reads the biographies or autobiographies of managers, one gets the sense that they enjoy meeting competitive challenges successfully. Many of them also seem to derive genuine pleasure from the development of subordinates and from maintaining or expanding company traditions. It is interesting that a great number of academic studies have been done on a wide variety of topics relating to management and leadership, yet there are very few studies on what motivates managers, other than those that study compensation in its various forms.[39]

There is a large amount of writing on leadership. Almost none of it refers to complying with the law as a characteristic of a successful leader. It is assumed that good leaders do not run afoul of the law, but it is not at all assumed that compliance with the law is the same as good leadership. Not all managers are leaders, but both managers and leaders have interaction with others as a significant part of their job. How we interact with others has already been defined as central to ethics. Good leaders, like good managers, are generally viewed as having a concern for the total impact of their actions. They are generally thought to carry out their own duties and to show concern for the rights of others. Fairness is high on the list of traits of both good managers and good leaders. These characteristics of good leaders and good managers have already been identified as central to the three basic approaches to ethics. It should not be surprising if we define good leaders and good managers as ethical individuals. Being ethical does not, by itself, make one a good leader or manager, but being unethical might be argued to prevent one from being either a good leader or a good manager.

There are unethical managers. Some of the executives of the companies involved in past scandals enriched themselves by tens or hundreds of millions of dollars while managing their companies in ways that were dishonest and value-destroying for stakeholders. Jimmy Cayne, the chairman of the board of directors of the large investment bank Bear Stearns, spent the last week of the company's independent existence, while it was fighting for its life, at a bridge tournament. He had to be summoned from a bridge game to vote (by phone) on approving the company's bankruptcy.[40] Some of these managers were simultaneously lying to their own directors, to regulators and to others about the true state of their companies. It certainly appears that much of the conduct of the top managers of these companies was unethical. For a period of time, their companies were widely praised and held up by the business press as models for others to follow. In the end, though, a manager who lies, enriches himself at the expense of stockholders and lenders, and manages his company into bankruptcy cannot be judged to be either a good or an ethical manager. This judgment holds true even if such a manager is never found guilty of breaking any law.

In describing previously the basic approaches to ethics, virtue ethics was briefly mentioned. As indicated there, we will not consider this as a basic approach to ethics for purposes of this book because virtue ethics has major difficulties in showing what the ethical action would be in a given situation, and why. However, there is one point from the virtue ethics approach that bears on our current discussion. Virtue ethics defines the moral act as the act that a virtuous person would perform. In some ways, this appears to be a case of circular reasoning. However, when we say that an unethical person who is not found guilty of breaking the law still cannot be judged to be a good manager, we are using the approach of virtue ethics.

Aristotle, the first proponent of virtue ethics and still the most quoted on this subject, said that the virtuous person is the one who does virtuous things. His point here is that we can discern a person's ethics by observing that person's actions over time. Many philosophers would set out to discern a person's ethics by discussing this subject with the person, asking both about his theories of ethics and how they might be applied in particular situations. In fact, all three of the approaches to ethics that we will consider at length in the following chapters concern themselves either with individual acts and their consequences or with the way that systems distribute resources. Aristotle concerned himself with people. In his major work on ethics, *The Nicomachean Ethics*,[41] Aristotle described the virtuous person as the one who observes moderation in all things. He discusses at length such virtues as courage, liberality, self-restraint and friendship. Throughout his discussions of the virtues, he uses examples constantly, showing what the courageous person or the true friend would do. The basis of all his discussion is that the virtuous person will show consistency and moderation in his actions.

Managers, as noted above, play various roles in their lives. Psychologists and social theorists tell us that individuals have trouble dealing with inconsistency. It is hard for the same person to be warm and nurturing with spouse and children, and cold and impersonal with subordinates at work. The ethical or virtuous person, according to Aristotle, is the person who shows consistency and moderation in all their dealings with others, be they family or friends, or peers, or subordinates. This is a point worth considering. We will examine, in the following chapters, specific instances of decisions managers must make that have moral implications. Some will involve the hiring or terminating of employees, others the evaluation and rewarding of the work of subordinates, and others the respect for or invasion of the privacy of others. In all these individual cases, we will ask how each of the three major approaches to ethics would determine whether a given act is moral.

There is a tendency, in examining isolated acts, to ignore or forget that the same human makes the various decisions that we will examine, and many others. Yet, when we reflect on ourselves as individuals attempting to be moral, we find that consistency or its lack is a major issue. How can we be caring and sympathetic in one situation and rational and emotionless in another? How can we be seriously concerned about telling the truth to our spouse or children, yet go to work and mislead others? How can we balance the time demands of our job with the time demands of our family? To Aristotle, these were important and reasonable questions. Yet, in much of the writing on business ethics, such questions are nowhere to be found.

Humans are sometimes inconsistent. Aristotle recognized this. Many of the best plays and novels ever written have this as a central theme. Totally predictable individuals are not generally valued as friends or as advisors. After all, if someone is totally predictable, once we have gotten to know them, we know in advance what they will say or recommend in any situation. Most people are not totally predictable. In other words, most people are, at least sometimes, inconsistent. We cannot predict their response in every situation because they cannot predict their response. However, most people do show patterns in their behavior and in their decision-making. These patterns are the basis for virtue ethics as an approach to morality. The just person typically acts justly. Typically does not mean always, but it does mean that a pattern of just actions can be perceived over time, and so for the other virtues. If individuals are truly free to choose different courses of action at least some of the time, then the pattern of their choices helps us to decide whether they are virtuous. As we examine individual choices in the following chapters, this is an important point to bear in mind.

Most people would not praise a person who habitually acts with no thought or concern for the consequences of his actions. We would apply terms such as thoughtless, heedless and reckless to such a person. None of these terms is complimentary. As we examine utilitarianism in the next chapter, we will see that the central point of this approach to ethics is concern for the consequences of actions. Most people would also not praise a person who habitually acts with no sense of responsibility toward others. We might apply such terms as selfish, uncaring and egomaniacal to such a person. Again, none of these terms is complimentary. In the chapter where we examine rights and duties, we will see that the central point is that other individuals do in fact have rights and that these rights often impose duties on us to take their concerns into account. Finally, little or no praise will come to the individual who habitually acts with no concern for the relative impacts of his actions on some people versus others, and with no sense of proportion between actions and their consequences for others. In the chapter where we examine fairness and justice, we will see that the relative impacts of our actions on others constitute a central concern of ethics, along with a sense of proportionality.

We have now considered a number of concepts concerning what ethics is, and what it is not. As a branch of philosophy, ethics shares the basic concerns of philosophy for clear thinking and accurate naming of things and for using reason rather than emotions or authority (divine or human) in reaching conclusions. We have seen that ethics often involves values that are shared by religious and legal systems, but that it is not identical with either of these kinds of systems. In the next three chapters, we turn to a more detailed examination of each of the three approaches to ethics that will be used in the remainder of the book to analyze areas of managerial decision-making.

four

Utilitarianism

Throughout the history of philosophy, thinkers have addressed the question of what makes an act moral or immoral (for purposes of this and the following discussions, we will use the terms "moral" and "ethical" interchangeably).[1] A variety of answers have been given. In this and the following two chapters, we will consider in some detail the three most common answers to the question. In this chapter, we examine the approach to ethics or morality known as utilitarianism.

The Greatest Happiness or Greatest Good

Utilitarianism is the philosophical approach which says that the moral act is the one that creates the greatest happiness or good for the greatest number of people. Because this approach judges morality based on consequences, it is classified as teleological. Are the greatest happiness and the greatest good the same thing? Broadly speaking, utilitarians answer yes. In the last chapter, we saw that Aristotle discussed ethics at length, principally in his *Nicomachean Ethics*.[2] In the first chapter of that work, he asks what might be the ultimate reason to do something. I might practice the flute because I want to be a better flute player, but a further logical question is why I want to become a better flute player. Finally, there must be something which people pursue for itself (an ultimate end) and not just because it leads to something else (an instrumental end). After discussing various possibilities, Aristotle concluded that humans pursue as their ultimate end "eudaimonia."[3] This Greek word has no exact English translation. It literally means good-spiritedness. It is sometimes translated as "happiness" but this does not capture the full flavor of the idea which Aristotle described. The term does not simply refer to an emotional state, but also has the sense of well-being of the spirit.[4]

Different philosophers have provided different answers to this question of the ultimate end of human action. For Kant, it involved doing one's duty with a good will. For others, it involves being fully rational. Still others would describe it as acting in accord with one's own nature, without influence from social conventions. The two philosophers most often associated with utilitarianism were both Englishmen: Jeremy Bentham (1748–1832) and John Stuart Mill (1806–1873). Bentham was particularly interested in the reform of British law. In 1789, he published *Introduction to the Principles of Morals and Legislation*,[5] which is perhaps the clearest statement of his views on utilitarianism. Chapter 1 opens with this statement:

> Nature has placed mankind under the governance of two sovereign masters, pain and pleasure. It is for them alone to point out what we ought to do, as well as to determine what we shall do. On the one hand the standard of right and wrong, on the other the chain of causes and effects, are fastened to their throne.[6]

He defines the principle of utility as follows:

> By the principle of utility is meant that principle which approves or disapproves of every action whatsoever, according to the tendency which it appears to have to augment or diminish the happiness of the party whose interest is in question: or, what is the same thing in other words, to promote or to oppose that happiness.[7]

John Stuart Mill's work, *Utilitarianism*, was first published in 1861. In this extended essay, he develops further and comments on Bentham's writing on the subject. In Chapter II, Mill says the following:

> The creed which accepts as the foundation of morals, Utility, or the Greatest Happiness Principle, holds that actions are right in proportion as they tend to promote happiness, wrong as they tend to produce the reverse of happiness. By happiness is intended pleasure, and the absence of pain; by unhappiness, pain, and the privation of pleasure. To give a clear view of the moral standard set up by the theory, much more requires to be said; in particular, what things it includes in the ideas of pain and pleasure; and to what extent this is left an open question. But these supplementary explanations do not affect the theory of life on which this theory of morality is grounded—namely, that pleasure, and freedom from pain, are the only things desirable as ends; and that all

desirable things (which are as numerous in the utilitarian as in any other scheme) are desirable either for the pleasure inherent in themselves, or as means to the promotion of pleasure and the prevention of pain.[8]

Results Orientation

Although it could be interesting to actually sit back and think about what our ultimate ends might be, in most cases we make decisions based on more immediate concerns—what philosophers would call instrumental or inter-mediate ends. We approve adding six new salespeople because we are per-suaded that the additional revenue they generate will not only cover their own costs, but also provide an increment of profits to the company. We choose to go to the dentist and have a root canal performed not because we enjoy pain as an ultimate end, but because the temporary pain of the dental procedure will result in a longer pain-free period afterward. We promote this person rather than that person not so much because it will make either us or them happy (although it may do both) but because we expect that they will perform well in their new job and thus produce desirable results.

When we decide on the morality of an action based on the results that will be achieved, we are engaging in utilitarianism. This is different from choosing an action because it is simply the right thing to do. The charge is sometimes raised that utilitarianism is wrong because it is based on the notion that the end justifies the means. This is a saying that is often quoted and seldom analyzed. It is true that utilitarianism is based on ends justifying means. Because an action will cause the greatest good for the greatest number (our end in taking the action), the means to that end are justified or found moral. Without examining what we are doing, we often make decisions on precisely this basis. The decision to pursue an MBA degree may mean that, for the next two years, the student will have less time to spend with family and friends, less money to spend on clothes or a car or other desirable things, and less energy left over for recreational pursuits or even for work. What justifies these results?

In the prospective student's mind, the knowledge and skills gained in an MBA program, or the higher level jobs open only to individuals with this degree, or the increase in career compensation that the degree will bring, or all of these factors justify the time spent in studying and the pleasures fore-gone during the MBA program. In other words, the end justifies the means. Suppose we consider this same investment from a different perspective. If I ask whether it is ethical for a man to choose to spend a good part of every weekend for an extended period sitting alone reading or typing on his com-puter, while depriving his wife and child of his company, you might answer that it is certainly not ethical. At least not if he is reading about the history of the National Football League and its teams and players, and typing his entries in a fantasy football league. In both cases, the man spends his weekends reading and typing, but in one (pursuit of an MBA) both the man and his wife may agree that the end (obtaining an MBA and the career opportunities that it will bring) does justify the means. In the other case, where the end is improved performance in his fantasy football league, perhaps no one except his fellow players will agree that the end justifies the means.

To many people, the statement "the end justifies the means" is the same as "a good end justifies any means." Increased profit for my business is a good end, but it does not justify my employing eight-year-old children for twelve hours a day and paying them a dollar an hour. It also does not justify ignoring safety concerns and selling a product or service with a high likelihood of harming or killing my customers. However, if my employees are seriously overpaid and my company is about to go bankrupt due to uncompetitive pricing caused by labor costs, reducing either wages or staff, or both, may well be justified in order to keep the company operating and prevent all employees from losing their jobs. Truth might be better served by re-phrasing the principle to say "ends often justify means."

Most actions of managers cause more than one result. Quite often, significant managerial actions cause happiness for some affected individuals and unhappiness for others. This would be true if no one had ever identified a certain approach to ethics as utilitarianism. It does not matter in terms of the results whether the manager intended or was aware of them or not. When ocean surf is breaking near the shore, it is sometimes possible to stand waist-deep in water and have approaching waves break over one's head. If the swimmer faces the waves, she can choose to dive into the next wave, or move quickly back toward shore, or swim out beyond where the waves are breaking. If the swimmer stands facing the shore and refuses to acknowledge the waves, the next one that breaks over her head will knock her off her feet, tumble her around a bit and provide a less-than-pleasant experience.

A manager can look forward, consider the consequences of a proposed action and perhaps take one of several actions to change those consequences, up to and including not taking the proposed action. Or, the manager can refuse to face the consequences.[9] However, refusal to face them does not usually change consequences. More often it results in being knocked off one's feet, tumbled around a bit and enduring a less-than-pleasant experience. Utilitarianism maintains that the moral thing to do is to face the consequences and to act in ways that will maximize the happiness or the good that will result from an action. The recent Great Recession might have been avoided or at least mitigated if managers at financial firms had faced the likely consequences of their actions and changed their behavior accordingly.

The statement was made in the introductory chapter that this book has two purposes: to make the reader aware of the ethical consequences of managerial actions and to provide tools for thinking through difficult ethical questions. Utilitarianism as a perspective on ethics performs both of these functions. If we consider whether an action will provide the greatest good or happiness for the greatest number of people, we automatically must think about what people will be affected, for good or for ill, by our action.

Consider the action of laying off employees. Some employees who now work for the company will be told they no longer have jobs. The reason is not that they have performed badly enough to be fired or have committed offenses that make it impossible for them to continue in their jobs. Rather, they are being laid off because the company has more employees than it needs, and they have been chosen for termination. Obviously the laid off employees are affected by this decision. More than likely, so are their families. What of their fellow employees? Someone will have to do the work formerly done by those laid off, and the prime candidates are their fellow employees. It is logical that other employees who were formerly comfortable in their positions will now fear for their jobs. Morale among these employees is likely to go down. If work is not done as well following the layoffs, customers may be affected. If the layoffs and resultant decrease in cost have their desired effect, profits may rise, the stock price may go up and stockholders may benefit.

The results described above will occur whether or not the manager deciding on layoffs foresees them. Some people will benefit, some will be burdened. Whether the net result is the greatest good for the greatest number or not, a number of individuals and groups will be affected by the decision that the manager makes. Utilitarianism requires that the manager thinks about these results and calculates their net impact before deciding. Obviously no one can mathematically calculate the total impact on all parties, but the manager who fails to consider and estimate the various impacts of her action is not being moral, according to utilitarianism.

Not everyone does take such consequences into account. Financial analysts generally applaud layoffs. When a company announces that it is laying off employees and taking a one-time charge to cover the costs of these layoffs, it is often the case that the company's stock rises immediately following the announcement. The logic that seems to lead to this result involves the conclusion that layoffs mean fewer workers, less labor cost and hence more profits. The impact on laid-off workers and on remaining employees, and the possible consequences of being understaffed and having employees whose morale is reduced by layoffs, does not seem to be factored into the analysis that leads to increasing stock prices as a result of layoffs.[10]

Cost-Benefit Analysis

Cost-benefit analysis is a utilitarian approach to evaluating proposed expenditures in business or in government. The basic concept behind cost-benefit analysis is that spending money, time and effort might be justified by the results to be achieved, but it also might not. Since this sort of analysis is future-oriented, it will necessarily be less precise than analysis of expenditures that have already been made and results that have already been achieved. As we will see in the chapter on ethical analysis of financial reporting, it is somewhere between very difficult and impossible to give a fully accurate financial picture of a company or a division even using skilled accountants and analysts and the best tools available. If this is true of events already past, the degree of accuracy obtainable about the future is obviously even less.

Cost-benefit analysis conceptually underlies the whole process of budgeting. It does not make good business sense to plan to spend money, under either expense or capital budgets, that will not yield a benefit at least equal to the expenditure. The budget process is often conducted with a good deal of politics involved and, as the saying goes, the devil is in the details. However, when money could be spent in one of several ways, but not all of them, then aiming to get the biggest bang for the buck is not really different than aiming to create the greatest good for the greatest number, at least in principle.

While cost-benefit analysis is utilitarian in spirit, it is more narrow in scope. Whether in business or in government, the most common benefit weighed against costs is financial in nature. If a project or an addition to staff will either generate enough revenues or reduce enough future financial cost, then it is approved. The principal metric used in cost-benefit analysis is efficiency—will the expenditure in question generate the most output with the least input? While it might legitimately do so, cost-benefit analysis does not always take into account impacts beyond expenses and revenues. To give one example frequently raised in business ethics textbooks, a cost-benefit analysis of a plant closing in a small town might not address the impact on the town's unemployment rate or tax base, while a utilitarian analysis would also factor in these issues

Cost-benefit analysis, by its nature, stresses quantifiable factors. However, projects or expenditures are sometimes approved on the basis of necessity rather than amount of dollar benefits. One relatively small hospital group with which I am familiar recently decided to spend tens of millions of dollars integrating its more than twenty software systems so that medical and financial information would be available to everyone involved with a patient from pre-admission medical work-ups to post-discharge follow-ups. The executives of the hospital group felt that they simply could not continue to provide adequate service without such systems integration. The project was approved on the basis of necessity rather than of quantified savings or additional revenue and profits. It appears that, in deciding to spend this amount of money on systems integration, they were aiming in a broad sense to achieve the greatest good for the greatest number.

Utilitarian analysis certainly takes costs into account. Spending money that could be spent in other ways does not, by itself, create happiness or good for anyone except the recipients of the money. The spending is justified only if the money, time or other resources spent create more good or happiness than they amount to in cost. By its focus on impacts, and its method of identifying and justifying them, utilitarianism provides a way for managers both to be aware of the impacts of their actions and to think through the moral issues involved in a course of action.

It is good to remember that acts that are morally right can also be right in other senses. For instance, if we consider that the goal of for-profit companies is to make a profit (by selling airplane rides, or audit services, or blue jeans), then acts that lead to or increase profits are strategically right for these companies and their managers. If the acts are also moral (in the present case, if they lead to the greatest good for the greatest number), then strategy and morality coincide. If the acts are immoral (for instance, lying in financial reports), they may lead to greater profit and hence appear strategically correct, but they are not morally right. We will see in the chapter on financial reporting that lying on financial reports does not create the greatest good for the greatest number.

Two Important Criticisms

Two major criticisms have been made of utilitarianism as a way of viewing morality. The first is that it is simply impractical. For most decisions that a manager makes, there is not time to do any sort of serious analysis of the possible impacts. Some managerial decisions have very little impact beyond the immediate and obvious. Others are simply decisions to continue a decision process. Major decisions are often preceded by numerous partial decisions, small steps, decisions to investigate further, and so on. In fact, by the time a major decision is made, these smaller partial decisions may have shaped the process in such a way that there is only one viable option left, and what appears to be the final decision is actually anticlimactic.[11]

Difficulty of Implementation

If a major decision point is clearly present, the direct and indirect impacts are likely to be such that it is difficult or impossible to quantify them even to a reasonable degree of approximation. The time to conduct such an analysis may not be available. Decision processes, particularly in large organizations, often have timetables that are not determined by key participants or final decision-makers. An issue not clearly dealt with by most utilitarians is whether to simply count those affected positively and negatively or to also assign weights to the degree of happiness or unhappiness that various individuals will experience as a result of the decision. Obviously this is an important point in determining the morality of an action by means of a utilitarian analysis. If no weight is given to degrees of happiness or unhappiness, the analysis clearly ignores an important element of the decision and its consequences. An individual who will suffer a momentary bit of unease counts as much as one who will experience deep and lasting anguish. Yet, if weights are to be assigned to varying degrees of happiness and unhappiness, an almost overwhelming complexity is added to an already difficult calculation.

Jeremy Bentham, the earlier of the two major utilitarian philosophers, proposed a detailed method for calculating the greatest good for the greatest number. He did assign degrees of importance to various forms of happiness and to the likelihood that an act would produce these forms. His so-called felicific calculus, or method for determining degrees of happiness, is quite complex. As he presents this calculus in the *Introduction to the Principles of Morals and Legislation*, he identifies fourteen kinds of simple pleasures, seven kinds of simple pains and seven circumstances affecting the value of a pain or pleasure considered by itself.[12] Bentham did indicate in the same work that it is not necessary to perform a full calculation before each action. He says that, once a person becomes used to the method of calculation, he will do it almost automatically and without long formal process, except perhaps for the occasional major decision with clear widespread impacts.

Writing some fifty years later, John Stuart Mill, the second major utilitarian philosopher, had the advantage of hindsight. Bentham's work had been taken seriously and among the most serious criticisms leveled against it was the lack of practicality. Mill suggests another way of determining which of two pleasures or pains is greater. His approach is to ask those who have experienced both of the pleasures or pains under consideration and to accept their opinion on the ranking of the pleasures or pains in question.[13] This approach is experience-based and does not depend on theorizing. It is also open to the charge of impracticality, since few decisions are worth the effort or can be postponed until the opinions of several experienced persons can be gathered.

All of this may make it seem that utilitarianism is a hopelessly impractical approach to ethics. Yet, in spite of the difficulties of doing a complete analysis, the emphasis of utilitarianism on the consequences of acts is an important element in thinking about managerial morality. If those who packaged and repackaged subprime mortgages had considered who would benefit and who would suffer as a result of their actions, it would have been clear quite quickly that many investors, lenders, business partners and others would be hurt with very few people deriving benefits. Even a very rough utilitarian analysis is sometimes sufficient to make clear which course of action is ethical and which is not.

Some Conclusions Seem Unethical

Besides the difficulty of accurately calculating the sums of happiness and unhappiness that an act might produce, the second major objection to utilitarianism in practice is that it sometimes declares acts to be moral that would not be approved as moral by the other two approaches to ethical reasoning, or by most people's basic sense of right and wrong. For instance, if I start a business, hire nine other people, and the ten of us are doing quite well, what sort of response can I morally make if one of my employees leaves and starts a competing business? Can I hire someone to kill my former employee? Burn down their place of business? Tell lies about them and their product to keep my customers from switching to them? Set my prices below theirs, even if I temporarily lose money, in order to drive them out of business and then raise my prices?

We will see in the next two chapters that neither rights and duties nor fairness and justice condones killing business opponents or burning down their place of business. These actions would also violate almost everyone's basic sense of right and wrong.[14] Yet, if my employees and I would all benefit from the elimination of competition from my former employee, and only the former employee (and perhaps his family) would suffer, at least a surface reading of utilitarianism indicates that the greater good for the greater number would come about as a result of murder or arson. There are ways to modify utilitarianism to deal with this kind of problem. The most obvious is to assign weights to the good and harm caused by an action, as well as simply counting those affected. We saw above that this was proposed by Bentham and has been criticized as creating a system which is practically impossible to use. However, we also suggested above that even a very crude calculation using rankings of the good and harm created might suffice to provide a clear answer.

Another way to deal with this problem is to switch from act utilitarianism, which judges the morality of individual acts, to rule utilitarianism, which judges the morality of following a rule by whether the rule results in the greatest good for the greatest number. One of the issues that we will see again and again in the applied chapters of this book is that individual actions create patterns. For instance, a manager who fills ten openings in a row within his department by internal promotion has in fact created a pattern of excluding outside candidates, perhaps not from consideration but indeed from being hired. Which of the ten individual hiring/promotion decisions created this pattern? No one of them, but all of them. A manager who overhears one racist or sexist remark from one of her employees to another and takes no action has not created or allowed a pattern of discrimination. However, if she overhears ten such remarks within a month and takes no action, there is a pattern of at least tolerating discrimination. Was it the second remark overheard without reaction that created the pattern? The fifth? No one by itself created a pattern, but all of them, taken together, did.

Utilitarianism, at least indirectly, takes this issue of individual actions and patterns into account when analyzing managerial decisions. Philosophers elaborating on the utilitarianism of Bentham and Mill have identified two ways of viewing the subject: act utilitarianism and rule utilitarianism.[15] Act utilitarianism asks the basic question of the greatest good for the greatest number about the results of an individual act. This approach has as one of its major drawbacks the fact that it does not deal well, if at all, with the problem of patterns of behavior because it concentrates its analysis only on a single act. Rule utilitarianism, in contrast, asks what the results would be in terms of the greatest good for the greatest number if a given rule were followed. By doing so, this approach is able to deal with the problem of patterns of behavior. However, it adds a major level of abstraction by introducing a generalized rule that may or may not cover an individual act, and may cover some acts more completely or partially than others.

This view is consistent with Bentham's writings on utilitarianism. His major work, referred to above, is titled *Introduction to the Principles of Morals and Legislation*. Bentham was very interested in reform of England's legal system. His view was that morality and law should be very closely joined together. A law should be passed or kept on the books only if it created the greatest good for the greatest number. John Stuart Mill wrote a famous essay, *On Liberty*.[16] He saw liberty as the most basic good and explained that all law is bad in that it constrains liberty. However, because some selfish individuals would interfere with the liberty of their fellow citizens, some laws are necessary to prevent them from doing so or to punish them and provide retribution when they have done so. The test of a good law is simply the utilitarian principle: does it provide the greatest good for the greatest number? If it does, it should be passed or maintained. If it does not, it should be amended or abolished.[17]

If we take this view one step further, and say that such an approach should also be applied to rules of behavior that are not laws, we arrive at something very much like rule utilitarianism. This approach to determining morality is almost identical, in one respect, to that taken by Immanuel Kant, the most famous proponent of a duty-based approach to morality. As we will see in the next chapter, Kant bases his view of morality on asking whether an individual act complies with a rule that could be made universal. There is a major philosophical difference, though, in how we arrive at this point. Kant starts from the premise that acts are moral if they comply with our intrinsic duties, and without regard to their consequences. Bentham and Mill start from the premise that acts are moral if they produce the greatest good for the greatest number of people, without regard to their intrinsic rightness or wrongness.

It may well appear to the practical manager that we have now reached such a point of useless abstraction that we will soon be discussing how many angels can dance on the head of a pin. However, the way we arrive at a basic approach to ethics matters a lot. If you as an individual feel that results are what matter (and it is hard to be an effective manager without such a view), then you may find talk of intrinsic duties to be somewhere between irrelevant and repulsive. If, on the other hand, you as an individual feel that an excessive orientation toward results brought us Enron, WorldCom and an irrational emphasis on "making the quarterly numbers," then considerations of intrinsic duty may have a good deal of appeal.

Any theoretical basis for morality is not going to affect the actions of individuals unless it is something with which they are at least somewhat comfortable. The sort of discussion being conducted here of how we reach rules of conduct is going to be very important in later chapters when we discuss whether and when it is good to require drug tests of employees, or to indulge in creative accounting, or to lay off "excess" workers. We will talk then of patterns of behavior and their results, and of the rights of employees, and of the duties of managers. Such talk will not have much meaning unless we have paid serious attention to the bases of moral and immoral decisions, and how to tell them apart.

An Ethic Based on Prediction

The two major criticisms of utilitarianism discussed above have been widely proposed and discussed. There are ways to at least lessen its alleged impracticality, and by focusing on rules instead of individual acts and on the quality as well as the mere fact of pleasures and pains, the problem of the tyranny of the majority (let's kill him) can be eased. There is, it seems to me, a third objection that can be raised against utilitarianism, and it is one that might be of particular concern to managers. If the morality of an act (or a rule) is determined by its impacts in the future on persons and groups known and unknown, the basis for deciding morality seems rather frail. Both the physicist Neils Bohr and the baseball manager Yogi Berra are reputed to have said, "predicting is always difficult, especially about the future." If a manager, who must make a lot of decisions and very seldom has full information on which to base them, wants to be ethical and tries to be ethical, but may or may not succeed in being ethical because she lacks the ability to see the future, have we really provided her with any help at all?

The central point of utilitarianism as an approach to ethics is the fact that actions have consequences. Looking forward to an action being contemplated, this approach requires that the manager who wants to be ethical in his actions think through the impacts or consequences of that action. Since the manager cannot see the future with certainty, there is room for two individuals each doing the best job they can to disagree about a utilitarian analysis. An individual can also be honestly mistaken in his analysis of impacts—intending to create the greatest good for the greatest number, and choosing one action rather than another for precisely this reason, he might end up being wrong and doing more harm than good. A manager, according to this view, might be immoral or unethical by failing to do an analysis of the impacts of a projected action. He might also be immoral by failing to do an honest or a competent analysis. But if he does analyze the impacts of his actions to the best of his ability and subsequently proves wrong, he cannot really be held to have failed morally.

While this point is often missed in explanations of utilitarianism, it is an important one. It might be more accurate to amend the definition given at the beginning of this chapter to the following: according to utilitarianism, an act is moral if its intended consequences following careful analysis create the greatest good or happiness for the greatest number of people. The message for the manager wishing to be moral, then, is that accountability matters. You need to think in advance about consequences, immediate and remote, of your actions and to balance the good that they might do with the harm that they might create.

Thinking about consequences, immediate and remote, coincides nicely with an approach to strategic management known as stakeholder theory that was mentioned briefly in the previous chapter. First elaborated by Richard Freeman in 1984,[18] this theory is intended as a balance to the view that the sole proper concern of managers is to maximize the wealth of the owners (stockholders) of the corporation for which they work. The stakeholder view asserts that there are a number of groups of people that either affect or are affected by a company, and that it is the responsibility of managers to consider and balance the interests of these stakeholder groups.

To take one example, as we will see in the chapter on financial reporting, there are different groups that rely in various ways on the public financial reports of corporations. These groups include current and potential stockholders, creditors, regulators, taxing agencies of various governments, and others. Each group is affected by the financial reports of the company and makes important decisions based at least in part on these financial reports. Most of these groups can and sometimes do have a major impact on the success or failure of the company. Therefore, managers who do not take these various stakeholder groups into account when making decisions (in this case, when preparing financial reports) are ignoring a part of reality that should not be ignored. Since it is usually not possible to please all of these groups simultaneously (taxing agencies want more tax revenue, employees want higher wages, stockholders want more profits), deciding on the greatest good for the greatest number is one way to approach the demands placed on managers who consider the stakeholder view. In this sense, the stakeholder view is at least compatible with utilitarianism.

A manager who makes no decisions does not earn her salary. Decision-making is that basic to the work of the manager. It is not her only task, but it is absolutely, fundamentally one of her tasks. Whether she manages accountants, sales clerks, nuclear physicists or bus drivers, she must make decisions to do her job as manager. So, a book on managerial ethics, such as this one, cannot escape the serious consideration of managerial decision-making. Is the premise that you may or may not have been ethical in your decision-making—wait and see—the best that utilitarianism can offer?

Once upon a time, there was a program for evaluating and compensating managers known as Management by Objectives. The program has largely gone away; the idea and the practice are still very much alive.[19] The basic idea was as follows. At the beginning of some period (usually a calendar year), the manager and her boss would sit down together and discuss what the manager could contribute in the following period to the progress of the organization. If she managed the mailroom, the objectives might involve timeliness of mail handling, cost of operation of the mailroom, success in supporting the new business brought in by the sales goal of 15 percent more customers and personal growth in the manager's business knowledge. These might all be agreed to be worthy goals, and objectives that would help the boss help the company with its overall objectives. The goals would then be specified and, to the extent possible, quantified. They would be put in writing.

A year later, the manager and her boss would sit down for a performance evaluation or appraisal. The agreed-upon goals would be brought out and discussed. If the manager met or exceeded her goals, she would be praised and rated highly and, at least in a good year, properly compensated for her fine performance. The interesting question is what happened if she did not meet or exceed one or more of her goals. She would undoubtedly plead unforeseeable circumstances, or inadequate resources, or failure to cooperate by other managers whose input was essential to her goals, or bad karma, or almost anything except personal failure. If the discussion remained rational (not always the case), the manager might successfully plead that, in light of unpredicted and unpredictable circumstances, her performance had been heroic. She might argue that, but for her outstanding managerial efforts, the results would have been even worse, as indeed they were for the company's three main competitors.

Her boss might argue that, but for her lack of foresight in making predictions, the manager would have met and, indeed, exceeded her goals. However, this is a tricky argument for the boss to make, especially if he signed off on the objectives a year ago. The boss might argue that the objectives were sound, but the manager's decisions through the year as to how to meet the objectives were a wee bit shaky (or perhaps, spectacularly dumb). If the boss was not asked to approve these interim decisions, he can argue more firmly as to their inadequacy.

There are several things to note here. The stakes are relatively high. The manager may receive a lower raise, or no raise, or a negative performance appraisal that not only offends her personally but remains permanently in her personnel file. The boss may have a difficult interview with his boss because the manager's failure to achieve objectives has now become the boss's failure to achieve objectives. The basis for judgment is predictions. As it turns out, the future was indeed difficult to predict. The present argument turns on that very point. Things change over the course of a year—any year. If the manager and the boss are being even semi-rational, they will both acknowledge this. The key issue is whether the changes could or should have been foreseen, and what reaction was appropriate once they came into evidence.

In this scenario, performance is being evaluated not on the basis of morality, but on the basis of practical achievement or non-achievement of stated objectives. The criterion of evaluation is not morality but efficiency, or economic soundness, or some other roughly quantifiable basis. However, we can note several similarities to our earlier problem with basing moral decisions on future events. The manager's job includes prediction of the future. When she and her boss sit down to set the next year's objectives, it is assumed that, whatever happens next year, it will not be an exact repeat of this year. History does not repeat itself in this way. It is also assumed that everything will not be different. Some of the same products or services will be sold to some of the same customers using some of the same resources to deliver the goods. The basis for next year's goal-setting is rational analysis, not poetry or science fiction or astrology.

Managers take it for granted that it is both possible and useful to think about the future using the past as a guideline. Similar thinking can be used for the predictions necessary to make moral judgments using utilitarian principles. It is reasonable to assume that employees laid off from their jobs will find this disrupting to their lives. Unless there are special circumstances, it is reasonable to assume that they will see the layoff as having a negative impact on them or, in our present terms, as creating unhappiness rather than happiness. It is possible that one of these employees who has been deeply dissatisfied with his job may find the layoff to be the stimulus to find a new and more suitable job, thus seeing the end result as producing more good than harm for him. In spite of this possibility, it is reasonable for a manager trying to sort out the morality of layoffs to predict that, for the employees involved, the action will create more unhappiness than happiness.

Management by Objectives is not as widely popular a program as it once was, but the principles embodied in it continue to be used in management planning. Budgets, whether expense, capital or sales, are standard tools. In a real sense, a budget is a means of setting and monitoring objectives and progress toward them. Since managers are routinely expected to predict the future economic impacts of their decisions, it seems reasonable to ask that they also predict the future moral impacts. Thus the objection to utilitarianism that it makes morality depend on results in an uncertain future can be dealt with. Any system of ethics, including the ones we will examine in the next two chapters, is useful only if it helps to analyze the future impacts of proposed actions. A system that could only analyze the results already achieved of actions already taken might provide an interesting historical perspective, but could not really guide the decision-making that is an essential part of a manager's job.

Usefulness of Utilitarianism

Utilitarianism is one of three perspectives on morality that we consider at length in this book. It is not an easy system to use, especially for a time-constrained manager who does not have the luxury of reading great books and thinking great thoughts. It does have a tendency, at least in some of its forms, to find morally acceptable acts that most of us would instinctively agree are morally repugnant. If it were the only way to assess the moral validity of our proposed actions, it would leave us in deep trouble some of the time.

Given all of that, this approach to morality does something valuable and provides insights that might not otherwise be seen. With its focus on the results of our actions, it makes us examine the likely impacts of our choices, including those we might prefer not to think about. Earlier in the chapter, the analogy was used of a swimmer who can face the waves and deal with them, or face away from them and be tossed by them. Utilitarianism, with all its imperfections, requires us to face the waves. To use an example we have been citing, consider the decision to implement layoffs. If we confine the analysis to financial results, layoffs often look desirable. After all, fewer employees means less labor cost, and less cost usually means more profit. Utilitarianism does not automatically bar layoffs, but it makes us consider that, among the results of our managerial decision to reduce staff, one certain consequence is unhappiness on the part of those laid off. As we will see in a later chapter, this may be an acceptable price to pay for the continued employment of the rest of our employees. Nonetheless, the consequence is real, and utilitarianism requires us to consider it as one element in our decision-making.

It is not always moral to make people happy or immoral to make them unhappy. If we reduced prices by 50 percent across the board and raised wages by a similar amount, we could create happy customers and happy workers, at least for a short while. Why not do so? We would almost certainly create a bankrupt company, with fewer (or no) workers, very unhappy investors and lenders, and longer range happiness would be pretty much limited to bankruptcy attorneys. Most managers instinctively know this, so we do not see many companies simultaneously slashing prices and inflating wages.

Sometimes industries, especially if they have strong labor unions, get caught up in the situation where they take actions almost certain to produce long-term unhappiness for many individuals. Tens of thousands of retired American auto workers now receive health insurance and pension benefits that create enormous burdens for the companies paying them, and for their current workers, investors, lenders and customers. Even though they were threatened with very costly strikes at the time these retiree benefits were granted and augmented, it might be that the greatest good for the greatest number in the long run would have been achieved if executives had denied or limited these benefits. It was undoubtedly easier for managers to grant these benefits because of the practice of pattern bargaining, by which benefits gained by the union at one company were automatically granted by their competitors in the same industry. Similar issues exist as local and state governments strain to fund retirement benefits for public employees. This is another example of the importance of patterns of decisions, as well as individual decisions.

In the second chapter, we said that ethics has to do with social interactions. We have seen that the nature of managerial work requires such interactions, no matter what industry the manager works in or at what level the manager is situated. One of the more interesting issues in organizational theory is the question of what it means to say that an organization decided something or did something. Ultimately, organization decisions are human decisions. Managers, alone or in groups, decide how an organization will acquire and use resources, what it will sell, to whom it will sell it and how all of this business will be conducted. These decisions have consequences. Utilitarianism helps managers to think through the ethical consequences of their decisions. This is no small contribution.

five

Rights and Duties

The second of the three major approaches to ethics that we consider in this book is that of rights and duties. This title refers to several somewhat different ethical views, and the works of many philosophers can be included under this title. Broadly speaking, the rights and duties approach focuses on doing things that are right in themselves, rather than right because of their consequences. This approach says that the moral act is the act which recognizes the rights of others and the duties that those rights impose on the actor.

Americans are perhaps the most rights-oriented people in history. We speak of having a right to free speech, a right to public education, a right to our place in line and a right to health care. We often do not give much thought to these rights, but simply proclaim them. A right is worthless if no one has a corresponding duty. My right to free speech imposes a duty not to censor my comments or writings. My right to privacy imposes a duty on others to leave me alone. If I have a right to health care, someone or some organization must have a duty to provide it, or else my right is worthless. It is a commonplace of contemporary culture in many countries that people are far more conscious of and insistent on their rights than they are on their duties.

Definition of Rights and Duties

While rights are often proclaimed, and duties sometimes acknowledged, there is often a lack of clarity in the discussion of rights and duties once it proceeds beyond proclamation and acknowledgement. Just what are rights and duties? One common approach divides rights into claims and privileges.

A worker who starts a job with a company at an agreed-upon salary has a right to be paid that salary as long as she is performing the job adequately and the agreement is not changed. That right is a claim on the employer to pay the specified salary to the worker. The same worker has a right to walk on a public sidewalk on her way to a nearby restaurant for lunch, but it is difficult to define this right as a claim against someone or some organization. It makes more intuitive sense to think of this right as a privilege, but it can be seen as a claim against government to honor her freedom to public access.

Philosophical discussion of rights frequently involves discussion of liberty. Isaiah Berlin, in a very famous essay on "Two concepts of liberty," defines what he calls positive and negative freedom or liberty. He says that the positive sense of liberty "...is involved in the answer to the question 'What or who is the source of control or interference that can determine someone to do, or be, this rather than that?'" He says that the negative sense of liberty "...is involved in the answer to the question 'What is the area within which the subject—a person or group of persons—is or should be left to do or be what he is able to do or be, without interference by other persons?'"[1] Positive liberty might be viewed as corresponding to claim rights, and negative liberty to privilege rights.

Rights can also be defined using logic to identify situations where one person or group has a claim on another. This approach is almost mathematical in nature and makes extensive use of definitions that include such terms as "if and only if..." This approach lends itself more to legal than to ethical analysis. It appears to follow the goal of clear thinking, which is characteristic of philosophy, but its main goal is precise determination of who has rights rather than definition of what they are.[2]

Duties are sometimes defined simply as the other side of rights. This approach makes sense especially with claim rights. If I have a right to be paid for my work, my employer has a duty to pay me. Somewhat more generally if I have a right to be considered as a job applicant without regard to my race, any employer to whom I apply for a job has a duty to consider me without regard to my race. More generally still, if I have a right to walk on a public sidewalk, government in particular and people in general have a duty to let me walk there unimpeded.

Some philosophers, such as Immanuel Kant, begin from duties and reason their way to rights. Kant emphasizes the duty to be consistent in our ethical rules and to treat all humans with proper respect. We discuss Kant's views in more detail later in this chapter. Some natural rights philosophers put at least as much emphasis on duties as on rights. This involves a difference in emphasis, but such reasoning often ends up with the same ethical conclusion as an approach that emphasizes rights and views duties as the logical consequence of someone having a right.

It is generally agreed that groups as well as individuals can have both rights and duties. As we will see below, some rights are granted by governments to their citizens. Each individual citizen of the United States has a right to free assembly, but an assembly by its nature involves a group. Companies, which are legal persons, have both rights and duties as a group of employees. One of the difficult questions in analyzing rights and duties is the extent to which groups rather than individuals have rights and duties. We will discuss this issue further in the second part of the book when we take up particular issues of discrimination.

Sources of Rights and Duties

There are four basic sources of rights. Some rights we have as humans, without regard to position or citizenship, or wealth or skill. Some rights we have by law. Some rights accrue to us by reason of our position. Finally, some rights have their source in contracts. Rights from each of these sources imply duties. Depending on the source of the rights, the corresponding duties fall upon individuals or groups that might be in daily contact with us, or might be quite remote from us. In order to understand how rights and duties can serve as a basis for ethical judgment, we will now consider each of the four sources of rights.

Human Rights

Human rights is a term that is used very loosely.[3] The concept has roots extending back hundreds of years and is built into the American legal system as a foundation. The Declaration of Independence says that, "We hold these truths to be self-evident, that all men are created equal, that they are endowed by their Creator with certain unalienable rights, that among these are life, liberty and the pursuit of happiness."[4] Almost 100 years later, at a battlefield in Gettysburg, Pennsylvania, Abraham Lincoln said, "Four score and seven years ago, our fathers brought forth on this continent a new nation, conceived in liberty and dedicated to the proposition that all men are created equal."[5] One hundred years later, in a historic speech to a quarter million of his fellow citizens gathered before the Lincoln Memorial, Martin Luther King said:

> When the architects of our republic wrote the magnificent words of the Constitution and the Declaration of Independence, they were signing a promissory note to which every American was to fall heir. This note was a promise that all men would be guaranteed the inalienable rights of life, liberty, and the pursuit of happiness.[6]

Another approach to defining rights comes from the theory of natural law. According to this view, an individual who reasons correctly about the nature of humans and their relation to each other and to the rest of the world will identify and recognize rights that all humans have, and the duties that correspond to those rights. This approach refers to the natural law in the sense that all humans have a special nature that sets them apart from other living things and from inanimate objects.[7] For instance, humans, because of their ability to reason, have a right to think and to speak freely and should not be owned as slaves.

What are these natural or inalienable rights, and are they American or are they human? The most basic right that a person can have is the right to life. In this context, we are not using the phrase as code for an anti-abortion position, but rather we are talking of the right not to be randomly killed. As far as I am aware, no society has ever condoned random killing—the taking of another's life for no reason at all. If someone said to us, "I hope Steve feels better tomorrow—this morning he woke up grumpy and killed the first three people he met," we would not accept this as a fact of life like the weather. If Steve killed even one person just because he was grumpy, we would find him and incarcerate him.

Different societies and cultures have different concepts of what makes a serious enough reason to take another person's life. Capital punishment is hotly debated in the United States and is abhorred in some parts of the world, but underlying the debate is the question of whether the state can take a person's life because of any crime they have committed, no matter how serious.[8] Through most of history, most people have felt that it was moral for combatants in war to take the lives of enemy combatants. There has been considerably more debate about whether it is moral to take the lives of civilians on the other side in a war. Self-defense is generally considered to be a valid reason to take an attacker's life.

Because ethical systems, religions and legal systems all treat many of the same values, it should not be surprising that all major religions have some form of "thou shalt not kill" as part of their commandments or behavioral codes.[9] Similarly, all of the major legal systems proscribe murder and define the illegal taking of human life, along with its prescribed penalties. Using induction, the method of reasoning that proceeds from specific examples to form general rules, it seems clear that the right to life is not based simply on societal norms, or legal systems, or religious belief, but is fundamental to human value systems and has been throughout known history.[10]

The next human right is called by various names and is sometimes identified as several different rights. We will simply call it the right to dignity. This encompasses the right to some freedoms, to truth-telling and to privacy. Various arguments can be made for why all humans have the rights included under dignity. However, as K. Anthony Appiah has stated:

We do not need to agree that we are all created in the image of God, or that we have natural rights that flow from our human essence, to agree that we do not want to be tortured by government officials, that we do not want our lives, families, and property forfeited.[11]

A number of philosophers have noted that human rights can be grounded in several different theories and that it is a sign of the strength of the argument for human rights that different approaches lead to the same conclusions.[12]

While it may seem strange at first glance, a very strong case can be made for including truth-telling as part of the right to dignity.[13] There are two ways to establish such a right. One, using the deductive approach, is to consider the fact that ongoing significant interaction between humans is impossible if there is no distinction made between lying and truth-telling. There are certainly instances where lying is expected—consider the rituals of early claims and demands in labor-management negotiations—but if lying is as likely as truth-telling, discourse breaks down very quickly. We do not often think about this, but in normal human discourse the default setting is truth-telling. Otherwise, "are you lying to me?" would be a meaningless question, since the answer would have an equal chance of being the truth or another lie.

The second way to establish a human right to truth-telling is to consider that religious, legal and moral systems all deal with this issue as an important one, and all start from the basis that it is wrong to lie. Using inductive reasoning, we can conclude from this large and diverse body of value systems that truth-telling is a central value. No religious, legal or ethical system starts from the premise that lying is neutral or positive. Most systems provide at least some circumstances when lying might be acceptable (although some are absolute in their prohibition), but none treats lying as a valid starting point and then asks when it is acceptable to tell the truth.

The human right to dignity also includes protection against such things as slavery and torture, and some right to privacy. The frequent appearance throughout history of both slavery and torture, and various violations by many societies of even rudimentary individual privacy, make the argument here more difficult. While it is hard for contemporary citizens of the United States to imagine a satisfactory life without such a right, our previous method of establishing rights inductively by finding universal or near-universal examples does not work so well here. However, as noted above, the fact that some individuals find the basis for such rights in one theory and others in other theories does not weaken the argument for such rights.

Legal systems deal in various ways with the elements of the right to dignity. Just what the right consists of is a difficult question to which no generally agreed-upon answer has been found. Most philosophers agree that liberty is part of this concept.[14] The reason why such an issue matters is that rights that are fundamental to all humans will provide an important starting point in dealing with issues concerning multi-national business practices. It is one thing to establish that a given society or country disapproves of bribery or full-time work by twelve-year-olds. It is another to establish that a given practice violates fundamental human rights because these rights do not depend on the laws or even the customs of a given country or society.

There is almost certainly a human right to own property, although there is a small body of evidence to the contrary. Thomas Hobbes was an English philosopher who influenced many of the Founding Fathers of the United States. He maintains in his famous work *Leviathan*[15] that, without some arrangement to keep the strong from taking whatever they want from the weak, there would be a constant war of all against all, and life would be "solitary, poor, nasty, brutish, and short." Human history is full of examples of individuals and groups who were not satisfied with "their own" food, property, wives or slaves and took "someone else's" without permission or compensation. However, in those societies where the norm has been to simply answer in kind, life has typically degenerated to a point where Hobbes' description seems accurate.

Again, religious, legal and moral systems all deal with some variation of "thou shalt not steal." The exception referred to above is that some examples exist of groups that do not allow for individual ownership of any property. Economic communism maintains that society should operate on the basis of "from each according to his ability; to each according to his needs."[16] For the most part, countries under the political system of communism have modified this pure economic theory to varying degrees, but they have functioned, some for several generations, according to this basic principle. Needless to say, this principle does not easily co-exist with private property. Some religious groups, such as Catholic religious orders, have practiced a very pure form of economic communism for hundreds of years. Each member of the group takes a vow of poverty and all property is owned by the group rather than by any individual member. Various utopian groups have lived more or less without individual property in different countries at different times.

In spite of the exceptions cited above, the overwhelming majority of people throughout history have recognized some form of individual ownership of property. This is true at least in the sense that something (food, clothing, a hut or house) is mine or yours, but is not anyone's simply for the taking. Under varying conditions and to varying degrees, humans have been viewed as property and have come under property laws, but this is a complex issue not directly relevant to contemporary managers.[17] Again, religious, legal and moral systems all deal with some variant of "thou shalt not steal." Such prohibitions are meaningless if no one owns anything. This, then, is evidence that in most religions and societies through most of recorded history, there has been an acceptance of the notion that individuals own things.

Human rights, then, if carefully examined, are relatively few but very important. Of course, it is not necessary that all humans everywhere agree that something is a human right for it to be so. There is a tendency to widen the range of human rights when discussing this subject. It is important to remember that rights are practically useless without corresponding duties. Perhaps some people who are quite free in listing a wide range of human rights would be somewhat more cautious in this endeavor if they gave full consideration to the range of human duties that they are simultaneously positing.

Legal Rights

The second source of rights is legal rights. These are rights granted to citizens of a government unit by law.[18] They are enforceable through court systems. Some legal rights embody human rights; others do not. There is both a legal right and a human right to life, which manifests itself in a duty not to randomly kill people. We showed above why this is a human right. It is also a right in legal systems, although different legal systems have different definitions of random killing. There is a legal right to drive at the posted speed limit, but it scarcely qualifies as a human right. In contrast to human rights, which are the same everywhere, legal rights vary by place and time. As we will see in Chapter 9, companies in the United States have fewer legal restrictions on terminating employees than companies in many European countries.

Different jurisdictions can and do grant different legal rights, but the hierarchy of jurisdictions is made clear by legal systems. In the United States, the Federal Constitution spells out the areas in which federal laws take precedence. Generally speaking, areas not specifically reserved to the federal government are open for law-making by states and lower governments, such as counties and cities.[19] In some countries, there is a single state religion, and religious authorities also make and interpret the laws. The United States, more than many other countries, is very careful to recognize the separation of church and state. Perhaps this is because, from its founding, the United States has been a pluralistic society, accommodating individuals of many different beliefs and of no belief. The first ten amendments to the U.S. Constitution, generally known as the Bill of Rights, guarantee freedoms to American citizens that are greater than those provided under many other governments.

We may well ask where governments get the power to grant rights and impose duties. In a democracy, the standard answer is that governments derive their power from the people. Some individuals are elected by the voting citizens to represent them (the voters) in deciding what government shall do, and how it shall do it. If these elected representatives do not in fact represent the people at large in a satisfactory way, they can be voted out of office at the next scheduled election. In extreme cases, they can be removed before a scheduled election by impeachment or by recall. In a monarchy, government power resides in the monarch. He or she may hold that position by heredity or by force, but the literal meaning of democracy is rule by the people, while monarchy means rule by one. In a government of religious establishment, the leader or leaders derive their power from God.[20]

Social contract theory is a view in philosophy that explains government power by saying that it is as if all the citizens yield by contract some of their individual rights in order to obtain the benefits of social stability available only through a recognized government.[21] It fits best in discussing democratic governments. Thomas Hobbes, cited earlier, is one of the early proponents of this theory. It was his view that people contemplating life without government and foreseeing a war of all against all willingly cede some of their individual liberties in order to provide an organized check against man's baser impulses. John Locke was another English philosopher who held the social contract theory.[22] These two, along with several French philosophers, strongly influenced the founders of the American government and legal system.

According to social contract theory, each of us gives up some rights to government and in return gains some rights that we would not otherwise have. Again, rights are worthless without corresponding duties. Citizens who have agreed to give up some rights to strengthen others also take on some duties as part of the social contract. Just as others are obliged to respect my private property, and the state will enforce this right for me, so I must also respect the private property of others. If the state is to provide for common defense against aggressors, and I have a right to be defended, then I also have a duty to provide some share of the cost of providing such defense. We buy products or services from brokers, or dealers, or retailers. We buy common defense (and other common goods) through taxes and sometimes through serving in the government.

Obviously all citizens do not sign social contracts, individually or collectively. This view of social rights and duties is on an "as if" basis. It is sometimes referred to as a thought experiment. It does make a certain sense as an explanation of why government has rights, why individuals are designated or elected and have position rights as agents of government, and why government has duties to respect and protect the rights of its citizens. Distinguishing democracy as practiced in the United States from other forms of government, it is sometimes said that ours is a government of laws rather than of men. This means that individuals hold government power and enforce it under the constraint of law, and that a change in the individuals in power will not change the laws or rules of government.[23]

Do legal rights have a place in a discussion of morality? As we indicated in Chapter 3, there is a starting assumption in most moral systems that civil laws are to be obeyed. In other words, it is moral to be legal. While this assumption is not universally true, we will argue that it is unethical for a manager to violate the law and cause her company to face legal penalties. Thus legal rights can and do impose moral as well as legal obligations on companies and their managers and employees. Note that, because we have a government of laws, when we say that it is moral to follow the law, we are not saying that it is moral to follow the political leader.

Position Rights

A third source of rights is position. If he has probable cause to do so, a policeman has the right to stop a motorist, require him to get out of his car, make a physical search of his person, handcuff him and take him to jail. These are powerful rights. An accounts payable clerk may have authorization to spend a company's money without further approval up to $1,000. The chief financial officer may have similar authority up to $100,000. A manager has the right to hire one applicant while denying other applicants the job. She has the duty by her position as manager to do this fairly. She also has the position right to terminate an employee for unsatisfactory performance, as well as the duty to do so. We will explore these issues further in the second half of the book.

Again, there is some overlap between classes of rights. The policeman has his authority by law as well as by position, but there is no law authorizing chief financial officers or accounts payable clerks to disburse certain amounts of company funds.[24] Rights by position are just that: they accrue to holders of certain positions while they are in those positions. A former police officer does not have arresting authority, nor does a former chief financial officer any longer have company disbursement authority. We hope that the holders of positions granting rights have the knowledge and skills to exercise the rights appropriately, but knowledge and skill by themselves do not carry these rights.

Positions carry duties as well as rights. Financial advisors have a fiduciary duty to their clients. Employees have a duty to carry out the responsibilities of their job. Government officials have a duty to uphold the Constitution. Managers have a number of duties. We will explore some of these duties in detail in the chapters comprising the second half of this book. One individual can have multiple duties because of the different roles that he plays in life. He can have spousal and parental duties at home, managerial duties at work, fiduciary duties as treasurer of his church and coaching duties as a Little League baseball coach.

According to the rights and duties approach to ethics, an individual's actions will be moral if he recognizes the rights of others and observes the duties imposed on him by those rights. Everyone has a duty not to randomly kill other people. Not everyone has a duty to prepare accounting reports in accordance with Generally Accepted Accounting Principles, or to show up thirty minutes early and bring the bats and balls for a youth baseball game. However, some individuals do have these duties and, under this view of ethics, they are morally obliged to carry them out. By becoming a manager, one takes on position rights and duties, and ethics for managers must take this fact into account.

Contract Rights

The fourth and final source of rights is by contract. My wife has no right, as a human, by law or by her position, to collect $100,000 from Metropolitan Life Insurance Company. Correspondingly, the company has no duty to pay her this amount (or any amount) of money. However, if I purchase a life insurance policy from Metropolitan Life, they will agree to pay my designated beneficiary (in this case, my wife) a given amount of money if I die while the policy is in force. The contract is what establishes the right and the duty. It is a legally enforceable contract, but this is not a right of citizenship or a legal right in the sense discussed above.

Contracts are agreements between two or more parties. The agreement of both parties to the contract initiates rights and duties spelled out in the contract, and they will remain in force as long as the contract is valid. This description of how contracts work is vastly simplified, but it is not false. Contract law is extensive and well developed, and contains precedents for an extremely wide variety of contracting situations and disputes.[25] Nonetheless, the basic idea of contracts is simple enough. It is important for the rights and duties view of ethics because contracts create both rights and duties where none existed before, and would not exist except for the contract. In the chapter on ethics and employment, we will see that some people work under explicit employment contracts. The question of whether others work under an implicit employment contract, and what rights and duties such an implicit contract might impose, is a particularly troublesome one.

Contracts obviously play an important role in managerial ethics. Labor-management contracts spell out the terms and conditions of employment for employees who are covered under a collective bargaining agreement. Such contracts typically oblige managers to pay certain wages and benefits, provide certain working conditions and refrain from firing employees except under specified circumstances. Contracts may also affect relations with customers, suppliers and other company stakeholders.

We have now seen four sources of rights and their corresponding duties. Before we leave this subject, some general observations are in order. Perhaps the most fundamental is that no right is absolute. The most general or universal rights are human rights because they are not dependent on a given legal system, position or contract. The most basic of human rights is the right to life. However, there are times when even this right does not prevail against all other considerations. If you are actively and immediately trying to kill someone else, a policeman is morally justified in taking your life to prevent you from committing murder. A soldier in battle may not leave the field because he fears for his life. Since this most basic of all rights can sometimes be over-ridden by other considerations, it stands to reason that other rights also have less than absolute strength. Clearly, if the most basic of all rights can be out-weighed by other considerations, lesser rights are also subject to prioritizing. Finally, since some rights are granted by law and others have other sources, it is clear that law and ethics are not identical.

Kant's Duty-Based Approach

Immanuel Kant is the philosopher most often associated with the rights and duties approach to morality. He wrote a number of widely cited works, some of which are difficult to read and some of which are nearly impossible. A flavor of his approach can be obtained by reviewing some of his titles. Among his most noted works are the *Critique of Pure Reason*,[26] *Critique of Practical Reason*[27] and *Groundwork of the Metaphysics of Morals*.[28] While his writings are difficult, his influence on subsequent philosophers has been great.

Kant emphasizes duties rather than rights. He identifies two kinds of rules (he calls them "imperatives"), hypothetical and categorical. Hypothetical imperatives are conditional. If you want to be a good flute player, then you ought to practice every day. The categorical imperative is not conditioned: it applies always and everywhere, according to Kant. He phrases this categorical imperative in three different ways:

1. Act only according to that maxim whereby you can at the same time will that it should become a universal law.[29]
2. Act in such a way that you always treat humanity, whether in your own person or in the person of any other, always at the same time as an end, and never as a means.[30]
3. Therefore, every rational being must so act as if he were through his maxim always a legislating member in the universal kingdom of ends.[31]

The first phrasing is perhaps the easiest to understand. Kant gives the example of a man who borrows money, but then has difficulty coming up with enough to pay it back. The question Kant poses is whether this individual can morally fail or refuse to repay the borrowed money. He explains that a universal rule that says "repay loans only if it is convenient" could not work because no one would lend money under such circumstances. The same sort of analysis would apply to a rule that said "lie when it is inconvenient or embarrassing to tell the truth." The categorical imperative imposes duties on everyone, all the time.

Kant is more rigid in his interpretation of universal duties than most other philosophers. If we consider the different kinds of rights enumerated above, we will see that the universal duty required by the categorical imperative fits best with human rights because they are not dependent on anything else to be applicable. One could form a universal rule to obey the tax laws of the countries where your business is conducted, but this already introduces a certain degree of contingency. Even here, though, Kant's approach seems to many to be too rigid.

Suppose that I am home at night reading a novel and my next-door neighbor knocks frantically on my door. When I open the door, she has terror in her eyes and asks me to hide her because her husband is trying to kill her. I tell her to hurry upstairs and go in the room to the right. One minute later, her husband pounds on my door. When I open it, he asks me where his wife is because he wants to kill her. Is the moral answer "upstairs to the right"? Most people would say not. This brings us back to the point made earlier, that no right is absolute. His right to be told the truth is not as great as her right to life.

This seemingly simple example has profound consequences. Since we have established one time when it is moral to lie and immoral to tell the truth, we must at some point enter the swamp of real life and sort out when else it might be moral to lie. While something like the categorical imperative has a certain conceptual attractiveness to many people because of its simplicity and its message of universal duties, in the real world where managers make decisions, simple universal rules do not always work. In other words, real-life rules for morality cannot be simple and universal. From this, it does not follow that everything is always up for negotiation. It does follow, though, that some decisions will not be easy to sort out from a moral point of view and that the comfort of certainty may not always be obtainable.

General Observations

Another general point about the rights and duties approach to ethics is that it is not completely different from the utilitarian approach. One could argue that we have a duty to perform those actions that will result in the greatest good for the greatest number of people. However, the emphases of the two approaches are notably different. Utilitarianism focuses on the results of actions and determines their morality by calculating those results (or a prediction of them). Rights and duties calls attention to obligations to act in a certain way. These obligations do not arise from the projected results of our actions but from intrinsic rights or duties. One other general point about the rights and duties approach to morality should be noted. There are important areas of life and human relations where this approach is not enough, or perhaps sometimes even appropriate. Family life is one such area. If a husband and wife, or mother and child, deal with each other on the basis of rights and duties, the relationship will lack important elements that ought to be present. Certainly the rights and duties approach has something to say about family relationships. Each spouse does have a right to some time alone, or to pursue their own interests, and children do have some rights (as they are quick to remind parents). Laws govern the property rights of each spouse, and parents have a legal obligation not to neglect their children. However, the love that motivates spouses and parents is really not captured in a discussion of rights and duties.

Churches and religious organizations have rights and duties regarding their members, but again this is not the kind of discussion that captures the actions and relationships of pastors and church members most of the time. Volunteer groups of many kinds use the time and skill of members. Boy Scouts and Girl Scouts, youth sports activities and homeless centers all flourish largely because individuals are willing to give their time and talent without employment relations or direct compensation. Again, some basic rights and duties do exist, but this form of discussion does not begin to capture the full scope of human relations that exists in volunteer groups. Even in work situations, it is not rights and duties that causes people to organize pot-luck luncheons or take up a collection for a co-worker about to get married.

In the workplace, where managers have specific roles to play, rights and duties often provides an appropriate language and set of concepts for thinking about the morality of actions. The whole stakeholder approach to business deals with issues of what individuals or groups that affect or are affected by organizations have rights or duties with regard to those organizations. Within the organization, managers have duties both to their bosses and to their subordinates, as well as to their peers. These duties exist because all three of these groups have fundamental human rights and because all three groups also have position rights. These rights impose duties on managers. In the chapters that make up the second part of this book, we will examine in some detail several of the kinds of rights and duties involved in being a manager within an organization. First, though, we need to consider the third basic approach to ethics, that of fairness and justice.

six

Fairness and Justice

Like the rights and duties approach, fairness and justice is an approach to ethical reasoning that includes several somewhat different concepts under one umbrella. This approach defines the moral act as the act that treats similarly situated people in similar ways with regard to both process and outcome, and with a sense of proportionality. Richard DeGeorge, in a widely used textbook on Business Ethics, lists four kinds of justice. He says that:

> *Compensatory justice* consists in compensating someone for a past injustice or making good some harm he or she has suffered in the past. *Retributive justice* concerns punishment due a law-breaker or evil-doer. *Procedural justice* is a term used to designate fair decision procedures, practices or agreements. *Distributive justice* involves the distribution of benefits and burdens, usually by the state.[1]

Since our discussion is in the framework of managerial ethics, we will focus on the last two, procedural justice and distributive justice.

Fairness in Daily Life

We do not often reflect on the complexity of the society in which we live and work. Each of us depends on others for many things that sustain our lives and make them good.[2] In a developed country today, very few individuals could provide all of their own food, clothing and shelter directly. Division of labor is here to stay. Organizations are formed and maintained in order to attain results that individuals, each acting alone, could not attain.

Most of us were born in organizations (hospitals), learned much of what we know in organizations (schools), work in and are compensated by organizations and, when we die, will very probably be buried or cremated by an organization. We play on teams, sing in choirs, purchase goods from stores and keep our money in banks. We are protected by military and police organizations, treated and healed by medical organizations, and comforted and inspired by religious organizations.[3]

In all of these contacts between individuals and organizations, there is some sort of exchange. We exchange labor for wages and pension benefits. We exchange taxes for protection and other governmental services. We exchange money for goods and services. Our interactions with organizations and the people who constitute them are basically unceasing. In all of these interactions, we have expectations both for what we will give and for what we will get. When these expectations are met, we feel good about the exchange. When they are not met, we are disappointed, or angry, or sad. Our lives are affected, on a daily basis, by the terms of exchanges.

One of our most basic expectations in the wide variety of exchanges that make up our daily lives is that we will be treated fairly. We know that this will not always happen, but we want it to happen, we receive satisfaction when it does happen and we have negative reactions when it does not happen. Since each of us as an individual is embedded in these organization–individual exchanges, we also meet or fail to meet the expectations of others. In one sense I work for a company, but in another sense, just as real, I work for my manager. I buy a shirt from a large department store chain, but I also buy it from a sales clerk. My salary is determined by my company in response to economic conditions, but it is also determined by my boss who conducts my performance appraisal and recommends my raise.

Meanings of Fairness

One of the first complete sentences spoken by many children (particularly if they have siblings) is "That's not fair!" A central issue in considerations of justice is the issue of what we mean by being fair. Is it fair to provide equal opportunity to all, even if the outcomes are unequal? Is it fair to distribute some resources (welfare benefits, charitable donations) based on need and other resources (high salaries, prestigious positions) based on merit? Is it fair to give preference to an individual now because she is a member of a group that was denied equal treatment in the past? To illustrate the difficulty of deciding what is fair, Amartya Sen tells the story of three children and one flute. One child claims that she should have the flute because she is the only one of the three who knows how to play it. The second child maintains that he should get the flute because he is the only one of the three who is so poor that he has no other toys. The third child argues that she should get the flute because she has invested many hours of work in actually making the flute.[4] The definition provided at the beginning of this chapter indicates that both procedures and outcomes must be taken into account in determining whether justice and fairness have prevailed. If all applicants have a right to be considered for open positions, and indeed all applicants are considered, but the only ones hired are white males (or black females, or disabled veterans) we intuitively say that fairness and justice have not been accomplished.

Among the dictionary definitions of both "fair" and "just" are the terms "equitable" and "impartial." The dictionary also defines "fair" as "just" and "just" as "fair."[5] The meanings, then, seem to be essentially the same. In common speech, the word "justice" carries more of the flavor of legal proceedings or decisions than does "fairness." In this discussion, we will use the words interchangeably, but with the caution that our discussion is philosophical, so the word "justice" is not limited to legal justice. Central to the concepts of fairness and justice is the idea of distribution, either of benefits or burdens, among more than one party.[6] In other words, I cannot be fair to one person without the context of my treatment of at least one other person. Utilitarianism, with its emphasis on the greatest number, is also a contextual concept, like fairness and justice. Rights and duties, on the other hand, can and sometimes does involve one person's dealing with one other person, without concern for any wider implications of the action.

Much of the writing on leadership emphasizes that a good leader must not only be fair but be perceived to be fair. That is why we include both procedural justice and distributive justice in our discussion. It may not be good policy or smart leadership to be unfair, but why is it unethical? Underlying this whole approach to ethics is a sense that individuals, in their dealings with one another, have a right to be treated fairly, and therefore we have a duty to treat them fairly. If there were no such right, the best argument that could be made for fairness is that it is useful for attaining some end, such as the greatest good for the greatest number, or the loyalty of one's subordinates, or the return of favors by those to whom we have given favor. These are not bad reasons for being fair. However, if we question whether we are morally obliged to be fair or simply free to choose fairness or unfairness as it suits our purposes, then a different and more fundamental justification for fairness is required.

In a basic sense, rights and duties and fairness and justice are related. A number of the topics we will examine in the second part of this book involve distribution of benefits and burdens on the part of managers. Employment situations involve a job that several applicants want to have, but only one will get. The same holds true of promotions and, to a different degree, of raises and bonuses. Termination situations, including layoffs, involve a job that current holders want to keep. Privacy issues involve the perceived benefit of privacy of the employee being weighed against the need to monitor activities that is inherent in the manager's position. Financial reporting involves the degree to which knowledge possessed by the manager should be disseminated to other interested parties, especially when the dissemination is apt to have negative consequences for the manager. All of these situations can be viewed as questions of who has a right to something and what duty that right imposes on the manager in terms of fair distribution.

Fairness and justice both have "equitable" as one of their meanings. Equitable can mean equal distribution of benefits or burdens, but it does not necessarily mean that. If two of my students both do excellent work throughout the semester, it is equitable for me to give them equal grades. If, however, one does excellent work and the other does work of a distinctly mediocre quality, it is not equitable for me to award them equal grades. In other words, equal treatment is sometimes fair and sometimes not. This may seem elementary, but in much of the discussion of affirmative action, comparable worth, welfare benefits and other approaches to distributing desirable resources, equitable and equal are often taken to mean the same thing, without any real analysis of whether this is correct or not.

Our intuitive sense of fairness tells us that sometimes it is fair to treat everyone equally and sometimes it is not.[7] It is fair to give each voter in a municipal or national election one vote and unfair to give several votes to an individual because she is better informed than other voters, or smarter, or richer, or has better family connections to power.[8] It is fair to allow only those who are trained and certified in medicine to perform surgery in a hospital and to deny the opportunity to perform surgery to all who lack such training, even if they have very steady hands and a sincere desire to heal the sick. In a broad sense, all men are created equal, but not all have equal talents, skills and knowledge. Because all men are created equal, it is wrong for one human to own another human, in the sense that one owns land or clothing or money. However, even though all men are created equal, all men should not be allowed to pilot jet planes, or teach university courses, or play professional basketball.

It is an interesting historical fact that Thomas Jefferson, who wrote the Declaration of Independence containing the famous "all men are created equal" phrase, owned slaves and continued to own them after signing the Declaration.[9] At the founding of the United States, the right to vote was limited to white, male property owners. Plato and Aristotle are arguably the two most influential philosophers in the history of Western thought. Both lived and wrote in Athens at a time when this small city-state was considered to be a model of Western civilization. They were able to spend their days teaching and discussing philosophy because much of the labor in Athens was performed by slaves. What, then, do we mean when we start with the premise that all men are created equal?

Through much of recorded history, societies have considered slaves, or women, or foreigners, or all of these to be less than human. The important point here is that various groups have not been considered to be different kinds of humans, but less than humans. The logical conclusion was that equality of treatment (as one kind of fairness) simply did not apply to slaves, or women, or foreigners, because they were not created equal. During much of the political debate leading up to the Civil Rights Act of 1964, politicians, journalists and others (especially from Southern states) argued that it was of great importance to prevent "the mixing of the races."[10] The implication in this argument is clear: there is not a single human race, including whites and blacks, but there are (at least) two races, the white race and the black race. School systems in many parts of the United States, including many universities, were described and defended as "separate but equal." This meant that there were separate schools for whites and for blacks and that as long as they were "equal" (which in many cases was simply not so) then fairness was achieved.[11]

Such recent history is important for understanding the role of fairness and justice in managerial ethics because much of the law and many of the regulations governing employment issues are a direct outcome of the debates of the 1960s.[12] Many of today's managers either lived through those debates or are the children of parents who did. In the contemporary world of business, there is no longer a serious question about which applicants or employees are to be included as human in the sense of all men are created equal. There is still evidence of discrimination against some classes of people for some jobs. Of the 500 largest companies in the United States, fewer than twenty have female CEOs. We will discuss this further in the chapter on employment issues, but it is clear from the numbers that something other than random distribution is occurring here.

John Rawls on Justice as Fairness

The twentieth-century philosopher most associated with issues of fairness and justice is John Rawls. He taught philosophy at Harvard University for many years and died in 2002. His most famous work is titled *A Theory of Justice*.[13] In 2001, he published a briefer commentary on the topics of his original work. This update is titled *Justice as Fairness: A Restatement*.[14] The basic issue that Rawls addresses is how a society should distribute benefits and burdens in order to achieve fairness. He specifies that the society he is considering is a pluralistic democracy, with rule by elected representatives and citizens who hold differing views on religion and politics.

One of the best-known ideas from Rawls' analysis is that of the veil of ignorance (he usually refers to this as the "original position"). Briefly, the concept is this. If you want to decide what would be a fair way for a society to distribute benefits and burdens, you will probably favor a distribution that most helps you as you are situated in that society. The rich, for instance, would favor low taxes because they would have to pay the most. The poor, on the other hand, would favor higher taxes (at least on the rich) because they would receive the most. Merchants would have one view of consumer protection laws and those injured by products a quite different view. To escape this bias, Rawls proposes that the individual mentally place himself behind a veil of ignorance. He says:

> In the original position, the parties are not allowed to know the social positions or the particular comprehensive doctrines of the persons they represent. They also do not know persons' race and ethnic group, sex, or various native endowments such as strength and intelligence, all within the normal range.[15]

They will know that they desire to have freedom to pursue and accomplish the basic goals of life, such as a sufficiency of food and shelter, as well as more advanced goals, such as education and self-fulfillment.

From behind the veil of ignorance, the individual now thinks about how to distribute benefits and burdens. Should the society tax all workers to pay for medical care for all its elderly members? Should its laws be restrictive or permissive regarding such things as race or gender discrimination? Should employers be able to terminate employees easily? What Rawls proposes is that we think first about what constitutes distributive justice and try to answer this question from a neutral position, rather than one that will maximize our own benefits. Having decided the basic pattern of distributive justice, we would then ask what kinds of procedural justice will result in this pattern. While Rawls makes clear in the *Restatement* that his proposed system is limited to political systems and is not meant to be a more general statement of morality, his ideas are useful for thinking about the relations between procedural and distributive justice.[16]

Procedural and Distributive Justice

As we will see in more detail in the chapters that follow, there are two key points at which fairness and justice become central to managerial decision-making. One is the design of systems and procedures for distributing benefits and burdens; the other is the decision by an individual manager in an individual case. Often the individual manager's decision is constrained by the system involved. The kinds of systems under discussion are not information technology systems but such things as standard hiring procedures, compensation systems such as salary ranges and guidelines for increases or stock option awards, and company-wide directives for the conduct of layoffs. These various systems can be seen as rules for procedural fairness, whereas individual decisions by managers about resource allocations can be seen as examples of distributive fairness.[17]

In our discussion of what philosophy is, we noted that a key issue in many philosophical discussions is the transition from general rules to specific applications. It is much easier to get agreement on the rule "do good and avoid evil" than it is to get agreement on whether it is good for the company to pay its chief executive several hundred times as much as the pay earned by low-level workers in the same company. At the more general level of company systems, we are closer to the "do good and avoid evil" level. A starting premise that this year's guideline for pay increases should be both economically reasonable and fair to all employees is not usually the point at which arguments arise. A more detailed premise that executive increases can be up to 20 percent of base salary, while clerical increases can be up to 5 percent may generate more discussion. The application, that Sam Smith has done a truly outstanding job but cannot be awarded more than a 5 percent increase, is where discussion is apt to become heated and emotions are apt to run high. If Sam's increase is not fair, who is to blame?

Individual managerial decisions are constrained in varying degrees by organizational systems. If employee salaries are governed by a negotiated labor-management contract, then a supervisor has no real impact on the amount of an individual employee's salary increase. If the company has a general rule to the effect of "hire the best qualified applicant" then the hiring supervisor has considerable discretion in deciding which candidate is the best qualified and will therefore get the job. The important consideration at this point in the discussion is that the fairness and justice of an individual managerial decision is often determined, or at least influenced, by the rules governing that type of decision.[18] Another way to say this is that procedural justice (systems and rules) influences or determines distributive justice (outcomes).

Procedural justice is intended to achieve distributive justice. In other words, the ultimate concern when using fairness and justice as an approach to ethics is with results—how do resources end up being distributed, and is this distribution fair and just?[19] Procedural justice is instrumental, in that it is concerned with achieving some result. The importance of establishing fair systems for distribution of resources was mentioned earlier in this chapter. It is possible to achieve fair and just results without using fair and just procedures. A monarch who is unusually sensitive and intelligent might distribute resources quite fairly (as, for that matter, might a manager possessing similar virtues) using a procedure that simply consists of individual decrees. Procedural justice serves two important purposes: it makes it more likely distribution of resources will occur and it encourages the perception that results are fair because procedures were fair.

Obviously not all procedural systems will be equally fair, and some may be patently unfair. A system that grants options for large amounts of stock to a few senior managers and none to anyone else is at least open to a charge of unfairness. A system that grants a greater chance for admission to a selective university to children of alumni readily creates a perception of unfairness on the part of applicants and their parents who are not alumni. It is important, then, in considering fairness and justice, to consider procedural systems. On the other hand, even a fair system can be abused, and many systems of general rules leave room for some interpretation at the individual level. It is also important, then, to consider how a procedural system is applied in individual cases and to consider whether the results constitute distributive justice.

Discussion of procedural systems and procedural justice seem quite abstract and far removed from the busy world of managing, where decisions often must be made quickly using whatever information is available and hoping for satisfactory outcomes. Let us see how the abstract theory links to the real-world decisions. Almost all managers operate within the confines of an expense budget. An expense budget is a procedural system for distributing financial resources. One of the duties of managers is to hire or participate in the selection of new employees. Employment rules and procedures are a procedural system to govern the awarding of the resource known as a job. Almost every manager, sooner or later, is put in the position of terminating an employee. Company rules and procedures governing termination are a form of procedural system (denial of resources, such as a job, involve distribution just as much as awarding of resources).

Jobs and compensation are important resources that managers control, at least to some degree. A negotiated labor-management contract specifies procedural systems in considerable detail. Such contracts often reduce greatly the amount of discretion that managers can exercise in distributing resources. The negotiation of such contracts, then, is a particularly important management function. Normally this negotiation is not open to most managers, but is conducted by a small designated group and requires top management approval before a contract is accepted and made operative. Such contracts are especially important in terms of reaching distributive justice.

During the recent financial crisis, General Motors and Chrysler declared bankruptcy. It is widely thought that unsustainable labor costs were a significant contributing cause in their failures. With a major reduction in labor costs, they were able to emerge from bankruptcy with what now appears to be a more sustainable business model. While workers at these companies were receiving very high wages and benefits, stockholders saw their investment steadily reduced in value, and lenders and vendors received only partial payment under the terms of the bankruptcy settlement.[20] Shortly before the companies went bankrupt, workers on their automobile assembly lines earned approximately $70 per hour in combined wages and fringe benefits. Fairness did not seem to prevail in the distribution of benefits and burdens among the companies' various stakeholders.

To a considerable degree, the kind of distributive justice that will ultimately be accomplished is determined by the procedures set up. Some people think that the truly fair way to distribute compensation involves equal pay for all doing the same job. Others think that those who do a job better than others doing the same job should be better compensated. Still others think that those who have been doing a job longer (and thus have more seniority) should be better compensated than those who have been doing it for a shorter time.

Different compensation systems reflect these differences. Labor unions generally favor contracts that require equal compensation for all workers in a given job classification, or equal compensation for all in the same classification with extra compensation for seniority. They generally oppose any form of compensation in which those identified as performing a job better are paid more. Managers often favor some form of merit pay system because they believe they should have the discretion to reward those who perform best with extra compensation. Merit systems certainly can be and have been abused, but their basic premise is different from those systems based entirely on job classification and longevity. Even in organizations where merit systems are in place, it is not unusual to find cost-of-living increases as part of the compensation package. These systems reward all employees, regardless of performance. Under almost any compensation system, most people feel that increases in compensation are fair, while decreases are not. The fact that many people favor one system while many others favor a quite different one is indicative that there are different views, widely held, of what constitutes distributive justice.

Many procedural systems are designed to assure compliance with laws and regulations, particularly in areas relating to human resources. While it is certainly important to comply with the law, both in the design of procedural systems and in their application, doing so does not necessarily guarantee that decisions will be moral. Fairness in the distribution of important information is a matter of concern to investors, regulators and others. In areas regarding financial reporting, there has been considerable recent evidence that it is possible to comply with at least the letter of the law while still providing reports that are essentially lies, and quite possibly unethical. Recent changes in the law, such as the Sarbanes–Oxley Act, have made this a bit more difficult.[21] Because the financial stakes are very high, and the technicians involved in these areas (accountants, attorneys, financial analysts) are numerous and very bright, it seems likely that changing the law will not, by itself, assure an improvement in the level of morality reflected in decisions about financial reporting.

Similarly Situated Individuals and Similar Treatment

In the final analysis, any procedural system is general and individual distributions of resources are specific.[22] The ethical sensitivity, or lack thereof, of the individual manager making an individual decision is important to the ultimate attainment of distributive justice. In other words, ethical managers are required in order to have ethical decisions. In order for a manager to make decisions that are ethical according to the perspective of fairness and justice, she must be able to determine who are similarly situated individuals and what constitutes similar treatment. Sometimes this is easy, and sometimes it is not.

If there are twenty applicants for an open position and twelve of them meet the minimum qualifications (e.g., a Bachelor's degree in accounting and three years of experience), it is easy to decide that all twelve will get further consideration and the remaining eight will not. However, each of the twelve has different experience and background, yet only one of them can be hired for the position. Deciding which one is not so easy. As long as all twelve are considered, is any hiring decision fair and just? What if one has significantly more work experience than the others, another has a higher college grade point than any of the others, and a third is a disabled Hispanic woman? Now what is fair? The goal is not only to treat all applicants fairly; it is also to hire the person who will do the best job in the open position. As we will see in the chapter on employment issues, there is no guarantee that a given person will perform in a given way. There are indicators, especially past performance in similar situations, that have proven to be better predictors than others.

This point is worth noticing. The ultimate goal in managerial decisions is not fairness. Managers are hired to oversee the work of others (again, to plan, organize and control) in such a way that the organization's performance will be improved. This is the goal that justifies minimum requirements of applicants for a position, or paying some people more than others, or relocating a plant from one city or country to another, or laying off some workers whose performance has not been lacking in any way. Sometimes in discussions of fairness this point is missed, and the tone of the discussion would lead one to believe that managers are hired to be fair. Managers are hired to oversee part or all of an organization, and the organization has goals other than fairness. Corporations aim to make a profit by producing and selling cars, or software, or airplane rides. Schools aim to educate students, and hospitals to treat the sick.

While corporations usually address profits specifically in their goals, other organizations also operate with economic goals and constraints. While school districts and public hospitals are not-for-profit organizations, taxpayers generally prefer that they also be not-for-loss. School superintendents and hospital administrators are not praised for losing money and encouraged to lose more in the following year. Thus, managers in both corporations and not-for-profit organizations who strive to be ethical are constrained in their decisions by economic concerns. Some philosophers seem to feel that this is an unfortunate fact and that somehow the business side of organizations is less noble than the lofty personal or spiritual side.

A moment's thought will show the flaw in this view. Healing the sick and educating the young are noble enterprises. However, the sick, the young, the healers and the educators all have to eat, all need clothing and all would like to have more rather than less of the good things of this world. Organizations make possible both sophisticated healing and comprehensive education. Few would choose to return to the days of "healers" selling snake oil from the backs of wagons (and even they charged for the snake oil) or all-purpose teachers in one-room school houses. Well-run organizations provide the possibility of modern life, with its many blessings. Evening study is more attractive from a comfortable chair under a good lamp than sprawled on the dirt floor in front of the light from a fireplace. Without furniture makers and retailers, and the power company, we would be back on the dirt floor in front of the fire.

Fairness and justice, then, like the other approaches to morality, must be situated in the confines of the real world if they are to help people who live in that world to make decisions. At the point where theory meets reality, some of the most difficult issues arise. We can establish theoretically the principle that it is moral and fair to treat similarly situated people in similar ways. We can only determine who is similarly situated in the practical world because the facts of a given case are what tell us what "similarly situated" means in that case.

Are all women similarly situated? By itself, this is a meaningless question.[23] Are all women who apply for a given job similarly situated? Probably not. Some will have more advanced education than others, some will have more relevant work experience than others, and one may be the friend of the hiring manager. All of these characteristics may well come into play in the determination of who gets the job. If the goal is seen as filling the position with the person most apt to perform well in it, then relevant work experience should weigh more heavily than being a friend of the hiring manager. In most cases, being a woman should have little or no weight. However, if the job is topless dancer or guard in a women's prison, being a woman may be a requirement of the successful candidate.

In a general way, the difference between laws and regulations stems from the distinctions we are making here. The law may say that it is illegal to discriminate in employment based on gender. This is a general principle. The regulations detailing what companies may and may not do in their hiring practices, or what conclusions can be drawn from the current composition of their workforce, are normally much more specific and detailed. The manager who is trying to make an ethical decision must be familiar with applicable laws and regulations or seek advice from a specialist who is. However, that is not enough. The manager must also be able to analyze a decision between two or more options, each of which is allowed by the law, or to choose in a case where there is no specific law or regulation. That is where ethical reasoning comes in, and a basic understanding of fairness and justice can be helpful.

So far, we have concentrated on the question of who is similarly situated. We must also consider what it means to treat people in similar ways. The first obvious point is that similar ways does not necessarily mean identical ways. In some types of managerial decisions, similarity or disparity of treatments is obvious. In hiring situations, Sam or Sally either gets the job or does not. But in other situations, results are not so clear. One employee may get a 4 percent raise, another a 6 percent raise. Are these close enough to be called similar treatment? While it is clearly individuals who finally do or do not receive similar treatment, these individuals are sometimes not the best judge of a situation.

Consider two managers, each of whom earns $80,000 a year. Each receives a performance bonus at the end of the year. One receives $10,000, the other $9,000. Have they been treated in similar ways? The one with the $9,000 bonus may feel that she has been slighted, treated in a non-similar way, and may be sure that such negative treatment came about because of her gender, or race, or because of some other obvious bias on the part of her boss. An impartial observer may conclude that, given the performance of each manager during the previous year and the size of the available bonus pool, the awards constitute similar treatment of similarly situated people because both performed well, but one performed slightly better.[24] Was the decision fair and just?

The point is that equal treatment is relatively easy to measure. Similar treatment is not. Yet, as we saw earlier in the chapter, equal treatment is sometimes not appropriate, or is impossible. Ten candidates for one position, each reasonably well qualified, cannot finally receive equal treatment because there is only one position available. In the selection process, each can be given equal consideration, in the sense that each application is reviewed with equal care. The top three or four might receive further equal treatment in that each is interviewed in person. Ultimately, all but one receive one kind of treatment (rejection) and one receives a different kind of treatment (they are hired for the position).

In a real sense, then, all applicants are similarly situated, as applicants. All qualified applicants are similarly situated, as qualified applicants. All finalists are similarly situated, as finalists. At each stage, similar treatment is in order according to our formula for fairness and justice. However, at each stage, similar treatment means something different. Consider the interview stage, for finalists. Similar treatment means that each is interviewed and treated in a similar way during the interview. One does not receive a five-minute interview, while another receives two hours. One is not asked hostile, challenging questions, while another receives only friendly, supportive inquiries. However, similar does not mean equal in every respect. If one is interviewed for an hour and another for fifty-five minutes, or one is inter-viewed in the morning and another in the afternoon, their treatment has been similar.

Who decides which individuals are similarly situated, and what consti-tutes similar treatment? Sometimes a procedural system specifies these decisions and sometimes the individual manager has considerable freedom in deciding. A system for termination that requires progressive discipline spec-ifies things that might otherwise be left up to an individual manager. Such a system might require that, except for certain specified very serious offenses, any employee whose performance is unsatisfactory must be informed of the problem face to face and in writing. The employee must be given a specified period of time to reach a specific improved level of performance. If this is not achieved, the employee must be given, in person and in writing, a final warning of pending termination. A second review must occur and, if the specified performance improvement level has not been reached, only then can the employee be terminated.

Such a system might be designed by human resource specialists to help the company defend itself against legal claims for wrongful terminations. At the same time, the system defines who is similarly situated (any employee whose performance is deficient to a specified degree) and what precisely con-stitutes similar treatment. This removes from the manager discretion to decide how bad is bad enough and whether to warn before firing, and if so how often and when. Even as the system removes discretionary judgments from the individual manager, it imposes certain obligations on him to identify unsatisfactory performance and to take specific steps at specific times in order to deal with the employee in question.

Sometimes there is no definition by the system and the manager is left to his own devices in determining who is similarly situated or what constitutes similar treatment. In many cases, perhaps most cases, no conscious analysis is done. Managers make many decisions each day. Most of them are rela-tively simple and relatively routine. Many of them can be reversed later if need be and, since the consequences are small, the time invested in deciding is proportionately small. What, then, separates the manager who is fair and just from the one who is not?

Evaluating Managerial Fairness

Almost every manager thinks of herself as fair and just. Yet subordinates and superiors might have a different judgment. Two different approaches can be taken, both of which contribute insight, to deciding whether a manager is fair. One is to stand back from the individual small decisions and examine the pattern of these decisions. When employees say that their boss is unfair, they sometimes elaborate by saying that she often favors one individual or group over another, or that she does not give equal consideration to the efforts or accomplishments of different employees. The word "often" is important. In these situations, the employees are not bemoaning one major decision that they think was unfair. Instead, they are making a judgment that the pattern of many small decisions is such that similarly situated people are not treated similarly.

Even though the individual small decision does not and should not (and given the time constraints on managers, probably could not) receive full analysis, it is important from time to time to examine the pattern of these decisions. If one's employees think that she is often unfair, then there may be a pattern of unfair small decisions, each one made without much conscious consideration. The instinctive reaction of most managers, if confronted with what seems to be a pattern of unfairness, is self-defense. While this response is instinctive, it is not usually enlightening. If the manager does, in fact, often make small decisions that involve unfairness, the only way to confirm this is to examine a number of decisions in retrospect. Because these decisions were made without much reflection or analysis, retrospective consideration may or may not support the charge of unfairness. If a manager wants to know whether there is substance to a charge of frequent unfairness, there seems to be no other way except to be as open as possible in examining some of these past decisions.

A second approach to determining whether a manager is fair in decision-making is to look carefully at the relatively few major decisions that he makes. Since major decisions usually have major impacts, they are apt to be noticed by more people and examined more carefully, both for process and for outcomes. One major decision that is widely perceived to be unfair can stand out in the minds of bosses and subordinates more than many small decisions. In fact, it can color their judgment of the many small decisions because of the impression that is made. A manager is more apt to be analytical and to take the time to examine a decision carefully when it is recognized as having major consequences. Even so, it is possible for a manager to miss important considerations or to misjudge factors that are consciously examined.

As with the question of frequent unfairness in small decisions, the only way to determine whether a major decision that is perceived as unfair by others is so in reality is to attempt a calm and dispassionate review of the decision and its impact. This is not the natural human tendency. When accused of unfairness in a major decision, most of us are inclined to immediate self-defense rather than to calm analysis. Self-defense may well be in order. The manager often has more facts than those criticizing, and major decisions often have significant negative consequences for some interested parties, making it harder for them to reach an objective judgment about the decision. However, if the manager is honestly trying to determine whether he was fair in his decision-making, he might do well to listen to those who perceive unfairness.

There is a further consideration here. We defined the moral act under fairness and justice as the act which treats similarly situated people in similar ways with regard to both process and outcome. At the time a major decision is made, the process can already be examined, but the outcome is yet to occur. The only way, then, to examine the second element of the definition is to examine the outcome at some point after the decision has been made. It is possible for procedural justice to occur (the process is fair) but distributive justice not to occur (the results are unfair). To take an extreme example, we could grant fair and speedy trials to those accused of embezzlement in both Boston and Los Angeles. Procedural justice is accomplished. However, if we fine those found guilty in Boston and hang those found guilty in Los Angeles, distributive justice has not been accomplished. One could argue that, in this case, the sentencing procedure was not fair, so neither procedural nor distributive justice was accomplished. This simple, and absurd, example illustrates how quickly the appearance of fairness can dissolve.

Given the way things actually work in organizations, especially in competitive business organizations, a manager who responds to any charge of unfairness by saying "you may be right" might be perceived as unusually open and praiseworthy. However, she might also be perceived as impractical, indecisive and easy to manipulate. Constant reviews of the fairness of managerial decisions both large and small may well lead to paralysis by analysis. On the other hand, a manager who will never listen to the views of others who think her unfair, or will never reconsider a decision once made, exhibits a self-confidence and a rigidity that may not serve her well. The middle path seems to involve an occasional review of the pattern of past small decisions and a more frequent review of major decisions at some point after they have been made and their results can be seen.

Some individuals can spend ten years in the same job and not be any smarter about the job after the tenth year than they were after the first year. Other individuals learn from experience and adjust their performance accordingly. The difference lies in self-reflection. Some people keep repeating the first year's experience without learning from it because they do not think about it, or look for patterns, or ask what results might have occurred if they had done things differently. Other, self-reflective people learn from both their successes and their mistakes. These people tend to advance in management (although this is by no means a universal rule). If fairness is a characteristic of good managers, then thinking about the fairness of one's own actions and their results might well lead to improved management skill, as well as leading to more ethical decision-making.

The final element in the definition of fairness and justice given earlier in this chapter is "with a sense of proportion." This element is included because otherwise the similar treatment of all similarly situated individuals, no matter how outrageous the treatment, would be defined as fair and just. To take an extreme example, if all employees who showed up late to work were promptly imprisoned, the similar group (all tardy employees) would receive similar treatment (imprisonment). Yet, common sense cries out against labeling this treatment as fair. In a broad sense, this last part of the definition maintains that punishment must fit the crime and, similarly, that reward should fit the performance that earns it.

This element of proportion not only tailors the basic definition in such a way as to avoid extreme negative consequences being considered as fair and just, but also limits positive consequences. If a CEO earns, in salary and stock options, one thousand times as much as an average worker, some people would consider this justified as long as other CEOs in comparable positions earn comparable amounts. In fact, this approach is sometimes used by boards of directors to justify very large salaries and stock grants. However, the introduction of the sense of proportionality allows for at least raising the question of whether such compensation is fair.

While the argument is anecdotal rather than scientific, many people have questioned whether Martha Stewart's prison sentence for her relatively small financial gain from insider stock trading and the subsequent cover-up was fair when CEOs of several commercial and investment banks that failed or were forced into mergers received severance pay in the tens of millions of dollars. Whatever one thinks of this argument, its basis is proportionality.

We have now completed our analysis of ethics as a branch of philosophy. We have seen how the general rules and procedures of philosophy apply to ethics and how ethics is both similar to and different from law and religion. We have examined each of the three major approaches to ethics and discussed some of the most important philosophers associated with each approach. We now turn our attention to practical applications of ethics. In the remaining chapters, we will use the three basic approaches to think through some of the ethical issues that arise in the course of the work of managers.

Part II
Applied Business Ethics

seven

Ethical Analysis of Employment Issues

One of the tasks of managers is to choose new employees from a pool of applicants. If there is one open position and there are several applicants, then a valuable resource (the job) will be awarded to one applicant and denied to others. Anyone who has anxiously awaited the results of their application and interview for a job knows that what happens here matters. There are consequences that make the successful applicant happy and satisfied, and the unsuccessful applicants unhappy and dissatisfied. The manager who has the open position may be constrained in various ways by company policies in choosing a candidate. As long as the manager makes the choice, he is making a decision, in the role of manager, that has ethical implications both for the new employee and for the rejected candidates. In this chapter, we examine the ethical implications of this choice and some of the common kinds of situations that raise moral concerns in making the choice. We will show how each of the three major approaches to ethics can be used to analyze the manager's decision.

The Hiring Process

In order to keep the decision under analysis relatively clear and to keep the example close to what actually happens in the real world of managers, we will start with certain assumptions. Let us assume that the open position is one that already exists and that its scope is already determined. Let us also assume that minimum qualifications for the job have been established and have been made known to the applicants. Let us further assume that the open position has been advertised or posted in some manner and that a number of individuals have applied for the position. Finally, let us assume that more than one applicant meets the minimum qualifications for the job. There are obviously cases where one or more of these assumptions will not hold true, but the assumptions as stated will let us make an initial examination of the issues without too many complicating factors.

The discussion that follows describes the hiring process as it is conducted in relatively large firms, where there are a number of managers who sometimes hire their subordinates. In such firms, at least in the United States, it is typical to have a human resources department which sets and monitors overall company practices with regard to hiring. The role of the human resources department in an individual case varies from company to company. In order to establish consistency across the company, human resources specialists are often involved in preparing salary ranges for each position and in establishing minimum qualifications for each job. They may also draft, or at least approve, any advertisements for the position. It is also fairly common to have the human resources department screen applications to eliminate those who do not meet minimum qualifications before the applications are presented for consideration to the hiring manager. Finally, a human resources representative may prepare and extend the offer of employment to the chosen candidate.[1]

In a small business, where the owner is often the only manager and there are no human resource specialists, all of the steps described above will be carried out, formally or informally, by the manager. Some anti-discrimination laws and regulations do not apply to small businesses in the United States.[2] In some cases, there is no advertisement of the opening or formal search for applicants—the manager simply invites an acquaintance to assume the open position and agrees with the sole applicant on a salary and any other relevant provisions of employment. Obviously, if there is only one applicant, and that one is an applicant by invitation, concerns about fairness and justice or the rights of applicants and duties imposed by those rights on the hiring manager are moot. Nonetheless, even small businesses sometimes advertise or otherwise publicize an open position and consider a number of applicants before choosing one. In this case, the description of the process that follows is applicable.

Let us begin by revisiting an observation made in the chapter on fairness and justice. The primary reason why a manager has her job is not to be fair, but to contribute through her section or department or division to the success of the company. So, when a manager is in the position of selecting a new employee from a pool of qualified candidates, the primary goal of the decision is to contribute to the success of the company. The hiring decision has two broad implications for the unit's and the company's success. One is that the person chosen should be the one most likely to perform well in the job for which he is being hired. The other is that the pattern of hiring decisions, in the unit and in the company at large, should be such as to contribute most to the company's success.

We will assume for the sake of this discussion that the job has been properly designed and the minimum qualifications properly specified. This is not always the case, but job design and the specification of minimum qualifications are separate topics. Much has been written about these topics and we will not try to add here to what is known on the subject.[3] If the hiring manager knows what he is looking for, then he has a better chance of finding it. As a start, the candidate should be able to perform the technical tasks required of the job. This may involve processing accounts payable, or designing marketing campaigns, or greeting customers and answering the phone. It is standard practice to use education level and work experience to establish these abilities, although specific tests of task performance can also be used.

Once we have established that the minimum qualifications are met, there may still remain a pool of applicants from which to choose. In many cases, the qualifications of these remaining applicants will vary significantly. The next step in the selection process is to select a final pool of applicants from the total group that meets the minimum qualifications. If one is much more qualified than another, logic suggests that the more qualified applicant is more likely to perform the job well and to make the hoped-for contribution to the unit's business performance. One immediate problem is this: how much is a significant difference in qualifications? If one candidate has the required minimum of six months' relevant experience and another candidate has five years, this is probably significant. However, if one has nine months and the other has seven months, this probably constitutes a distinction without a difference and does not really matter. Obviously, how much difference is enough to be significant is a judgment call, and the hiring manager usually gets to be the judge. If there is a significant difference in the levels of qualification, this is clearly relevant information.[4]

In Chapter 2, we noted that one of the characteristics of philosophy is an emphasis on clear thinking and calling things by their correct names. If there is no real difference, then claiming a difference and basing the hiring decision on that claimed difference does not square with the philosophical approach. It is a tempting solution because it provides an apparently objective reason for hiring one candidate and rejecting another. Nonetheless, claiming a difference when none really exists does not qualify as an ethical approach to decision-making.

Once the most qualified candidates have been identified, the hiring manager still must make a decision. From conversation with hiring managers, with human resource directors and from my own experience as a manager, such decisions are often made based on what is called "chemistry." This seems to mean personal intuition, in practice. In other words, there are no objective, measurable job-related criteria on which the candidates differ, yet something tells the hiring manager to offer the job to one candidate rather than to another. Suppose that he prefers working with women and one of the qualified applicants is a woman. Is it morally acceptable for him to hire her on this basis? Note that we are not discussing legal requirements here. If his department or unit has very few female employees, or for that matter, very few male employees, there may be considerations of equal opportunity that could legally impact his decision. We will discuss this issue later in the chapter. Assuming that such constraints do not apply here, can our manager hire the female applicant and be ethical in his decision?

What if the situation is the same in all respects, except that our hiring manager prefers to work with attractive females and one of the qualified candidates is an attractive female? Is he ethical in his decision-making if he hires her because she is an attractive female? What if he prefers white males over fifty years old who graduated from Ohio State, or avid football fans, or Republicans, or Presbyterians, or some combination of the above? As long as the candidate who meets his preferences is also among the most qualified for the job, is there any moral problem if he uses his preferences as the final criteria for hiring? What if he prefers working with Caucasians?

Problems arise if a series of hiring decisions is based on these personal criteria. Suppose the manager who prefers working with attractive women has, over a period of time, seven different hiring decisions to make as natural turnover occurs. On each occasion, there are several qualified candidates and one of these in each case is an attractive woman. Eventually, this manager will be presiding over a work unit made up entirely of attractive women. There now appears to be a pattern of discrimination against males and less attractive women. Which decision created this pattern? The first? The third? The seventh? In a way, each did because each contributed to the pattern. In addition to the pattern of discrimination, we should ask, at least in passing, what will happen if this manager leaves his position and is replaced by one of the attractive women working in the section? Suppose she prefers working with attractive males. Will the next seven hires be attractive males, and what sorts of interesting dynamics will occur in the section while this transition is in progress?

The key point here is that individual decisions are parts of patterns of decisions.[5] Particularly in terms of fairness and justice, as we will see later in this chapter, patterns are important. They occur as a result of individual decisions, and sometimes these decisions are widely separated in time. Nonetheless, in considering moral decision-making in employment-related matters, we must examine not only the individual hiring decision, but also the pattern which a number of these decisions create. There is no other way to account for patterns in employment practice except to analyze individual decisions from the perspective of their part in forming a pattern.[6]

Affirmative Action and Diversity

Under each of the three perspectives on ethics, we will need to deal with the issue of affirmative action. This term has taken on a variety of meanings and a good deal of emotional weight in light of legal requirements spelled out in Title VII of the Civil Rights Act, of subsequent legislation in this area and of multiple regulations promulgated by the Equal Employment Opportunity Commission.[7] The term affirmative action has four basic meanings. It is important to be clear about what is meant when discussing affirmative action because the same term can mean quite different things, and some managers taking it to mean one thing might automatically either defend or oppose it, while other managers or employees, giving the same term a quite different meaning, might take a different position without taking the time to be sure they are discussing the same thing.

One meaning of the term affirmative action in employment is the removal of barriers. If a company conducts all its employment interviews at its offices in an area of town not served by public transportation, prospective applicants who do not have cars may not be able to apply. A requirement that applications be filled out online means that those who do not have access to computers with internet connections cannot apply. Removing such barriers requires that companies do something different (take affirmative action) in terms of applicant access to the employment process. Such steps to diversify the pool of applicants are often simple for the company and do not involve the ideological debates that accompany other meanings of affirmative action.

A second meaning of the term is changing managerial attitudes to eliminate bias and its effects. This might involve such simple steps as providing printed material to all managers about the company's hiring policies and the reasons for them. It might involve either optional or required classes or training sessions for hiring managers. It might involve meetings either between a hiring manager and his supervisor or between the hiring manager and a human resources representative when a pattern of apparently discriminatory hiring is identified. Whatever steps are taken in this category, the specific meaning here of affirmative action is that the company does something or some things to address the attitudes of hiring managers.

A third meaning is to recognize under-represented groups and facilitate applications from these groups. Typically the recognition that one or more groups is under-represented will not be the job of the hiring manager, but of the human resources department. It may also be that a department, such as marketing, will recognize that it would be more effective if it had more employees who were similar in some respect (age, ethnic origin, etc.) to the target market for the company's products or services. However the recognition occurs, facilitating applications from the under-represented group will usually be the task of the human resources department rather than the individual hiring manager. In some ways, this facilitation will be similar to the actions described under the first meaning of affirmative action, but will be more targeted to increasing applications from a given group or groups.

The fourth meaning of affirmative action is to give preferential treatment to some individual applicants because they are members of some group. This grouping could be based on age, gender, ethnic background or other characteristics. This is the most controversial kind of affirmative action. In the United States, recent changes in law due to court decisions have tended to make this form of affirmative action illegal. Its opponents argue that discrimination of this sort is wrong, even though it is intended to make up for the results of past discrimination against members of the favored group. Many managers identify this fourth meaning as the only meaning of affirmative action and, based on this identification, are strongly opposed to what they think of as affirmative action.[8] It is important to distinguish among the four meanings when trying to decide whether a hiring decision or practice is ethical.[9]

Affirmative action is aimed both at insuring fairness to individual applicants and at creating diversity in the workforce. An argument can be made for many organizations that they will function better if they employ a diverse workforce. This diversity extends to age, to gender and to ethnic background. Such diversity helps a company to serve a diverse customer base. It provides differing viewpoints that can prove valuable in responding to changes in the world in which it operates. Diversity in age of employees can provide a balance between innovation and stability, as well as providing a somewhat orderly rate of turnover and retirement.

A diverse workforce is sometimes important because of a diverse customer base. Upscale hotels in major cities serve clients from all over the world. If they employed only people of one nationality, they would have a harder time recognizing and serving the diverse needs of their clients than if they had a workforce with different national backgrounds. It may be necessary for their employees to be fluent in different languages and knowledgeable about different customs. All of this could be done with a homogeneous workforce, but diversity in the workforce is more apt to help the hotel function at a high level of service for a diverse customer base.

One does not have to be a manager in an upscale hotel to deal with these issues. Police departments, school districts, retailers and organizations of many types are finding that, practically speaking, they can operate better in serving their diverse clientele if they have diversity in their workforce. Diversity is a requirement for many kinds of workforces. A further argument can be made as follows. Diversity often stimulates innovation. A group of individuals that is very much alike is less apt to come up with different and better ways of dealing with situations than a group of individuals with differences in characteristics and outlook. Many organizations require at least some innovation in their products, services and operations in order to succeed. Thus, diversity in their employees will help them in this respect and assist the organization in generating and accepting useful innovations.

Not everyone will agree with this assessment.[10] Some will argue that a homogeneous, or non-diverse, work unit will actually perform better, since energies can be focused on getting the job done, rather than on getting along. Diverse people, by definition, are not the same. They will have different assumptions, different values and different ways of doing things. If coordination within the unit is important, then sameness will be preferable to diversity. None of these arguments is universally true for every organization at every time. Diversity is sometimes a necessity, sometimes a benefit and sometimes a detriment for good performance. However, there are enough reasons why it is useful to good performance to make it a desirable goal in many situations.

There are easy cases in analyzing the morality of employment decisions. If there is only one qualified candidate, the choice is straightforward. If the hiring manager chooses to hire his unqualified daughter instead of the qualified outside candidate, the decision is obviously wrong. If the manager clearly indicates that members of one race or religion need not apply because he would not hire them no matter how they ranked against other candidates, his hiring practice is clearly unfair. The easy cases are not usually the interesting ones. It is the difficult cases—where several qualified candidates with no significant difference in the level of qualifications present themselves, but the manager can hire only one and must choose on some basis other than the stated qualifications—where ethical analysis becomes both interesting and difficult. We turn now to the three basic approaches to ethics and investigate how each one can be used to sort through the ethical issues involved in hiring.

Utilitarian Analysis

Utilitarianism says that the moral act is the one that creates the greatest good for the greatest number of people. Using this approach, the manager who is trying to decide which hiring choice is most ethical will examine the impacts of that hiring choice. Obviously, the candidate who is hired will experience happiness and feel that she has been the recipient of good. If the manager feels that he has made the best choice, he also will experience happiness. There is no way to know for sure that any candidate will work out in practice, but if the manager is able to hire a candidate who meets the minimum qualifications for the job and appears to be the best candidate in the pool, there is at least a reasonable chance for success. The manager may also feel a certain degree of happiness because the search is over, the position is filled and he can get on with other things. Managers are partly evaluated on their ability to choose new employees, since this is a key part of their jobs. If the new employee succeeds, the hiring manager also gains by reason of having made a good hire.

The candidates who are not hired are also impacted by the decision. Even though they will probably feel unhappiness at failing to get an offer of the job, they may or may not find another job that suits them as well or better. It is good for the hiring manager to remember, though, that those rejected for the position will feel rejected. To the degree that they understand the hiring process, if they perceive that it was fair, their unhappiness at not getting the job may be somewhat reduced.[11] The other employees in the unit, who will work with the new hire, will gain happiness if the choice was a good one and the new employee proves to be successful. They will suffer unhappiness to the extent that this is not the case.

More care is needed with some hires than with others. A new mail clerk or fast food restaurant server may not have a significant impact on the company as a whole. The impact of their hiring probably does not extend much beyond the work unit into which they are hired. A new middle manager or executive, though, may have much more impact on the organization, or a significant part of it. The amount of good or harm created by a new hire in such a position carries more weight. The hiring manager, in this case, makes a decision that will create considerable good or harm and thus the hiring decision is more important.

The utilitarian approach requires the hiring manager to think about consequences that may extend for months or years after the decision is made, especially when the position being filled is at a relatively high level. This is a worthwhile perspective and one that is not always immediately obvious to a harried manager who is trying to complete the task of hiring while simultaneously doing a number of other things. It is good to remember that managers seldom if ever get to concentrate on just one thing at a time. While the manager is reviewing and considering candidates, he may also be doing some of the work required by the position that is now vacant, dealing with other employees, trying to meet a request from his boss for information and working on next year's budget. Under such circumstances, thinking about multiple impacts that are weeks or months away is not likely to be an automatic response for the manager. Yet the impacts are real, they depend to some extent on the present hiring decision and they do require his attention if he is to do a good job of hiring.

What does the utilitarian approach have to offer if a hiring manager is trying to consider patterns of decision-making as well as the immediate problem of which candidate best fits the open slot? As we discussed above, many thoughtful individuals have argued that a diverse workforce is important not only to comply with current American laws, but to adequately serve a diverse customer base. Further, many thoughtful individuals argue that it is not good business practice to exclude individuals from being hired because of reasons that do not relate to work. There is no intrinsic reason why a candidate cannot or will not do a good job simply because she is a woman, or he is a Muslim, or he or she fits any of the many categories into which we instinctively sort people. If the hiring manager excludes, consciously or subconsciously, individuals who are qualified and might otherwise perform well because they fit some category that is not actually work-related, then he lessens the chance of filling the position with the applicant who will perform best once placed in the job. He also makes it less likely that a diverse workforce will be achieved.

There are two issues involved here. One is deciding whether to hire a given person for a given job based on criteria that really do not affect or predict job performance. The other is the value of a diverse workforce and steps that might be taken to achieve such a workforce. The first issue is rather easy, at least conceptually. Hiring decisions should be made based on criteria that predict success in the job and should not be made based on other criteria, however much they may accord with the hiring manager's personal beliefs. The fact that there are fewer than twenty females among the CEOs of the 500 largest corporations in the United States cannot be the result of statistical chance.[12] It is the result of decisions by individual boards of directors, choosing to fill one opening at a time, to hire a male rather than a female candidate for CEO of a given company at a given time. Are there really fewer than twenty women qualified to be CEO of a Fortune 500 company? This is a difficult argument to make with a straight face.[13] It is hard to escape the conclusion that at least some boards of directors, faced with the task of hiring a CEO, have for whatever reason given preference to male candidates.

Given the tendency to litigation prevalent in the United States today, it is unlikely that any board member (or for that matter, any other hiring manager at whatever level) will be heard to declare that women are simply not fit to manage. Yet, looking at the numbers of men versus women in top management jobs, it is hard to escape the conclusion that some hiring managers do consider being female as a disqualifying factor for some management positions. Again, such exclusion of individuals based on non-job-related classifications is simply not good business and does not create the greatest good for the greatest number of people.

If indeed a diverse workforce creates the greatest good for the greatest number, then an approach to employment issues that results in such diversity is needed. As a general approach, this means that hiring managers in individual situations should not consistently favor applicants of one gender, or age group, or ethnic background. In some organizations, the location in which they operate will more or less automatically provide a diverse pool of applicants. In this case, all that is needed to achieve the benefits of a diverse workforce is to avoid discriminating against any one class of applicant. In other situations, though, the pool of applicants is not naturally diverse, or at least sufficiently diverse, and efforts to diversify the pool may be required if a diverse workforce is to be achieved.[14] Such efforts are usually not the responsibility of the individual hiring manager, but rather of the human resources department. In this situation, the ethical responsibility of the hiring manager is limited to avoiding discrimination based on non-job-related characteristics, except in small businesses where the hiring manager must perform the human resource functions.

Rights and Duties Analysis

In the chapter on rights and duties, we identified four sources of rights: human rights, legal rights, position rights and contract rights. In considering the rights and duties approach to employment situations, we will be concerned mostly with legal rights and position rights. To review, legal rights are rights that individuals have by reason of being a citizen of some political unit, be it a state, county or city. They are legal rights, which means that they can be found in the law and are enforceable by the mechanisms of law. They can vary from place to place because laws vary. There is no human right to a job. If there were, someone or some organization would have a corresponding duty to provide a job to each person. Position rights are rights that an individual holds by reason of their position, such as police officer or chief financial officer. The position of applicant does not entitle an individual to a job, although it does entitle an individual to be treated fairly in the selection process, and it establishes that employers have a corresponding duty to treat all applicants fairly. Finally, an individual can have a contractual right to keep a job once it is attained, but she does not have a contractual right to obtain a job.

Individuals do not have a legal right to be placed in a given job, but in the United States and some other countries, they do have a legal right to be treated fairly as applicants in the employment process.[15] The right of an applicant to be treated fairly corresponds to a duty of the hiring manager to treat all applicants fairly. There is also a duty of the human resources department, where one exists, to see that hiring procedures provide for fair treatment of all applicants and that these procedures are, in fact, followed by hiring managers.

One obtains the rights of an applicant simply by applying for a job. Fair treatment for qualified applicants is different from fair treatment for unqualified applicants. In the beginning of the process, anyone who applies for a job is an applicant, and the determination of who is qualified and who is not is part of the process of treating all applicants fairly. Correspondingly, one is governed by duties in this situation simply by being the hiring manager. Rights without duties are useless. The part of the manager's job that involves hiring brings with it automatically certain duties and, to the extent that the manager makes or influences the hiring decision, these duties cannot be assigned to someone else.

In Chapter 3, we made the argument that it is normally ethical to follow the law and that cases where ethics might require a person to violate the law are rare. There are numerous laws in the United States that address hiring practices, and in particular discrimination in hiring on a variety of bases. These laws impose duties on employers, and thus on hiring managers, to comply with legal requirements. Since many of these laws are interpreted in court decisions each year, and sometimes are changed by legislators, it would be impossible for each hiring manager to know all of the current provisions that affect their actions. However, ignorance is not an excuse under the law. Human resources departments in medium-sized and large companies have knowledge and expertise in this area, and the duty of the hiring manager is to follow procedures set up by these experts to assure legal compliance and to seek guidance in situations where legal questions arise. In smaller companies, legal knowledge and compliance becomes more difficult, and legal advice is still sometimes required.

Since the first set of decisions normally has to do with who does and who does not meet the minimum qualifications for a job, setting these minimum qualifications correctly is part of treating all applicants fairly. Minimum qualifications are not usually set every time a job opening occurs. When they are set, however, either because a new job has been created or because a review of previous standards is under way, it is important from the perspective of treating applicants fairly that the minimum qualifications be realistic.[16] It is also important from the perspective of the hiring manager that they not be too broad, in order to keep the number of qualified applicants who will receive further consideration to a reasonable number. Those applicants who meet the minimum qualifications will go through a further screening process before one is selected and offered the job. They also have a right to fair treatment as this screening is conducted.

We will explore in more detail below what it means to treat applicants fairly. In a broad sense, this means that screening processes and hiring decisions will be made based on job-related characteristics as much as possible and not on personal preferences of the hiring manager that are not job-related. Applicants have a moral right to be treated fairly; in many cases they also have a legal right to such treatment. One could also argue that applicants have a moral right to be treated with reasonable dignity. This would include such things as conducting interviews at the scheduled time and in a thoughtful manner, without constant interruption. It could also include keeping applicants reasonably informed about the progress of the job search. This would mean that it is not just good business to treat applicants with respect, but it is also the moral thing to do. Applicants also have some rights to privacy. We will discuss this issue further in Chapter 10.

Fairness and Justice Analysis

Under the ethical perspective of fairness and justice, we defined the moral act as the one that treats similarly situated people in a similar manner, with regard to both process and outcome. When applied to the employment decision, this is obviously a perspective that has relevance.[17] In our discussion in the chapter on fairness and justice, we said that similar treatment is not the same as exactly equal treatment. We also said that similar treatment is owed to similarly situated people, but not to everyone regardless of their situation. Let us examine how this might provide guidance to a hiring manager who is concerned that her actions be ethical.

Since the main reason for hiring a person into a vacancy is the expectation that the person hired will be the best contributor to the success of the work unit by performing well, it is reasonable to determine what minimum set of knowledge and skills the person hired should bring to the position. People who lack the minimum knowledge and skills to perform the job successfully are not similarly situated compared to people who have those skills. It is fair and just to make this distinction and to make it early in the hiring process. Some applicants who lack the required skills and knowledge will plead that they really can do the job, if just given a chance. The task of the hiring manager, though, is to hire the applicant most likely to succeed in the position. If the minimum qualifications have been determined reasonably, then using these as the first screen to eliminate unqualified applicants is quite fair.

It sometimes happens that a hiring manager will review a pool of applicants and identify one or two, saying something like this: "Gee, they don't meet the minimum qualifications, but they are very strong in some areas, and I know personally that they are really dependable, so let's include them anyway." A moment's reflection will show that what this actually means is that the minimum qualifications are really not that at all, but a sort of guideline to be ignored based on the manager's individual judgment of each candidate. While the setting of minimum qualifications is probably as much art as science, if they have any meaning for screening candidates, they must apply to all candidates. Perhaps they are set wrong and dependability should be allowed to substitute for education or experience. If that is the case, they should be changed and the new standards should be applied uniformly to the entire applicant pool. Otherwise, similarly situated people will not be treated in a similar way.

In the normal case, the original pool of applicants will be separated into two groups: those who meet the minimum qualifications for the position and those who do not. Since the two groups are not similarly situated it is fair to treat them differently. Those who do not meet the minimum qualification will be told that they did not get the job. Those who do meet these qualifications, assuming there is a sufficient number of such candidates, will undergo further screening as described elsewhere in this chapter. Of this group, a relatively small number of the most qualified will undergo still further screening in the form of interviews or tests, or both. The others, who are not as qualified, will be treated differently and told that they did not get the job. Finally, one applicant from the most qualified group will be offered the job and, assuming that this applicant accepts, the others will be treated differently and told that they did not get the job. At each step, if the process is done carefully, two groups will be identified that are not similarly situated and will be treated in different ways. This process meets the definition of fairness and justice.

What if a job search ends with no candidates who meet the minimum qualifications or the only qualified candidate does not accept the job offer? Would it be fair at this point to reconsider the applicant pool, but apply lower minimum qualifications? Since the purpose of the job search is to find an applicant who can become a successful employee in the open position, it is certainly reasonable at this point to reconsider the minimum job qualifications. If this is done, then fairness and justice would indicate that the new, lower minimum qualifications should be applied to the entire applicant pool. What actually happens at this point, often enough, is that the hiring manager simply reaches into the remaining pool of applicants, picks one based on intuition and quickly sets up an interview and makes an offer. This may or may not work out for the best, depending on the manager's intuition (and, frankly, depending on their luck). However, what occurs is no longer a fair and rational job search, but a quick casting about for an immediate solution to an immediate problem.

If we analyze the processes and recommendations described above, we see that a fair hiring procedure is basically a rational hiring procedure. No hiring procedure is foolproof. Any manager who has made several hires, or any human resources professional, will confirm that people who look good on paper, and who interview well, do not always perform well once they are on the job. It is also true that apparently marginal candidates sometimes turn out to be stars. In these cases, the hiring manager is sometimes found, well after the fact, to have shown marvelous insight into the potential of the candidate who turned out very well. As a general rule, though, a rational process based on an examination of the facts as they can be determined about each candidate, and treating those who appear to be similar in similar ways, has a better chance of succeeding in picking the best candidate than a process based on managerial intuition.[18] Such a rational process is also the only way to go if fairness and justice are important criteria for the search.

Special Cases: Promotion

We now turn from the basic hiring situation to two special cases of employment action. The first of these is the situation where a job opening is to be filled by promotion instead of by outside hiring. The issues are basically the same whether the company has a policy of only hiring from within for some jobs or whether the pool of candidates includes both outside applicants and candidates who already work for the company but seek to be promoted into the open job.

Suppose that the open position is that of supervisor. The hiring manager surveys the employees currently working in the section that has the open supervisory position, selects the best technician (accountant, claims examiner, engineer) in the section and promotes him to supervisor. This is a common scenario that occurs in many different companies in many different industries. What happens next, with depressing regularity, is that the newly promoted supervisor does not perform well as supervisor and ends up either being demoted to his former position as a technician or leaving the company entirely. The section has lost a good technician, at least temporarily, and gained a poor supervisor. What went wrong?

The job of supervisor requires different skills than the job of technician. A good technician, whether an accountant, a claims examiner or an engineer, is comfortable with detail. He knows a lot about some technical area and can apply his knowledge easily to the work at hand. It could be said that he works best in a world the size of a computer monitor. A good supervisor is aware of what is going on around him. He knows who is doing what throughout his section. He is comfortable interfacing with other supervisors, with bosses and with the people in the section. He switches easily from training a new employee to meeting with the department's other supervisors, to working on budget forms. He has a sense of how his section's work contributes to the larger efforts of the rest of the company. He is able to adapt to changing circumstances and respond to both opportunities and deadlines.

Some few individuals combine both skill sets to a high degree. However, most people do not, and herein lies the heart of the problem. The good supervisor has at least some technical knowledge of the work done in the section. He will have a very hard time doing his job without this. However, he does not have to be and often is not the best technician in the section. He is not paid to do the work of the section, but to oversee the doing of the work by the members of the section and to tend to the interfaces of his section with others within and outside the company. In other words, his job description is significantly different from those of the technicians in the section, and the minimum qualifications for the job of supervisor are significantly different from those of the technicians.

Ignoring these facts in the selection/promotion process is the mistake that leads to unhappy consequences. If a new supervisor fails to perform adequately, not only is he unhappy, but the boss who promoted him is also unhappy, the members of the section are unhappy and others inside or outside the company may be unhappy. These are rather severe consequences. To cause them by making the wrong promotion, based on the wrong criteria, certainly does not create the greatest good for the greatest number. In other words, according to the utilitarian perspective, it is not only bad business to promote the wrong person to supervisor when the likely failure is foreseeable, it is unethical to do so.

Suppose, though, that a technician does have the skills required of a supervisor, at least to a reasonable degree. Should he be promoted if the supervisor job is open? There is a strong argument for doing so. If he is the best-qualified candidate, then our previous analysis of the standard hiring process shows that he should be offered the position. There are additional benefits in the case of promotion. Many employees hope to rise one day to more responsible and higher-paid positions. When they see one of their own make this transition successfully, it gives them hope for themselves and makes them more inclined to stay with the company and to do good work in the hope of obtaining a similar promotion. If these employees are good ones, and indeed might be capable of moving up, keeping them happy and motivated creates a significant benefit for the company as well as for the employee.

A further consideration is that a supervisor who is rightly promoted from within the section will almost certainly have a shorter breaking-in period, since he already knows not only the technical work but the people he supervises and the company's practices and procedures. In this happy circumstance, when an employee in the section is qualified to be supervisor and is the best candidate, his promotion clearly achieves the greatest good for the greatest number. Some of these benefits can also be attained by promoting someone who is already an employee of the company, but does not currently work in the section where the supervisory opening exists.

Utilitarianism provides an interesting perspective here. If the unqualified or significantly less qualified employee is promoted, there is a reasonable chance that he will not perform adequately in the new job. If this occurs, it will result eventually in his removal from the job, after a period of poor performance. This period of poor performance will most probably be a difficult and unhappy time for the employee, for those he oversees and for his boss. If he does perform well, he may well have to overcome obstacles presented by the initial expectation of those he supervises that he will fail because he lacks qualifications. This period of proving himself will be a time of struggle for the new supervisor, which he may or may not enjoy. It will probably be an anxious time for those he supervises and for the boss who promoted him and is observing the struggle. In neither case is it likely that the promotion will result in the greatest good for the greatest number.

From the perspective of rights and duties, an employee does not have a right to a promotion simply by being an employee. He also does not obtain such a right by performing well in his present job. If managers had a duty to promote all employees who perform well, many organizations would soon become exceedingly top-heavy. Senior managers who performed well would have to be promoted to even more senior positions. Finally, what would we do with CEOs who perform well? As we have seen previously, employees have a right to be treated fairly if they apply for a promotion, just as other applicants for the position have a similar right. They do not have a right, by their position as employee, to extra consideration (unless being an employee is a legitimate qualification for the job) or to be awarded the job simply because of their status as employee.[19]

Under the perspective of fairness and justice, the issue turns on whether the current employee is similarly situated as an applicant with other applicants from outside the company. Again, assuming that the company does not have a policy of promoting only from within, and assuming that the similarly situated group is defined as those having similar qualifications, then the inside employee should be seen as a member of the applicant pool, or a qualified member of the applicant pool. If, for legitimate job-related reasons, inside candidates are preferred, then the employee is not similarly situated with outside candidates, and fairness does not require treating him in a similar manner in terms of the selection process.

Would it be fair to consider company employees, or employees of the section whose supervisory job is open, to be in a special class of applicants? This would mainly depend on whether some requirement of the job could be better met by insiders than by outsiders. This might legitimately be the case. Ideally, such a decision would be made before the pool of applicants is assembled. This is so because, once the pool of applicants has been assembled, the next step is to decide which applicants are similarly situated, and it is logical that the criteria for grouping the applicants should already be in place. There is much to be said for specifying additional experience or knowledge beyond the minimum qualifications as "preferred" in the job advertisement or posting. As long as the additional criteria are legitimately job-related, this provides useful additional means for further screening those candidates who meet the minimum job requirements.

Managers sometimes argue that present employees should be promoted as a reward for their good performance in their present jobs. This can be said of workers being considered for promotion to supervisor, or of those who already manage and are being considered for promotion to higher management positions. If the employee is the most qualified candidate, there is no question that the promotion is in order. This is not really a promotion-as-reward scenario, but rather a case of the best candidate getting the job. What happens, though, if the employee in question does not meet the minimum qualifications for the new job, or meets them but is significantly less qualified than another candidate? This is a case of promotion as reward.

Fairness and justice requires that similarly situated people be treated similarly regarding both process and outcome. What we have been arguing in this case is that current employees who apply for a higher-level position in their company are similarly situated with outside applicants for the same position. There are benefits to promoting good employees in terms of company loyalty and encouraging other present employees to work hard and strive for promotion within the company. Nevertheless, there are disadvantages to promoting unqualified or less qualified individuals to positions of increasing responsibility. It is fair to all applicants if the most qualified is offered the open position. It is unfair to offer the position to those significantly less qualified or unqualified simply because they currently work for the company and perform well in their present position.

Special Cases: Equally Qualified Candidates

At the beginning of the chapter, a set of questions was posed concerning criteria for choosing when more than one candidate meets minimum qualifications, but there is only one position open. In the course of the chapter, we have added the distinction that there can be significant differences in qualifications between candidates, both or all of whom meet minimum qualifications. While "significantly different" is a relative term, it is a concept with some meaning. If a position requires a Bachelor's degree in a given field, one candidate may have that degree, but another may have an advanced degree in the same field. This probably constitutes a significant difference. If six months' experience in a given position is a job requirement, a candidate who just meets this standard is significantly different in qualification from one who has five years' experience in the same position. On the other hand, the difference between a candidate with ten months' experience and one with a year's experience is probably not significant.

What should the hiring manager who wishes to be ethical use as a criterion for deciding between two candidates, both of whom meet the minimum qualifications and neither of whom differs significantly from the other in the specified requirements for the job? In times when the economy is good and unemployment low, this may not be a frequent issue. On the other hand, when unemployment is up, or when a job is particularly desirable, the situation may present itself often. In any case, the hiring manager faced with this case cannot decide what to do based on the information and analysis provided so far in this chapter.

Hiring decisions do have ethical implications. The present situation, because it is more problematic and less open to easy explanation, has added implications. If this situation is faced with some frequency, either by the individual hiring manager or by the company, the issue of individual decisions forming patterns also comes to the fore. While we are treating this as a special case of the general employment decision, it is in some ways the most difficult and the most symbolic case.

As a starting point, we can question what we mean when we say that two candidates are equally qualified. When minimum qualifications are specified, they are usually not intended to describe all of the knowledge and experience that will contribute to success in a given job. In defining minimum qualifications, it is useful to specify items that can be quantified or identified on a yes/no basis. A candidate either has a Bachelor's degree in accounting, or she does not. Her grade point either was 3.0 or higher, or it was not. She either has at least six months' experience processing accounts payable, or she does not. If she has more than six months' experience, we can specify how much more. Although other criteria are sometimes used, their measurement is either difficult or impossible, so that their application to a group of candidates is primarily subjective. How do you compare two candidates in terms of such criteria as "friendly and outgoing," or "responsible," or "detail-oriented"? It is possible and sometimes necessary to identify examples of these traits in interviews, but they are harder to judge than possession of a specified degree or period of previous work experience.

The economy of the United States, and of most other developed countries, is heavily service-oriented. More than four out of five jobs in the United States are in service rather than manufacturing industries. It is in fact important in service industries to have workers who are friendly and outgoing. It is important to have supervisors who are fair. When workers do not share the same physical location as their supervisors (bus drivers, field sales representatives, policemen), it is important that they be responsible. Human resources professionals often agree that the best single indicator of what an employee or applicant will do is what that employee or applicant has done. This does not deny the possibility that an employee will learn from experience and change their future behavior. It does mean that most of us are creatures of habit. If an applicant has been fired from his last three jobs because of attendance problems, chances are good that the next manager who hires him will have to deal with similar problems.

The hiring manager who is trying to decide between two candidates who are equal on the specified minimum qualifications for the job would be acting rationally and ethically if she reviewed other work-related factors to help in making her decision. The reasons why an applicant left his previous job or jobs might well be indicative of work-related issues. Even the number of previous jobs might be revealing. In an extreme case, a candidate who has three years' related work experience at the same company is probably more attractive than one who has the same amount of experience but acquired it by spending six months each with six different employers. Since the basic objective of the selection process is to hire the candidate who is most likely to perform well in the open position, a tendency toward attendance problems or job-hopping is certainly relevant in assessing an applicant's likelihood to succeed on the job.

So far, all of the ethical analysis using each of the three major perspectives that we illustrated earlier in the chapter still holds good. What happens, though, in the case where a reasonably diligent inquiry still does not reveal any job-related differences on which to base a choice between applicants? Very seldom are such decisions made by flipping a coin or putting both names in a hat and drawing out one to be the winner. What managers often say, when asked to describe their reasons in making such a choice, is that they were somehow more comfortable with one applicant rather than the other, or that it came down to "chemistry." What this seems to mean, when managers are pressed further to explain their decisions, is that I chose the candidate who was more like me. If this is indeed the case, is there anything morally wrong with using such a criterion as a tie-breaker in situations where there is no other clear reason to choose one candidate over the other?

Suppose that the position open is that of department manager. Suppose further that "more like me" in this case means that I, the hiring manager, am thoughtful and careful in analysis and decisive once the analysis has been completed, and so, apparently, is the chosen candidate. On the other hand, suppose that I, the hiring manager, am a conservative, well-dressed white male, and so, apparently, is the chosen candidate. To make an even more extreme case, suppose that I am a rabid fan of the Chicago Cubs, and so is the chosen candidate. In each case, I am more comfortable with the chosen candidate because he is more like me—we have better chemistry.

In the first case, the characteristics of thoughtfulness followed by decisiveness might be seen as job-related. A manager who does not give careful thought to his decisions, or who cannot make up his mind after conducting an analysis, may not be a successful performer in the job. Thus, we are not really dealing here with an instance of "chemistry", but with a subtle but important job-related characteristic. In the second case, being well-dressed may or may not be job-related, depending on the amount of dealings with customers, senior executives or others for whom appearance actually matters. The issue of being conservative is more subtle, harder to clearly identify from an application or in an interview and perhaps less likely to be job-related. Thus, if it is really being used as a key criterion for the hiring decision, caution seems to be in order. A conservative controller may be a good thing, while a conservative marketing manager may not. But for most positions, the meaning of "conservative" is too vague, and its connection to job performance is too tenuous. Being a white male may induce a level of comfort if the hiring manager is also white and male but, of the characteristics mentioned, it is least apt to be in any way job-related and, as we will see below when we discuss hiring patterns, it is most problematic. Being a rabid fan of the Chicago Cubs is a characteristic that really does not need a great deal of analysis, unless a propensity to support underdogs is a relevant job characteristic.

What we see from these examples is that some characteristics of applicants that might not initially appear to be job-related may actually turn out to be so, either directly or indirectly. Other characteristics that are in no way job-related appear silly on their face of it when provided as reasons for a hiring decision. Some characteristics are not really job-related, are not on the face of it silly, but are problematic. For instance, to continue the example, let us consider white and male.

It sometimes happens that a hiring decision comes down to two candidates, both of whom appear to be equally qualified on the basis of any and all job-related characteristics that can be assessed through the normal selection process. Only one of the candidates can be hired. The hiring manager may say something like, "This one just feels like the right one." Since the hiring manager presumably is in her position because she is qualified for the job, and she has followed the company's procedures for forming a pool of applicants and screening them based on job-related criteria, does it matter at all in a moral sense which one she now chooses, and why? Suppose she personally does not like men, or African Americans, or Catholics, and when we analyze with her why one "feels right," it turns out that this personal preference was the final criterion in choosing one candidate over the other. Is this morally neutral? Although it is unlikely, suppose that in three or four successive job searches, each time the choice comes down to two equally qualified candidates, and each time she selects the woman, or the Caucasian, or the non-Catholic. Are we still on morally neutral grounds?

Let us start to analyze this particularly difficult case by returning to a point made earlier in the chapter. Because the hiring manager controls a resource, namely, the open position, that is desired by several applicants, one applicant will gain because of the hiring manager's decision and others will lose. This is why there is an ethical component in the hiring decision, whether it is explicitly recognized by the hiring manager or not. The hiring manager's task is to select the candidate who is most likely to perform well in the open position. Further, as was stated earlier in this chapter, the hiring manager also has an obligation to observe the law in the selection process. There are two issues here that intertwine. First, is it moral to choose or deny a candidate because of gender, race or religion regardless of the law, and second, does it violate the law to do so?

The second question is the easier to dispense with. The short answer is yes, it does violate the law to discriminate in hiring based on a candidate's gender, race or religion. In the United States, such discrimination is illegal except for small employers. A manager has the authority and responsibility to hire one applicant and decline another because of her position as manager, unless she owns the company. Acting in her position as manager, if she breaks the law the company is made liable. She has an ethical obligation not to break the law and place the company in a position of liability. Therefore, she has an ethical obligation not to base her hiring decision on criteria that the law forbids her to use.

We said in Chapter 3 that, while the legal and the moral are often the same, they are not always the same. It might be legal for a company that employs fourteen people to discriminate based on gender, race or religion, but illegal for a company that employs sixteen people to discriminate on the same basis. It is very hard to build an argument that the morality of such discrimination depends on the number of people employed. This leads us back to the first question, namely, is it moral to choose or deny a candidate based on gender, race or religion, regardless of the law?

It is important for this analysis to view the individual choice as both a single event and as a part of a pattern. A work unit composed of all women or all whites or all non-Catholics gets that way as a result of a number of individual choices. A group of 500 CEOs of the largest companies in the United States that has fewer than 4 percent females got that way as a result of individual choices by boards of directors choosing one candidate at a time. There is, in fact, an ethical implication about patterns of hiring or promoting involved in each individual decision, whether the manager recognizes it at the time or not.

The fairness and justice approach, which seems the most relevant here, requires treating similarly situated people in similar ways, regarding both process and outcome. The heart of the matter is whether the two finalists, one of whom gets the job and one of whom does not, are similarly situated. Of course, no two people are exactly alike. If the two finalists are similarly situated in all relevant characteristics that can be determined in a reasonable screening process, then it will not be possible to treat them similarly in outcome, except on the basis of dissimilarities that are not job-related. This is true both for the individual decision and for the pattern of decisions of which this individual decision is a part.

Since the pattern issue is real and is hiring-related, what if we include this as part of the assessment of similarity for the two finalists now under consideration? In other words, if the two seem similar in all relevant characteristics for the job now open, what if we consider whether one is the better choice in light of patterns of hiring? What is suggested here is that if diversity is a good thing in the workforce, as we discussed earlier in this chapter, then it is a hiring-pattern issue. When every other relevant characteristic fails to identify one candidate as the better choice, then diversity could be a legitimate basis for choosing. The diversity issue could involve age, gender or any other issue for which diversity matters in the workforce. If this argument is valid, it stands whether the law mandates diversity or at least non-discrimination or not.

Note that the argument made here for diversity does not become operative unless and until a pool of applicants has been screened and the best two or more candidates have been found to be essentially equal in all relevant characteristics for the open job. Diversity thus becomes a tie-breaker, and only operates as a decision criterion if there is a tie. It is hiring-related in the pattern sense. Diversity as a tie-breaker is another way of separating two or more people who are otherwise similarly situated and providing a defensible basis for treating them differently in outcome (although the selection and screening process to this point will have treated them similarly).

If an organization is located in an area where the population is diverse, and it regularly finds that its applicant pools are diverse, then the opportunity will sometimes present itself to use diversity as one criterion for hiring. In these cases, the argument made above that diversity can serve as a legitimate tie-breaker in hiring situations holds true, and using it can achieve fairness and justice. The same can be said for cases where affirmative action is used to increase the diversity of applicant pools.

The argument for using diversity as a tie-breaker is essentially utilitarian. Recall that, according to the utilitarian perspective, the moral act is the one that creates the greatest good for the greatest number. When we consider what we have called the pattern perspective, the relevance of this definition becomes clear. The pattern perspective focuses not so much on the individual hiring decision by itself as on this decision as one of several, and the pattern that is created by the sum of these individual decisions. We showed above that a pattern of non-discrimination (here meaning non-discrimination on the basis of characteristics or criteria that are not job-related) creates the greatest good for the greatest number. If decisions are made based on job-related criteria first, and in cases where this does not identify the best candidate, then on pattern-related criteria, we have set up a means to the end of non-discrimination, in the sense described above.

The discussion of using diversity as a tie-breaker in cases of employment decisions has been framed as a choice between at least two candidates who are equally qualified. Earlier in the chapter, we discussed promotion as a form of hiring decision. We said there that, in some situations, being an internal candidate is job-related and can be a legitimate factor in choosing between candidates. If this is not the case, or if both finalists are internal candidates, then our discussion of diversity can apply to decisions to promote as well as decisions to hire.

There is one final possibility that we have not yet addressed. What if two or more finalists are essentially equal on all reasonable characteristics and diversity does not serve as a tie-breaker? This could occur either because diversity is not judged to be a desirable goal in the particular situation or because the candidates do not differ on whatever diversity issues are considered relevant. This situation is unlikely but possible. Now, finally, have we created a situation where the manager is morally free to hire the attractive female or the Chicago Cubs fan? There is no good answer here. The stated goals of this book are to help managers recognize the ethical implications of their actions and to provide them with some methods or tools for thinking through difficult moral situations. In the present case, the "right" answer is not at all clear, so no answer is provided. Rational analysis has taken us as far as it can.

eight
Performance Appraisal and Compensation

Various Approaches to Compensation

In the last chapter, we discussed the role of the manager in hiring and promoting, and some of the ethical issues involved. We turn now to the role of the manager in evaluating the performance of employees and determining their compensation. In a number of employment situations, performance on the job does not determine or even influence raises and bonuses. Under negotiated labor-management contracts, salaries and raises are determined by one's position and how long one has been in it (seniority).[1] Most employment contracts specify raises and bonuses in such a way that managerial performance appraisal does not play a role. Public employee raises are sometimes determined by legislative bodies rather than by managers. Raises and bonuses of various types for CEOs of public companies are determined by boards of directors, on the advice of their compensation committees and often with the input of compensation consultants hired for this purpose. While this group constitutes a small portion of all compensation decisions, it receives a significant amount of publicity and therefore shapes some people's view of the whole process of appraisal and compensation.

Several years ago, the legislature of the State of Nevada determined that faculty members at the state's universities and community colleges would not receive cost of living raises during the next fiscal period, but that a pool of money would be available for merit raises. This led to considerable discussion at the universities about how to structure merit increases. One faction felt that all faculty members, by the fact that they were employed as faculty members, were meritorious. They called for a distribution of the merit pool to all faculty members. Another faction felt that merit was not universal (at least, not equal merit) and that there should be differences in the amounts and percentages of raises granted different faculty members, with a significant minority not receiving increases. The legislature got wind of this discussion (or so it was rumored) and sent word to university administrators that if the merit raises were turned into cost of living raises, the legislature would simply withhold all funds for faculty increases. The merit pool was finally treated as such; some faculty members got larger percentage raises than others, and many got no raise at all.

This little story illustrates an important point about the connection between performance appraisal and compensation. An organization can choose to award compensation increases based on performance, or based on inflation, or based on position and longevity, or based on some combination of these factors.[2] However, these are different bases for making compensation decisions, and the organization needs to be clear about what it is trying to do in order to manage compensation rationally. Managers generally seem to prefer merit systems, whereby at least part of any increase in compensation is based on performance. Some workers, particularly those in union environments, seem to prefer some basis other than merit, so that individual managers will have no say in which workers receive how much increase in their compensation.

Since this book is primarily written for managers, I suspect that most readers will take it for granted that merit compensation is the right and natural way to go. But, as I regularly remind my MBA students, the whole world is not made up of people who think that managing is a fine and noble profession, and that it is so complex that an investment of time and money such as they are making is helpful in learning how to do it well. Less than three miles from the university where I teach is the world-famous Las Vegas Strip. There, in huge hotel-casinos, tens of thousands of union workers perform tasks that provide services to millions of visitors annually. Many of these workers have higher pay and benefits than they would otherwise have because of the influence of the Culinary Union. Ask these workers if management is a fine and honorable profession, and many of them will say no. One of the reasons that some workers pay union dues is their perception that they will fare better as employees with a union than without one.

Hotel workers in Las Vegas are not the only ones who hesitate to trust their managers to determine their salary increase. Many teachers throughout the United States belong to unions. These unions, almost without exception, have historically been opposed to any form of merit pay.[3] Their expressed feeling on the subject is this: if administrators, such as school principals, are allowed to determine salary increases, they will simply reward their friends and punish their enemies. They simply cannot be trusted to evaluate meritorious teaching and make compensation decisions accordingly.

Faculty in many American universities receive merit pay increases. However, the evaluation of meritorious performance is numbingly complex.

The faculty member must prepare a detailed package of documentation, often several inches thick, justifying an increase. The decision often involves the judgments of three individuals (department chair, dean and provost), two committees (department and college) and final official approval by the university president. After all of this, elaborate grievance procedures are in place for those faculty members who wish to question the collective wisdom of the entire process. A much simpler way for a faculty member to get a raise is to move to a different university and negotiate a higher starting salary.

There are, then, many accepted ways of approaching the issue of compensation increases. In most private businesses in the United States, where compensation is not governed by negotiated labor-management agreements, some form of merit compensation is the rule. This approach, whether for mail clerks or for CEOs, relates increases in compensation to an evaluation of job performance during the previous period. It is this approach that we will now analyze, along with the problems it presents for managers.

In the chapter on employment, we said that there is an ethical component in the hiring decision because the hiring manager controls a resource that is desired by several applicants, but will be awarded to one and denied to others. A salary increase or bonus or stock option grant also constitutes a valued resource, controlled to some degree by an individual manager and not awarded to all employees equally. We have the conditions, then, for an ethical component in the performance appraisal-compensation increase decision.

Merit-Based Compensation Decisions and Performance Appraisal

In the analysis that follows, we make certain assumptions. Compensation increases will be granted to some or all of the employees reporting to a manager, and the basis for such increases and their amounts will be the manager's evaluation of each employee's performance during a specified period. Since the most common period for such evaluation seems to be one year, we will use this period in our base analysis. We assume that the organization has specified some rules for how the process will work and has placed some limits or parameters on the amount and kind of increases that may be awarded. We will assume, finally, that both the manager and the employee have been in the work unit together throughout the period being evaluated.

What obligations does a manager have in doing that part of her job that relates to performance appraisal? First, let us agree that this is a part of the manager's job and that she is expected to do it competently and professionally. Much has been written about the task of performance appraisal and we will not attempt to add to this body of writing. One of the standard and primary recommendations for good performance appraisal is that it be done on an objective basis as far as possible. Obviously, if I am evaluating you, there is a subjective element involved. Nevertheless, if I am evaluating how many teller transactions you completed, or how many invoices you processed, or how many miles you drove your bus without an accident or a customer complaint, there is also an objective component to the evaluation.

In our discussion of the hiring decision, we said repeatedly that the manager's primary task is to obtain good performance from the unit that he manages. This perspective is also good to remember in discussing performance evaluation. There are several reasons why managers have as part of their job the evaluation of employees who report to them. One is related to compensation increases. Another is to identify workers who are not performing adequately and either help them to improve their performance or remove them from their jobs. Another is to identify particularly promising or high-performing employees and prepare them for promotion if they seem capable of performing in a higher position. Still another reason why performance evaluation is part of a manager's job is that almost everyone could do their job at least a little better. The unit that the manager oversees would perform better if everyone did improve by just a bit. Part of the manager's job is to do what she can to achieve this improvement.[4]

Our discussion of performance appraisal so far has perhaps given the impression that it is a once-a-year task, like preparing the budget. Much of the writing on performance appraisal makes it clear that this is an ongoing task, and it cannot really be done well if it is limited to one evaluation a year and one conversation a year to discuss this evaluation. It is pretty much standard wisdom in the writing on performance appraisal that nothing said in the annual formal interview for appraisal should come as a surprise to the employee being evaluated. Discussions between manager and employee, both about superior and inadequate performance, should occur regularly. Such a pattern of discussions is sometimes described as performance management.[5] In most companies, filling out an official appraisal form and discussing it with the employee is an annual ritual. The official form is not designed by the individual manager. Instead, it tends to be a one-size-fits-all form that actually does not fit any individual situation perfectly. It has the virtue of standardization and often involves assigning numerical ratings to a number of performance categories. Not uncommonly, the final evaluation is reduced to a single number on a rather limited scale. This makes it easy to compare employees' performance ratings; unfortunately, it is impossible to accurately summarize a year's work in a single number.

Unless a manager is in a position to change the system, she must work with her company's system. Because the allocation of valuable resources depends on her evaluation, there is an ethical component to the evaluation process. Obviously, the manager performing the evaluation has an obligation to do so carefully and thoughtfully. Another issue arises here that we have not previously discussed, namely, the obligation to be honest in appraising a subordinate's performance. But why would a manager be less than honest?

Lying and Truth-Telling in Performance Appraisal

Suppose that the employee being evaluated is a sixty-four-year-old woman who has announced her intention to retire next year. You have been her supervisor for one year, and you judge that her performance is below standard, but not bad enough at present to require termination unless she improves. When you review her personnel file, you find that her previous supervisor has rated her as satisfactory for each of the last three years. People who have been in the unit for a long time assure you that her performance has not changed this year. One final item of relevance is that she does not take criticism well. In fact, she tends to respond to criticism with tears and hostility. Should you rate her as satisfactory, as your predecessor did for the last three years, or should you rate her as below standard and endure the difficult interview that is sure to follow, with very little hope that her performance will improve before she retires? In other words, is it the ethical thing to make Granny cry, and if so, why?

If you evaluate her as satisfactory, fill out the form accordingly, sign it and put it in her personnel file, you have lied on an official document in your official role as manager. But it is just a little lie! First, some additional questions will help to shed light on the situation. Suppose Granny's situation changes, she decides not to retire and she will spend the next five years in your section instead of leaving next year. Should you still rate her satisfactory? What if you have two performance appraisals to conduct and the second one is for a forty-year-old male whose situation is similar to Granny's in terms of his performance and his previous evaluation? Should you rate him satisfactory also? If not, why not? Suppose your company is considering layoffs and the method of deciding which employees will have to leave is performance-based, with emphasis on the most recent performance appraisal? Suppose the other workers in the unit are becoming increasingly frustrated because they have to pick up the extra work due to Granny's failure to do her share, and they have expressed this frustration to you as their manager?

As with so much else in the work environment, individual performance appraisals are done within a wider context. A little lie, told to one employee and recorded in her file, has repercussions. Most employees consider performance appraisals to be important matters. They are often apprehensive coming into the interview, they care a lot about what their manager has written and how she explains the appraisal, and they go out either uplifted or downtrodden depending on the content of the appraisal. If a manager lies in an important matter, can it be a small lie? It seems not.

As we saw with employment decisions, performance appraisals must be considered both as individual actions, an interchange between a manager and an employee, and also as part of a pattern. The decision to lie on Granny's evaluation raises the question of what other lies might have been told or are going to be told on performance appraisals. Let us suppose that "little" lies like this one are told on one out of five performance appraisals. This means that anyone using performance appraisals to make any sort of decision has a one in five chance of basing their decision on deliberately erroneous information. Since it is inevitable that some performance appraisals will also contain information that is based on honestly mistaken judgments, there is now a better than one in five chance that the user of the performance appraisal will be using bad information.

What sort of uses might be made of performance appraisals? First of all, they may be used to determine compensation increases. They may also be used to identify promising employees in order to prepare them for higher positions. They may be used for progressive discipline (graduated warnings leading to possible termination for poor performance). They may be used in case of layoffs to determine who stays and who goes. They are regularly used in considering employees for either lateral transfers or promotions. In total, these uses of performance appraisals have a lot to do with how a company manages its human resources. If all of this is based on lies, things are clearly not as they should be, and smart managers will no longer rely on performance appraisals as a source of valid information. For this very negative consequence to occur, it is not necessary that all, or most, or even half of the performance appraisals contain lies. It is enough that lying is known or suspected to occur with some frequency for smart managers to decrease or cease their reliance on the whole performance appraisal system for information.

There is a further harmful effect from a pattern of lying on performance appraisals. Employees will sense that lying is occurring. If they are rated higher than their performance deserves, they are very unlikely to complain. They are more likely to make note of the fact that their manager is either too dumb to see their real performance or too dishonest to report it. Since performance appraisals are often the basis for compensation increases, and compensation increases often become known to employees, at least a general sense of what performance rating people received will also be known to employees. Since those who work with an employee in the same unit are apt to be quite accurate in judging that employee's performance, it is not a long stretch to conclude that those who work with an employee who is not evaluated accurately will know this. If they think the correct rating is obvious, they will conclude that the manager is either dumber than dirt or dishonest. Neither conclusion is conducive to positive performance or trust.

As we saw with employment decisions, each decision is part of a pattern, whether that fact is recognized at the time the decision is made or not. This same fact sheds new light on why it is important not to lie on an individual performance appraisal. Not lying by itself does not fulfill a manager's obligations with regard to conducting performance appraisals. The ongoing process of evaluating the performance of employees and discussing this with them as well as the formal annual review of performance are part of the job of managers. In most companies, the performance appraisal is directly related to the amount of compensation increase that an employee will receive. Since the two are linked, we can now turn to an examination of the ethical concerns in this process and see what each of the three major perspectives on ethics can contribute to analyzing this part of a manager's job.

Utilitarian Analysis

Once again, utilitarianism defines the moral act as the one that produces the greatest good for the greatest number of people. Appropriate compensation increases produce considerable happiness for many of those who receive them. Some employees will undoubtedly feel that they deserved a greater increase than they received but, on the whole, appropriate increases will produce employee happiness. Such increases will also tend to keep employees reasonably motivated and loyal to their employer. This is good for the organization as a whole. Shareholders might prefer lower or no compensation increases, but would favor higher profits. Customers might prefer lower or no compensation increases and instead would use the money to lower prices. This is the eternal triangle that challenges business strategists. The proper balance among the three is the one that keeps employees, shareholders and customers reasonably satisfied without doing so at the price of driving away one or both of the other groups. This is why the phrase "appropriate compensation increases" is used.

There is no magical formula for determining how much is appropriate when discussing compensation increases. In an open labor market, with unemployment relatively low, if compensation does not satisfy employees at one company, they will leave and work for competitors who offer better compensation. Likewise, shareholders can sell their stock or refuse to buy new issues if they feel profits are too low, and customers can shop elsewhere if they feel prices are too high.

Two levels of management decision are involved here. One is the organization-wide level where overall wages and policies for compensation increases are set[6]; the other is the individual level where a manager recommends or grants a specific increase for a specific employee. Most managers are not directly involved at the first level, but the implementation of these company-wide decisions is a responsibility of most managers. The greatest good for the greatest number of people is achieved if individual performance appraisals are conducted thoughtfully and accurately, and are communicated to the individuals being appraised in a manner that is both professional and sensitive. Most employees do not consider it professional or sensitive to be called into the manager's office and told to "read this and sign it—I have to turn it in this afternoon." It is not entirely uncommon for performance appraisals to be conducted in just this way, but it is unlikely to provide much happiness for anyone except, possibly, the manager.

From a utilitarian perspective, then, managers have an obligation to conduct performance appraisals in a professional and reasonable way.[7] From the same perspective, they have an obligation to be truthful on performance appraisals. This is where the pattern perspective comes in. It does not create the greatest good for anyone if the performance appraisal system is permeated with lies. As we saw above, this means that the system cannot be used reliably to identify fast-track employees, to judge appropriate compensation increases or to discipline or terminate non-performing employees. This last point needs a bit of elaboration.

In some companies, no employee can be terminated until the case is first reviewed by the human resources department. One reason for this is the complex laws and regulations that now govern employment and termination. We will examine this issue in some depth in the next chapter. The reason for raising the issue here is as follows. Human resources professionals say that it is not uncommon to have a termination case presented for approval with a personnel file indicating no negative evaluations or warnings of any sort. When asked the reason for termination, managers say something like this: "they just don't perform well, have not performed well, don't respond to suggestions for improvement, and, well, we can't tolerate this anymore." When asked why the verbal description differs so greatly from the written description in the personnel file, these managers become less articulate. When told they cannot proceed with the termination because the company does not have a legal leg to stand on and, in fact, would have to settle before trial for a large amount of money if the employee were terminated and subsequently sued, these managers become dismayed.

Both because law and regulation require it, and because professional management practice would require it even without laws and regulations, telling employees about unsatisfactory performance, documenting the conversation and offering suggestions for improvement are required. They are required, among other things, by a utilitarian analysis. This process relates to fairness, as we will see below. Nonetheless, an organization in which performance appraisals do not address the reality of poor performance, but poor performers are fired without warning is not an organization promoting the greatest good for the greatest number. We are not talking here about termination for cause or layoffs. In terminations for cause, an employee has done or failed to do something so critical that warnings are not in order. Examples might be physically striking a supervisor or embezzling company funds. In layoff situations, employees are terminated not because of seriously inadequate performance, but because of an urgent need to reduce total staff quickly.

Rights and Duties Analysis

The rights and duties perspective says that the moral act is the one that recognizes the rights of others and the duties those rights impose on the actor. The actor here is the manager, and the rights of employees being evaluated, as well as other users of the performance appraisal system, are at issue. We said in the chapter on rights and duties that humans have a basic right to be told the truth. There are exceptions to this rule, but it is the fundamental rule. If we accept this, then its application in the performance appraisal setting is clear. Employees, as humans, have a right to be told the truth about their work performance by their work supervisor. This right means that managers have a duty to tell employees the truth on their performance appraisals. Since most performance appraisal forms include a section called something like "areas needing improvement," most performance appraisal interviews will include some discussion that amounts to criticism of current performance.

This may be a small part of the overall appraisal, if the employee is generally a good performer. Unfortunately, most people do not receive criticism well, so this is often the most difficult part of the performance appraisal process. There are many ways to discuss performance and many ways to communicate what is lacking and how it might be provided in terms of the employee's job performance.[8] Unfortunately, many supervisors dislike confrontation of any sort and find it difficult to sit down one on one with a subordinate and initiate a discussion that may become confrontational. Some supervisors deal with this problem simply by not listing any areas needing improvement and not discussing performance shortcomings with their employees. It is at this point that the duty to tell the truth becomes relevant.

Not only do humans have a right, as humans, to be told the truth but also employees, by their position as employees, have a right to be told how they are doing and how they can improve their performance. Thus managers have a duty to tell employees these things and to discuss not only what the employee does well but also what the employee can do to improve his performance. The fact that this is not an easy conversation to have does not mean that the manager is justified in omitting it. From a pattern perspective, the manager has a duty, by her position, to obtain good performance from those people that she manages, or to remove them if they cannot or will not perform well. The only way that this can be done is one person at a time, and one appraisal at a time. The manager who refuses to discuss or document negatives in performance appraisals is almost certainly unable to maintain or improve the performance of her unit.

Discussing performance appraisal in terms of the rights and duties perspective may seem a bit abstract and perhaps even harsh. The point being made can perhaps be seen more clearly if we view it from the perspective of the employee being appraised. If the manager in question considers how she is evaluated by her own boss, this may cast things in a different light. While most people do not like to hear negative things about themselves, most managers do want to know how they can improve their performance in the eyes of their boss. If nothing else, the connection between performance appraisal and compensation increase makes this issue important. If I know what it takes to do my job better and get a bigger raise or bonus, then I can take action to accomplish this. If I know my boss is not fully satisfied with my performance and do not know why, then it is much more difficult for me to decide on a course of action for improvement, and for bigger raises and bonuses.

The rights and duties perspective on compensation increases ties in rather tightly with the fairness and justice approach. Indeed, the right of an employee is not to a certain amount of compensation increase (in a merit system) but to be treated fairly in terms of the amount of increase. We will discuss what this means in the next section. In systems that do not base compensation increases on merit, as determined through performance appraisal, the employees typically have contract rights to an increase in compensation. Typical union contracts, negotiated between labor and management, specify the amount and timing of increases both in salary and in benefits during the period that the contract is in force. Other types of employment contracts, such as those often held by entertainers, athletes and senior managers, either call for specific increases at specific times or else they spell out the terms under which increases will be granted.

Once such contracts have been negotiated and agreed to by both sides, they establish contractual rights that are enforceable through the legal system. They are somewhat different from other legal rights because they do not apply to all citizens of a government unit. The contract is what gives them the force of rights, but the legal system is the typical method for enforcing these contractual rights if they are disputed. In the case of labor-management contracts, individual managers normally do not have any role in determining salary increases. The contract spells out the details, and the payroll department implements increases as contracted.

In light of recent events, particularly in the automobile industry, an interesting question arises concerning the morality of large compensation increases. In mid-2009, both General Motors and Chrysler filed for bankruptcy. Subsequently, Chrysler was sold to Fiat, and General Motors emerged from bankruptcy after restructuring both its debt and its labor contracts.[9] Executives in the industry and commentators who follow the industry both feel that one of the major causes, if not the primary cause, of the financial failures of these companies was the level of wages and benefits paid to unionized workers under contracts approved by both labor and management.[10] If this is the case, can it be moral to pay a level of wages and benefits that results in the financial ruin and sale or bankruptcy of the company? It clearly isn't smart, but is it ethical? The same question arises in somewhat different form in a few other American industries that have traditionally been unionized and that have very large accumulated obligations to retired employees in the form of generous health insurance and pension benefits. These so-called legacy costs, approved by both labor and management, have hampered financial success in the steel and trucking industries in particular. Is it moral to pay such benefits when their total cost makes a company uncompetitive and perhaps eventually causes it to fail?

Our discussion of contractual rights indicates that employees and retirees do have rights to the compensation in question if it comes as the result of a legally negotiated labor-management agreement. It would violate these rights, and thus be immoral under the rights and duties perspective, if management failed to pay the compensation required by the contracts without first renegotiating the contracts. Yet, how can management be morally obliged to follow a course of action that results in the non-competitiveness and eventual bankruptcy of the company? If we examine this question at the point where generous contracts are in force and negative financial consequences are occurring, we have to recognize the binding effect of the contracts.

Under American law, in certain circumstances, a judge can approve the revocation of existing labor-management contracts when a company is in bankruptcy proceedings. Short of that, unless both sides are willing to renegotiate a contract that is in force, management is legally obliged to pay compensation according to the terms of the contract. Historically, unions have generally been unwilling to renegotiate contracts that are favorable to their members, even if a company is in severe financial trouble. There have been some exceptions, but for the most part it is extremely difficult to reach agreement to reduce compensation during the life of a negotiated contract.[11] It is also very difficult to negotiate reductions in salaries or benefits for either active or retired employees when contracts are due to expire and come up for renegotiation.

At an extreme point, such as that reached by the U.S. auto industry, the choice comes down to paying compensation as specified in an existing labor-management contract and going bankrupt, or violating the contract.[12] Since the contract is legally enforceable, this is truly a no-win situation. Two points are worth noting in trying to sort out the morality of possible managerial actions in this situation. One is that this is a classic case of the different perspectives on ethics giving different answers in examining the same situation. The other is that we are analyzing the situation of present management, but the management (perhaps the same individuals) that negotiated the contract, and the labor union that negotiated the contract on behalf of its members, also had a part to play in the development of the situation under analysis. Further, the labor union in this situation may also have moral obligations regarding the existing contract and its renegotiation.

The first point is that different ethical perspectives here provide different answers in the same situation. Under the rights and duties perspective, management is morally obliged to observe the terms of the existing contract. They are also morally obliged to do their best to provide satisfactory performance for the owners or shareholders, for the employees, for customers and perhaps for others, such as suppliers and lenders. There is no clear way that they can carry out all of their various duties at this point. Under the utilitarian perspective, the greatest good for the greatest number would be accomplished if the company did not go bankrupt, and especially if it did not cease to exist. This is so because bankruptcy causes harm for shareholders, lenders, suppliers, and usually for employees and sometimes customers. It ultimately also causes harm for employees and retirees because the company no longer has the funds to make payments under the terms of the contract and, even if a company successfully comes out of bankruptcy, it usually has significantly fewer employees. Finally, under fairness and justice, the analysis centers on the relative treatment of employees and retirees who receive high compensation under the existing contract versus others who also have a stake in the company's performance, such as shareholders and lenders, and are financially harmed by the status quo.

There are no clear or easy answers to the situation described above. Historically the situation is fairly rare. When it does arise, as in the U.S. auto industry, what has normally happened is that the situation remains difficult or impossible for managers until a company enters bankruptcy.[13] There have been instances in which labor unions have agreed to give back some of the benefits they had previously negotiated under an existing contract and cases in which terms are reached at contract renewal that allow a company to achieve financial success because of reduced labor costs. There have also been cases where no solution to contract issues was reached, even in bankruptcy, and judges have allowed management to void existing labor contracts and impose lower compensation levels. Even if this set of events occurs, problems are far from over because companies coming out of bankruptcy in this situation sometimes face labor unrest.

The second point indicated above is that the untenable situation of a company faced with compensation costs so high as to make it uncompetitive did not just suddenly appear. When labor and management meet to negotiate a contract, whatever they agree to will have force for the life of the contract (typically three years). If these consequences are negative, as they certainly are in the case of uncompetitive labor costs leading to bankruptcy, then the parties that negotiated the contract logically bear some blame for the results. This logical connection is often missed in analyzing such situations, but it is still valid. To deny this reality is to argue that major policy decisions are not ethically connected to their foreseeable consequences—a hard argument to make.

Fairness and Justice Analysis

In systems that do base compensation decisions on merit, what does the fairness and justice perspective tell us about managerial decisions? Basically, that managers must determine who is similarly situated. Our definition says that, under the fairness and justice perspective, the moral act is the one that treats similarly situated people in similar ways regarding both process and outcome and with a sense of proportionality. It does not say that everyone should be treated equally. To evaluate employees fairly means that their performance must be judged based on similar standards if they are similarly situated. This is not always an easy task.

A supervisor of bank tellers might establish that the main results desired from the work of the tellers involves speed, accuracy and courtesy. Speed is important to limit the number of tellers needed to serve a given number of customers, and ultimately both to satisfy the desire of the customers for expedited processing and to satisfy the desire of management to control labor costs. Accuracy is important both to customers, who want their transactions handled correctly, and to management, which wants to conduct the business of banking as accurately as possible. Courtesy is important to customers, who want to be treated with dignity and respect, and to management, which wants customers to go away satisfied so that they will come back and keep their business with the bank. So far, so good.

Speed can be measured fairly well by counting the number of transactions handled by each teller over some period of time. Accuracy can be measured because each teller is required to balance their cash drawer and transactions at the end of each business day. But how do we measure courtesy? If we are going to evaluate the teller fairly, and use this evaluation to determine the amount of his compensation increase, then we need a good way to evaluate courtesy. This, of course, is not just a problem in evaluating bank tellers. Many service jobs have a customer service component where courtesy, or customer satisfaction, or knowledgeable service, or some other intangible, uncountable component is an important part of doing the job.

This means that managers, who have performance appraisal as part of their job, must think about performance appraisal not just when they are filling out a form or doing an interview with an employee, but also when they are considering the basis for appraisal. If part of a service job is to satisfy customers during an employee–customer interface, there are various ways to measure how well the employee does this part of the job. Customer complaints or compliments provide one source of input. Supervisory observation is another. A supervisor of bank tellers spends much of her day, every day, on the teller line. Over a period of weeks or months, if she is at all observant, she gathers first-hand impressions of how each teller deals with customers. Secret shoppers are another way to obtain input regarding employee–customer transactions.

Whatever method or combination of methods is used to evaluate service performance, it is important that employees perceive it as fair. In the chapter on fairness and justice, we noted that both procedural and distributive justice are important. Procedural justice matters not only because it helps to achieve distributive justice, but also because it helps to create the appearance of fairness. One of the characteristics often cited in writings on leadership is that leaders are fair. It is also often remarked that leaders must not only be fair, but be perceived to be fair. If a benevolent dictator made decisions by himself with no input from others, he might make fair decisions. It is unlikely, though, that they will be perceived as fair by his subjects. If a supervisor makes decisions about performance and compensation entirely based on her own observations, the decisions might be fair, but they are very unlikely to be perceived as fair. The process of performance appraisal matters, as well as the results.

There is no way to avoid the fact that it is harder to evaluate how courteously a teller or a sales associate served a customer than to evaluate how many customers they served, or how many dollars in transactions they completed. If this is a significant part of the teller's or the sales associate's job, it is important to evaluate it and to do so in a way that is fair in procedure as well as in outcome. Because it is a hard thing to do, and subject to dispute, managers tend to minimize or avoid altogether this part of the evaluation process. They are not alone. Faculty, including business faculty, at universities are evaluated, among other things, on their published research. It is easy to count how many articles are published during the period under evaluation; it is considerably more difficult to evaluate the relative merits of different articles. Not surprisingly, many university evaluation systems give more weight to the number of articles published than to their quality or impact. If quality and impact are desired goals of research, they need to be fairly evaluated, even though this is harder than counting how many articles have been published.

Fairness requires that similarly situated employees be evaluated on similar criteria. Accomplishing this is a challenge for those who supervise service workers, but it is part of their job. A more difficult question still is how to reward or compensate similarly situated employees in similar ways. Part of deciding who is similarly situated involves setting up job descriptions. This is typically the responsibility of the human resources department, with input from the supervisor or manager of the unit where jobs are being evaluated. Once the job description is determined, jobs are often assigned a grade level, and salary ranges with minimum and maximum allowable salaries are determined based on the grade level. While such an approach is common and is designed to help achieve fairness, it often leads to complaints. Very dissimilar jobs (perhaps accounts payable clerk, warehouse worker and delivery person) may be assigned the same grade. Workers in these jobs may feel that the level of knowledge, skill and responsibility required of them make their job worth more than other jobs in the same grade.

If there is no system in place to establish job descriptions and grades, this task is left up to the judgment of some manager or managers in the organizations. If such a system is in place, it is obviously important that it be implemented carefully and thoughtfully. It is probably impossible to set up and use such a system perfectly. In the fairly recent past, there was a movement known as comparable worth that argued that all jobs in an employing unit as diverse as state government can and should be evaluated on a common scale.[14] This movement advocated position evaluation and grading for jobs as diverse as nurse, prison warden and truck driver. The obvious difficulty of finding common grounds for evaluating very diverse jobs meant that this movement did not achieve a great deal of progress, but the idea behind it is the same as that of establishing job descriptions and grades within a company. The ultimate stated goal of such systems is to treat similarly situated people in similar ways regarding compensation—in other words, to put into practice fairness and justice.

While fair grading of jobs is difficult for the positions of individual workers, it is even more difficult for the positions of managers. Managers are typically evaluated on the achievements of the units they manage, rather than on their own individual production. Since the job of a manager is not to make widgets or to service customers, but rather to oversee the work of those who do, it is reasonable to evaluate the manager on the basis of how well his unit has performed. It is harder to define the position responsibility of a manager, and hence harder to establish fair criteria for evaluating and compensating managers. Some managerial jobs are relatively easy to define and evaluate. A supervisor of ten bank tellers is responsible for seeing that the tellers in that unit meet standards of speed, accuracy and service. The supervisor may or may not be responsible for deciding what those standards are. She is also responsible for participating in the hiring process when there is an opening, for training new employees, for evaluating employees, for reporting on her unit's performance to her boss, for attending meetings, for solving customer problems, for assisting with budget preparation and monitoring, and for other duties as assigned.

If the manager being evaluated is several levels up the management ladder, his responsibilities and duties will be quite different from those of the supervisor just described. A chief financial officer may have among his duties interface with the information systems division to assure that all financial systems are capable of reporting data that is timely, accurate and secure. He may be responsible for dealing with regulators, investors, bankers and outside auditors. He may provide input on possible acquisitions and divestitures. All of these duties are very different from those of a teller supervisor. Both are in some sense managers, but they need different levels of skill and knowledge, different levels of business sophistication and communication skills, and they have very different levels of accountability and responsibilities. They spend their days differently and will be evaluated on different criteria. They do, however, have some things in common. Both have subordinates and both are responsible for evaluating and recommending compensation for these subordinates. Each has duties and each can be and will be perceived as fair or unfair based on how they carry out their duties.

Compensation of Senior Executives

All those who manage others in organizations that use any kind of merit system have moral responsibilities regarding the evaluation and compensation of their employees. There is another area of evaluation and compensation decisions that does not affect most managers, yet it is so much a part of the public perception of business that it deserves some comment. That area involves the evaluation and compensation of senior executives, and particularly of CEOs. This area of concern involves several related topics: the level of compensation, its form, its relationship to compensation levels of other employees and its relationship to company performance.[15]

Recent estimates have placed CEO compensation for large American companies at between 300 and 400 times the compensation of the typical worker.[16] This multiple is dramatically larger than it was ten to twenty years ago and is also dramatically larger than CEO compensation in other countries. As indicated earlier in this chapter, CEO compensation, and that of other senior executives, is not determined in the same way as that of other employees. The board of directors approves such compensation, usually following the suggestions of its compensation committee, which in turn often follows the advice of outside compensation consultants hired to assist the committee.

Many CEOs of major American companies have employment contracts that are negotiated as part of the hiring procedure. These contracts, approved by the board of directors at the time of hiring, have a significant influence on overall compensation levels for CEOs. Whether in the annual performance review and compensation increase or in the terms negotiated when hiring a CEO, the board of directors is responsible for the compensation level of CEOs. It is impossible to rationally discuss the amount of CEO compensation without discussing its form. In the last few years at least, the highest-paid CEOs in the United States have received far more compensation from exercising stock options than they have from their salary and bonus. This is not to imply that their salary-bonus compensation is negligible; in the last few years, this compensation has approached and sometimes exceeded $10 million annually for some major company CEOs.

Stock options, which are mainly but not exclusively awarded to senior executives, basically involve the right granted now to purchase a given number of shares of the company's stock at a specified future date or within a specified future time period at the price for which the stock is selling when the option is granted. Thus, if Giantco's stock is selling for $20 a share today and its CEO is granted the option to buy 500,000 shares of Giantco's stock three years from now at today's price, he will achieve a $5 million profit in three years if the stock is selling for $30 a share at that time and he sells. This example ignores transaction costs and taxes, but it is not uncommon for major companies to grant additional compensation to cover the executive's taxes on gains from stock options. The concept is fairly simple, but the variations that have been devised are sometimes quite complex.

Why grant stock options? The original motivation was to make executives think and act more like stockholders. If their compensation is tied to the performance of the company's stock, or so the argument goes, then they will act in the best interest of shareholders because that will also be their best interest.[17] If they do not benefit from increasing prices of the company's stock and suffer from decreasing prices, or so it is argued, then they will do things that help them personally but hurt the company's long-range performance. What has been clearly proven in the last few years is that some executives will do almost anything in the short range to raise the price of the company's stock and the value of their options, even if their actions are immoral, illegal and harmful to the company's long-term performance and continued existence.

Executive pay takes many forms. The most common categories include salary, bonus, stock option grants, perquisites ("perks" include such things as country club memberships, use of company aircraft, low or no-interest loans from the company, etc.) and severance pay. Much of the negative sentiment, particularly in the popular press, concerning executive pay seems to center on its total amount, some of the perks that are granted and severance pay. When Jack Welch, the much-admired former CEO of General Electric, retired, he was widely praised in both the business and popular press. His autobiography was a bestseller. Less than a year later, it became known that he was having an affair with an editor of Harvard Business Review, a woman some twenty years his junior. Shortly afterward, in the early stages of divorce proceedings from his current wife, it was revealed that his retirement benefits from General Electric included such items as continued use of company aircraft, cars, office, apartments and financial planning services. He was also allowed the use of the company's prime tickets for various sporting events.[18] The publicity that ensued, and his voluntary surrendering of most of these benefits, pointed up problems both with perks and with retirement income.

What is the ethical perspective on all of this? Chief executives and other senior executives of large companies have tremendous responsibilities. Their jobs require high levels of skill and knowledge. They work, for the most part, extremely long hours at high-intensity tasks. Their compensation can legitimately reflect these facts, and it should. The greatest good for the greatest number is achieved when these positions are filled by the relatively few people willing and able to perform well in these jobs. Whole companies can be and have been harmed when senior executives are not sufficiently skilled and knowledgeable to perform at the level their jobs demand. These executives have a right to be well compensated for the skills and knowledge they bring and the work that they do. They are not similarly situated with lower-level managers or workers, and their compensation should reflect this fact.

Boards of directors have a duty based on the nature of their positions to attract and keep top level executives to run their firms, and to reward these executives adequately. They also have a duty, which they are sometimes slower to recognize, to evaluate, guide and, if necessary, remove executives who are charged with running these firms. It seems clear, at least in retrospect, that directors at such companies as General Motors, Merrill Lynch and Countrywide did not do an adequate job of evaluating the executives who were pursuing failing strategies and guiding their companies toward bankruptcy. The compensation systems in force at these companies for senior executives appear to have encouraged the wrong kind of behavior, ultimately to the great detriment of the companies and their various stakeholders.

While CEOs and other senior executives have a right to be well compensated for carrying out their very difficult jobs, they do not have a right to unlimited compensation, either in amount or in form. Where are the moral limits on executive compensation? This is not at all an easy question to answer.[19] One approach is to start from an extreme point and work back. No individual executive of a public company has yet been paid $1 billion in salary and cash bonus for a single year. Would that be too much and, more importantly, how would we know?

One way to consider whether executive compensation in a given case is reasonable or unreasonable is to use a fairness and justice approach and compare it to that of other executives. If an executive's compensation is higher than any other ever paid, it would seem that some extraordinary justification would be needed for payment at this level.[20] Comparison to any other executive compensation ever might be a bit extreme. It would also be reasonable to compare the compensation of the executive in question with that of other executives of similar companies. A CEO's compensation package might be compared to those of other CEOs in the same industry or, even better, to CEOs in the same industry running companies of comparable size and complexity. This would approximate the question of whether similarly situated individuals are being treated similarly.

Stock option grants make it hard to compare one compensation package to another because there is no way to know when the options are granted what their worth will be when the time comes that they can be exercised. Until recently, companies did not record the grants of stock options as an expense. The reason most frequently given for not counting stock options as a corporate expense was the difficulty in valuing these options. In 2004, the Financial Accounting Standards Board ruled that stock options should be treated as an expense. Without going into details of the way they are treated at the time options are granted, their value to at least some executives is beyond dispute. Each year, Bloomberg Business Week presents detailed coverage of the highest-paid executives in the United States. For the last several years, the highest-paid executives have received far more from the exercise of stock options than they have from the combination of salary and bonus.

Another way to judge the reasonableness of an executive compensation package is to consider it as a percentage of the company's profits for the year in question. The highest annual net income ever reported for a corporation is approximately $40 billion. Only a very small number of American companies (fewer than twenty) achieve net income in excess of $10 billion in any given year. A compensation package of $1 billion, then, would amount to at least 2 percent and perhaps more than 10 percent of the total profits for a very large and successful firm. Is this too much? There is obviously no definitive answer. When one considers the number of individuals contributing to the success of a very large and profitable corporation, and the fact that some profits should arguably be shared with other executives, the rest of the employees, stockholders and others, it is not clear that one individual should be rewarded with as much as 10 percent of a company's total profits.

In this discussion, we have used the term "reasonable" to evaluate compensation packages. The greatest good for the greatest number is likely to be achieved by reasonable rather than unreasonable executive compensation.[21] Executives have a right to be reasonably compensated; they do not have a right to unreasonable compensation. Some argue that high compensation encourages executives to work hard and use all of their skills at a high level.

Others maintain that greater overall good would be accomplished if top executives were paid less and some of the money used for their compensation was used to benefit other workers or stockholders. Fairness and justice, as we have argued previously, involve reasonable treatment of similarly situated individuals. Thus, in a loose sense at least, it is ethical to compensate executives reasonably and unethical to compensate them unreasonably.

One part of the executive compensation package that is somewhat different in concept is that of severance pay. Golden parachutes are one form of severance pay, related specifically to contractual provisions obliging a company to provide certain compensation to executives if they terminate as a result of a change in control (if their company is sold). These became popular during the 1980s when many large corporations were purchased in hostile takeovers by so-called corporate raiders. The golden parachute in this case guaranteed substantial severance payments to executives who lost their jobs because of a change in corporate ownership. The term has since been broadened, at least in popular use, to include almost any contractual agreements for severance pay. In some cases, these contracts are binding on the company no matter why an executive is terminated, unless it is for felonies directly related to his job.

The amounts paid under various forms of severance agreements can be quite substantial, sometimes exceeding $10 million, in addition to a variety of perks such as free office space, one or more salaried assistants, use of corporate aircraft and apartments, and very lucrative consulting fees guaranteed in advance (sometimes guaranteed to executives who leave under circumstances that no one would even consider consulting with them).[22] These various forms of severance pay are in addition to the retirement benefits that executives receive from corporate pension plans and deferred compensation plans.

Since departing executives, especially CEOs, have usually been very well compensated by their companies during their time of employment, and since their retirement benefits often exceed substantially those of lower-level managers and other employees, it is difficult to establish a need for additional post-employment compensation. Such compensation is usually not tied to performance while in office. It is often negotiated at the time of employment and contractually agreed to by the executive and the board of directors. Our discussions of various compensation arrangements to this point have all related compensation in some way or other to performance. This link is missing in many of the severance or post-employment compensation arrangements negotiated by top executives.

It is often difficult to determine how much of an executive's severance compensation was previously earned in the form of stock options, deferred compensation and pension benefits and how much is specifically a payment for leaving. However, a number of widely reported severance packages in recent years seem, at best, difficult to justify. Michael Ovitz was terminated as President of Walt Disney after less than two years in that position. His reported severance compensation was $140 million. Robert Nardelli left as CEO of Home Depot in 2007 after losing the support of the board of directors. His severance compensation was reported as $210 million. Stan O'Neal was fired as CEO of Merrill Lynch when the company was about to be purchased by Bank of America because of its huge mortgage-related losses. His severance total was $160 million. Such widely publicized stories feed the public perception, rightly or wrongly, that companies are reckless and unethical in their CEO pay practices. While much of the compensation for departing CEOs has been earned in previous years, most readers probably do not make this link and assume that the entire amount is a sort of going-away present. Lavish retirement benefits which a wealthy former CEO could easily purchase for himself also cause perceptual problems.

It does not appear to contribute to the greatest good of anyone except the departed executive to lavishly compensate a former employee (albeit a former CEO) with money that ultimately reduces the current profits of a company. The arguments that we have made so far linking compensation levels to performance and the skills and knowledge needed for success do not apply to post-employment compensation such as we are now discussing. Although a contractual right to such compensation is created when such a contract is agreed to by the executive and the board of directors, it does not seem to be a right that would exist except for the contract. While the question is almost never raised, the board of directors does have a moral obligation to exercise restraint or perhaps even denial at the time of negotiating such contracts. Such lucrative post-employment compensation is fair only in the sense that other similarly situated senior executives have also managed to negotiate such contracts, but it lacks the sense of proportionality that is part of the definition of fairness.

The whole topic of executive compensation, whether in terms of level of compensation, liberal use of stock options or post-employment compensation, often seems to turn on what others are doing. Two defenses are frequently offered when executive compensation is challenged. One states that the difficulties faced by top executives in successfully carrying out their jobs are such that they deserve every penny that they get. The other is that the market for top executives is extremely competitive and, while we might prefer not to grant so much compensation, as a board our hands are tied by what others do. In other words, if we are to obtain competent senior executives, we have no choice but to pay them at the same level that other companies do. This second argument is perhaps the more persuasive one for generous post-compensation arrangements.

On closer examination, this argument has flaws. The whole issue of the market for top-executive talent is examined by Rakesh Khurana, who reviewed an impressive amount of data and concluded that the way the market for CEOs works now is not the only way it could work, nor is it for the best in most cases.[23] This may be small consolation for a board of directors negotiating compensation with a prospective new CEO. However, it is not beyond the realm of possibility that some boards could reverse the current trend, eliminate some of the excesses in compensation packages and still hire excellent candidates for open positions at the top of their companies. Khurana also raises the issue that promotion from within is an option not used frequently enough by boards of directors and an option that may make it somewhat easier to slow the acceleration in executive compensation packages from what appear to many to be unreasonable and unjustifiable levels.

Whether the issue is how big a raise to give to an accounting clerk or how many stock options to grant to a CEO, there are certain common elements in the ethical analysis of performance appraisal and compensation issues. Such issues, especially in medium and large companies, are normally dealt with within a framework that is set by senior management and/or human resources professionals. Starting compensation for a new incumbent in a position, whether and how often to increase compensation, how evaluation procedures and results affect compensation increases and what form such increases should take are all issues decided by individuals at some point in time. Managers at every level are charged with evaluating subordinates, at least in systems where compensation is merit-based. They have ethical obligations to be honest and thorough in performing and communicating their evaluations. Those who set up or modify compensation systems also have ethical obligations to set up and maintain such systems with due consideration for various individuals and groups affected by the systems. In the practice of management as it is actually done by managers, evaluation and compensation are part of the job and do have moral implications.

nine
Terminations

As we continue our review of selected managerial functions and their ethical implications, we turn now to the issue of terminating employees. There are various categories of terminations: termination for cause, layoffs, down-sizing, right-sizing, performance-related terminations, and others. To the employee who is told that they can no longer work for the company, there is a certain sameness regardless of the name given to the termination. One day the employee has a job, a steady income, benefits, a place to go on a regular basis to work with familiar people, an identity as an accountant, or sales manager, or vice president, and a source of stability. The next day, the employee has none of these. Further, there is the stigma that, whatever the company called it, the employee was actually fired.[1]

In our discussion of terminations, we will assume that the company, not the employee, has decided to end the employment relationship. The situation is quite different when the employee decides to resign or retire, and the manager's involvement in this situation is usually limited to replacing the employee. The issues involved here for the manager have already been covered in the chapter on employment.

Limits on Termination

There is a good deal of law to be considered when the issue of terminating an employee arises. For most of the twentieth century, the legal standard in the United States was employment at will. Beginning in the late nineteenth century, the law in the United States gave employers the right to "dismiss their employees at will for good cause, for no cause, or even for cause morally wrong, without being thereby guilty of a legal wrong."[2] This doctrine was based on the idea that the employment relationship was roughly equal. An employee could quit at any time and a company could terminate that employee at any time.[3]

The reality is that very few labor markets are so tight that employees and employers are on roughly equal terms. Beginning with the National Labor Relations Act in 1935, legal restrictions on the employment at will doctrine appeared. They were considerably expanded by the Civil Rights legislation in the 1960s and later amendments and expansions, to the point now that there are many reasons for which it is illegal for an employer to terminate an employee.

Many employees in the United States are covered by employment contracts or have been granted tenure in their jobs. About 12 percent of the U.S. labor force is currently covered by negotiated labor-management contracts.[4] These contracts typically provide limited grounds for termination of an employee by management. Except for these grounds, management does not have the legal right to terminate employees covered by the contract. Other employees also have contractual rights spelled out in employment contracts. Professional athletes, entertainers and senior executives often have employment contracts, giving them legal rights to retain their jobs for specified periods of time and permitting termination only under limited conditions. Even after termination, these contracts sometimes guarantee compensation for the period of the contract. Several years ago, the highest paid employee of the State of Nevada was a former university basketball coach who had been terminated with three years left on his contract. The state was obliged to pay him for the remainder of the contract for not coaching! This is not an unusual situation for athletes and coaches.

Tenure is basically a guarantee of continued employment, often for as long as the employee wishes to remain employed. Tenure is formally granted to full-time faculty members at most colleges and universities after a probationary period of about six years and after very detailed, formal review by faculty committees and administrators. Tenure is automatically granted to U.S. federal judges. Although it is not referred to typically as tenure, the job protection afforded to workers covered under the Civil Service in the United States bears a close resemblance in practice to tenure. School teachers in grammar, middle and high schools, once they have attained permanent status (often after one or two years of employment), have job protection that is similar in practice to tenure.[5] In many Western European countries, essentially all full-time workers are provided by law with a level of job security that resembles tenure.

Various reasons are given for the job security represented under negotiated labor-management contracts, other employment contracts and tenure. Labor-management contracts start from an assumed premise that management will not treat workers properly of their own accord. Workers unite (form labor unions) to assure that individual workers will be able to deal with management from a position of power rather than helplessness. It is assumed at the start of bargaining that the interests and desires of labor and management are different and that, through bargaining, a point can be reached that is at least tolerable and perhaps satisfactory to both sides. As we noted in the chapter on evaluation and compensation, labor does not trust managers to make individual decisions about compensation increases that are fair, so typically the contract spells out the timing and amount of increases. Similarly, labor does not trust management to be fair in matters of termination, so the contract typically spells out limited grounds that are the only allowed reasons for terminating any employee. Other employment contracts, such as those of athletes and entertainers, spell out in considerable detail the grounds for termination and benefits to be paid if termination occurs. While these contracts are not as firmly based in a theory of labor that distrusts management, the terms embodied in them often reveal a basic lack of trust.

It is often difficult for managers to accept the lack of trust embodied in labor contracts. After all, the manager knows that she is personally a fine and trustworthy individual with a profound respect for the role played by workers in the success of the organization. The manager sees herself as thoughtful, sensitive and humane. Very few managers will admit to being thoughtless, insensitive and inhumane! Given the sterling qualities of the manager, it is somewhat offensive that anyone would think otherwise and in fact insist on establishing rights contractually regarding employment matters. If the manager will give a moment's thought, she may realize that, while she is personally above reproach, she has known or perhaps worked for a boss who was a rude, uncaring clod. Many managers, at some time in their working lives, have been fired. On the day that this occurred, if they were asked whether workers and managers approached the issue of termination from equal power bases, or whether workers might need some sort of protection from arbitrary managers, the answers would almost certainly be no and yes, in that order.

Tenure is a somewhat different issue. In the case of judges, the alternative is periodic election. This presents its own set of problems, with judges running for office soliciting campaign funds from attorneys and other interested parties, and the question of whether the ability to win an election in any way correlates with the ability to serve as an effective judge.[6] Civil service employees have tenure-like job security because the alternative, evident before civil service laws were enacted, is a wholesale replacement of government employees after each election. A variety of reasons has been given for awarding tenure to college and university faculty members. Perhaps the most prominent of these is academic freedom—the tradition that professors should be free to research and teach, even in controversial areas, without fear of losing their jobs.

Most of what we know about organizational theory says that it is not a good idea to have a significant number of employees in any organization with guaranteed jobs for life.[7] This situation tends to decrease employee motivation and makes it difficult or impossible for managers to deal effectively with employees who cannot or will not adequately perform their duties. While this view is widely accepted by those who study organization theory in the United States, it is not shared by many European academics. Labor laws and practices in much of Western Europe are much more pro-employee and place many more restrictions on management than do corresponding laws and practices in the United States. Individuals who tend, from theory and personal experience, to trust managers to act reasonably toward their employees generally do not favor tenure and tenure-like arrangements. Individuals who tend to distrust managers and fear their power in employment situations tend to favor tight controls on management's ability to evaluate, compensate or terminate employees.

Employees at Will

Since more than half of the U.S. labor force does not have tenure, civil service protection or protection under a negotiated labor-management contract, we must deal with the situation where a manager can terminate an employee and consider the ethical implications of such a situation.[8] In many large companies, no manager is allowed to terminate an employee without the approval of the human resources department. Such rules are relatively recent and are still not prevalent in smaller businesses. The reason for such rules appears to be two-fold. One reason is that managers, like other humans, sometimes act hastily when emotions are high. An angry manager, deciding to terminate an employee immediately, may not be acting in anyone's best interests. By requiring that the situation be reviewed by a human resources professional, an element of objectivity is introduced. The second reason for requiring review by a human resources professional before terminating an employee is the legal complexity that now exists regarding termination. The manager is acting on behalf of the company and the company can be held liable for violation of a variety of laws if the termination is not proper.

We saw in earlier chapters that managers are generally obliged to follow the law and that they are morally wrong if they expose their company to legal problems. If a company is charged with wrongful termination under the law, or with violating any of the regulations prohibiting employment actions based on race, gender, age or other protected categories, the consequences for the company can be severe. Individual managers may not be aware of the various laws and regulations that affect termination of employees. Even if they are aware of them, individual managers may not know of recent court cases or regulations interpreting the application of these many rules. Professionals from the human resources department are expected to be knowledgeable in these details and to be qualified to keep the company from violating laws or regulations in a given case.[9]

Managers do have a moral obligation to obey laws and regulations, and sometimes they are unable to fulfill this obligation without professional help in understanding the application of laws and regulations to the particular case with which they are dealing. Thus, even if a company does not have a rule requiring that all terminations be reviewed by human resources staff, a manager still is required to take care and seek advice in such a complex area. However, managerial obligations do not cease with the determination that something is legal. In other words, the fact that one may do something does not necessarily mean that one should do it.

For the sake of the present discussion, we assume that a termination is not for cause. We will use this term to mean that the employee has done something or omitted to do something that is sufficiently serious and job-related that it is, by itself, grounds for termination. Such actions or omissions might include embezzlement, violence in the workplace, use of drugs or alcohol on the job or similar serious violations. Termination for cause is not the same as termination for unsatisfactory performance.

There is really not much to say about the moral implications of such situations. If an employee embezzles company funds, or physically assaults someone at work, or is guilty of a similar violation, prompt termination is in order. Termination in such cases constitutes the greatest good for the greatest number; continued employment does not. The employee, by their behavior, has forfeited the right to continued employment. The manager has a duty to remove the employee from the work situation. Employees who commit such acts are similarly situated, in the sense that there are not grounds for discussing circumstances, or establishing degrees of guilt, or warning of the future consequences of repeating such behavior. Termination in such cases is fair and just.

Most terminations that are not for cause fall into one of two groups. They occur either for unsatisfactory performance or because the organization has decided to conduct layoffs. This means that the company has chosen to reduce the size of its staff and is terminating employees whose performance is otherwise satisfactory.

Terminations for Unsatisfactory Performance

Let us first consider termination for unsatisfactory performance. In some ways, this is the reverse of compensation increases based on performance. As we saw in the last chapter, one of the duties of a manager is to evaluate the performance of his employees, at least in a system that considers merit in determining compensation. If an employee is performing well, the issue is how much of an increase in compensation is merited by the employee's performance. If an employee is performing poorly, there are two issues for the manager to deal with. One is how to improve the employee's performance; the other is what to do if the performance does not improve. Let us assume for this discussion that the manager has established or is using established performance standards for a given job.

Because of the importance of running public transit buses according to a published schedule, a bus company may establish a standard that drivers who are tardy by more than one minute in showing up for work more than four times a year will be placed on probation, and drivers who are tardy six times in a year will be terminated. This is a measurable work standard and is easy to apply uniformly. Suppose, though, that a sales representative is required to be professional in dress and demeanor. This is a work-related standard, but it is much more difficult to apply and there is plenty of room for honest disagreement over what constitutes professional dress or demeanor. In general, quantifiable standards are much easier to apply uniformly. In many service industries where most employees interface with customers, some important criteria for satisfactory performance will necessarily be more vague and less quantifiable.

Whatever the performance standards involved, some managers personally feel that it is wrong to terminate employees for any reason other than for cause. This may be a philosophical position or it may be that they are very much averse to confrontation. Not all termination interviews are confrontational but, in terms of interaction with employees, few situations are as difficult as a termination interview. It is not easy for most managers to close the office door, sit down face to face with an employee and tell them that they have been terminated. Grown men and women, when told that they have been terminated, sometimes cry, sometimes argue and sometimes plead. These are very difficult situations for most managers and, as a result, some managers will go to considerable lengths to avoid being placed in this situation.

The fact is that managers are sometimes obliged to terminate an employee whose performance is unsatisfactory and that it is wrong for a manager to fail to do so. We will examine below how each of the three perspectives on ethics approaches this situation, but when an employee is being paid and not doing the job they have been hired to do, it is the manager's job to correct the situation. One possible and desirable course of action is to help the employee to improve his performance to a satisfactory level. This may involve training in the skills of the job, or counseling with the employee, or referring the employee to someone else who can help. But if such efforts fail, the manager is faced with terminating the employee. At many companies, progressive discipline is practiced before an employee is terminated.

Progressive Discipline

Progressive discipline means that an employee is informed, clearly and formally, about their unsatisfactory performance, what it is that makes it unsatisfactory and what they must do by a certain date to reach a level of performance that will be satisfactory. For example, a bank teller might be told that he is only processing seventeen customer transactions per hour, when the standard is twenty-five. The employee would then be told that he must reach a level of at least twenty-two transactions per hour within the next thirty days or further action will be taken. He may be offered coaching or some other help to reach the stated goal. During this meeting, the manager will schedule the next meeting, for thirty days from now, and draw up a brief memorandum of what they discussed, with both the manager and the employee signing the memo. After thirty days, at the next meeting, if the employee is still short of the performance goal, he may be told that, unless he reaches the goal of twenty-two transactions per hour within two weeks, further action will be necessary and may (or will) include his termination at that time. The next meeting is scheduled and a memorandum recounting the conversation is signed by both manager and employee. After the two-week period, another meeting is held. If the employee still has not attained the production goal, he is informed at that point by the manager that he is being terminated for unsatisfactory performance.

Such progressive discipline serves several purposes. It lets the employee know clearly what is unsatisfactory about his performance, what improvement is required and when he must reach the specified level of improvement. It gives the manager a chance to discuss performance with the employee and learn of any facts that may be impacting the employee's performance. It establishes a written record of what has occurred that can be used later if the manager and the employee have different recollections of what was decided. It also establishes a clear written record that can be reviewed by a human resources representative if termination becomes necessary and by attorneys if subsequent legal action occurs. Finally, it provides an objective basis for discussing and acting on unsatisfactory performance. Instead of the manager saying that the employee has to work faster or become more productive, manager and employee both are on record with a clear standard and goal for performance approval.

Progressive discipline is easiest when the job has quantifiable goals that can be measured in ways that are clear to both manager and employee. It can also be used in other situations, with modifications as appropriate. A sales representative who has been reported as being discourteous to a customer could be warned that any other reports from customers or discourteous behavior observed by the manager within the next sixty days will result in further action. There is room for interpretation here because some customers are very difficult and expect a standard of courtesy that may not be realistic. Nonetheless, modified progressive discipline is still better than basing terminations on single occurrences or on anonymous or vague reports.

Given that an employee's performance may be unsatisfactory to the point that it is wrong for his manager to allow things to remain as they are, is there a moral obligation to warn the employee before terminating him? Legally, progressive discipline is not strictly obligatory. However, it has been adopted as standard policy by many companies at least partly as a way to avoid legal problems over wrongful or discriminatory termination. A utilitarian analysis of this question would favor progressive discipline, or at least some kind of clear and direct warning prior to termination for performance. Avoiding legal problems creates the greatest good for the greatest number, since it is better for the supervisor and for the company not to be sued, and it is better for the employee not to have to sue.

Discussing the employee's unsatisfactory performance and specifying what it would take to remedy the situation may lead to improved performance and to the employee keeping his job and performing it in a satisfactory fashion. This result would be better for the company than terminating and replacing the employee.[10] It would also be better for the employee than being terminated. If the discussion does not lead to improved performance or to performance that reaches the satisfactory level, then some time has been lost and the less desirable result still occurs. There is no way to be sure what the outcome of warning before terminating will be and, if improved performance does not occur, the delay of better performance and the eventual removal of the employee and search for a replacement make the situation worse than it would have been had the employee been terminated and replaced earlier.

The result of progressive discipline in a given case may lead to the greatest good for the greatest number, or it may not. If we take the pattern perspective and ask whether having a standard practice of progressive discipline for performance problems creates the greatest good for the greatest number, the answer seems to be in the affirmative. A pattern of terminating without warning for performance problems would make for a less secure workplace as viewed by employees. While some decisions made under this no-warning scenario would be correct, others might not be. Performance warnings sometimes reveal misunderstandings about what constitutes adequate performance, or what the employee's actual performance level is. Communication at this point can be enough to remedy the situation. Further, the pattern of progressive discipline as the company standard can be very helpful in defending against charges by regulators or against lawsuits that blame the company for wrongful or discriminatory terminations.

As we saw in previous chapters, managers have a duty to see that the work of their unit is performed in a satisfactory way in terms of both quality and efficiency. An employee who does not do his part to reach this goal is a problem for the manager to deal with. The manager has a duty to do something; the question is what. An employee who is not performing at a satisfactory level does not have a right to keep his job (we will deal later in the chapter with the question of whether an employee who is performing satisfactorily has any right to keep his job). The company that employs and pays the employee has a right to a reasonable day's work from that employee on a regular basis. This right of the company imposes a duty on the employee to perform a reasonable day's work. The relative rights and duties of manager and employee make it ethical, then, for the manager to take action when one of her employees performs in an unsatisfactory manner.

Does the employee have a right to progressive discipline? If so, the manager has a duty to carry it out. Legally, as we have indicated, progressive discipline for performance problems is useful but not required. Morally, the manager not only is within her rights to take some action to remedy the situation, but has a duty by her position as manager to do so. At the level of the individual case, one could argue that the employee has a duty to know what his job is and whether he is performing it satisfactorily. Managers are not in the position of baby-sitting for little children; rather, their job is to oversee and coordinate the work of responsible adults. Misunderstandings can arise between employee and manager as to what constitutes satisfactory performance, but as a general rule the manager has a right to expect such performance from each employee and the employee has a duty to perform at a satisfactory level.

At the system level, if progressive discipline is a company policy, the operating manager did not set this policy. She probably did not even have input into the policy. Nonetheless, the company does have a right to expect its managers to carry out its policies and the managers have a duty to do so. Notice here that the rights and duties analysis at the system level is not directly concerned with the individual employee, but with the respective rights and duties of the company and its managers. This is a legitimate level of concern, although not the only one. Employees, quite naturally, think that any analysis of termination situations should center on the terminated employee. Nonetheless, the larger picture is real and cannot be ignored.

Is it fair to terminate an employee for unsatisfactory performance without first using progressive discipline? The basic criterion for moral action according to fairness and justice is that similarly situated individuals are treated similarly regarding both process and outcome. For the situation under discussion, employees who are not performing at a satisfactory level make up the similarly situated group. But are they really all in similar situations? A whole range of behavior falls under the general term of unsatisfactory performance. In almost any job, there are degrees of success and degrees of failure in carrying out the functions that make up the job. A computer programmer who has excellent technical skills but is somewhat lacking in interpersonal skills might be overall a satisfactory or even superior performer if his job requires little interface with other workers or customers. A sales representative who is a bit weak technically but has outstanding interpersonal skills might be a more-than-satisfactory performer as long as technical knowledge is not a key to the job of sales associate.

Most people perform better on some days than on others. We all have days when physical fatigue or personal concerns impact our performance in negative ways. There are also days (perhaps not as many) when we wake up on top of the world and, without any particular effort or strain, perform in ways that far exceed our usual conduct on the job. Satisfactory or unsatisfactory performance, then, must be judged over some period of time. We are not discussing here the performance that is so bad that a given instance justifies termination. A sales associate who is fatigued and personally pressured cannot be excused on these grounds if he physically assaults a difficult customer. Within the normal range of better and worse days, some overall assessment of performance must be made. Just as there is a range of satisfactory performance, so there is a range of unsatisfactory performance.

A further factor that impacts the question of who is similarly situated is time on the job. A new employee in her first weeks on the job will not usually perform as well as someone who has been doing the same job for two years. This fact is sometimes recognized by different job grades (e.g., junior analyst, analyst, senior analyst). Still another factor that can affect the issue of satisfactory performance involves changing circumstances beyond the manager's or the employee's control. Performance requirements in a CPA office are very different in the week before the April 15 tax filing deadline from what they are in the middle of July. Sales associates in a department store have different performance requirements during a rainy week in October than they have in the last week before Christmas.

Do all of these conditions mean that no one is really similarly situated with anyone else, so fairness and justice is useless as a moral perspective? Not at all. There is a famous dilemma in logic that says that it is impossible to walk across a room. In order to do so, one would first have to walk across half the room. But to do that, one would have to cross half of that distance, and so on and on. There is an infinite series of ever smaller spaces that one would have to cross and, since no one can cross an infinite number of spaces, it is impossible to traverse the room. The answer to this logical dilemma is very simple: it is solved by walking. The point is that philosophers sometimes think themselves into absurdities, but eventually they have to get up from their thinking chair and go to the refrigerator for a beer or a soda, thus re-establishing contact with the real world. If we ask a reasonable manager whether they can tell satisfactory from unsatisfactory performance, and whether their unsatisfactory performers are similarly situated, the answers will very probably be in the affirmative.

Fairness and justice require that unsatisfactory performers, if they are similarly situated, be treated in similar ways. If one unsatisfactory performer is called in and summarily fired, while another is called in and given sixty days to improve and assigned a trainer to help them improve, we can reasonably conclude that the process was not fair. This conclusion can allow for differences in the situations of the employees or the dispositions of the managers. It is a system rather than an individual perspective, which is the only way to approach fairness and justice. A moral perspective that starts with the notion of similarly situated individuals obviously has a system aspect, but ultimately it makes judgments about the treatment of individuals.

On the whole, then, an ethical analysis of progressive discipline for unsatisfactory performance favors this process. Again, this analysis is separate from the question of whether progressive discipline is legally required. For managers who work in medium to large companies where such policies are not set by individual managers but by specialists from human resources, or by attorneys or by top executives, the question is not whether to follow the company's policy. The sort of analysis done here might make a manager feel better about such a policy, but in most cases when a policy is in place, it is not for the individual manager to decide whether to follow it. In small companies, where there is only one manager, or only a few managers but each one is free to make policy, the question is whether to adopt or keep a policy of progressive discipline. In small companies, problems tend to be more immediate and even one poorly performing employee poses a greater danger to the business.

Long-Term Employees

One category of termination for performance that we have not discussed but that presents particularly difficult problems is the long-term employee whose performance deteriorates due to issues outside of work. It sometimes happens that an employee who has served a company long and well shows either a gradual or a dramatic deterioration in performance. The cause may be alcohol or drug addiction, difficult personal circumstances such as divorce or the death of a spouse or child, or psychological problems such as clinical depression. In such cases, performance may be well below standard, but the long years of adequate or even excellent performance that preceded the problems seem to make this case different from those we have discussed before. This problem is even more difficult to deal with, in some ways, if the employee is in a managerial or executive position.

Some managers or executives respond to cases like this by insisting that everyone must observe the same standards and that every employee, whatever his rank or time with the company, must perform satisfactorily or face the consequences. This is not a response that can be dismissed out of hand. The performance of the whole company does depend on the perform-ance of the parts. The system perspective that we have repeatedly used to analyze ethical impacts and obligations requires that individual cases be viewed in a broader perspective. Yet, many managers, especially those who are themselves long-term employees, feel that there is something different about the kind of case described, and the usual solutions may not be the only ones here.

Let us start by returning briefly to our analysis of progressive discipline in cases of unsatisfactory performance. Underlying that analysis was the concept that adequate performance is the final standard. Progressive discipline involves identifying and dealing with unsatisfactory performance. Time is allowed for improvement and perhaps training or some other form of help is provided to the employee to help him reach satisfactory performance. However, the process is unbending. Satisfactory performance is defined, the gap between present performance and satisfactory performance is identified, the time in which the gap must be closed is specified and the consequences of not closing the gap are made clear. Finally, the termination of the employee results if the gap is not closed. We did not ask whether the failure to close the gap was due to the employee's lack of ability or lack of motivation. The only consideration in this analysis of the reasons for unsatisfactory performance was the possibility that lack of knowledge could be addressed by training.

In the present case of the long-term employee whose performance has deteriorated, lack of knowledge is unlikely to be the problem. Is the manager of this employee ethically obliged to consider what the problem is, or merely to address its lack of solution? In other words, is this case fundamentally dif-ferent from those we discussed above? Obviously, whether an employee is long-term or not, there are some issues that require termination. If perform-ance has become unsatisfactory, but there is no clear and immediate issue requiring termination (e.g., embezzlement, workplace violence), analysis of the individual case does not differ greatly whether the employee is long-term or not. However, additional time or consideration might be in order for the long-term employee.

Utilitarianism indicates that it may not create the greatest good for the greatest number of people to make extra allowances and prolong the period of unsatisfactory performance beyond what would be done for any employee under progressive discipline. The employee involved may benefit, but others who have to pick up the slack do not, nor do customers who are adversely affected by the poor performance. However, if the long-term employee has knowledge or skills that exceed those of other employees, pursuing a process that might lead to their improvement and retention might create additional benefit.

An additional factor comes into play with the long-term employee if we take the system perspective rather than the individual case perspective. People notice how a company treats its employees. If it especially values its long-term employees, this fact encourages current employees to stay. If they are good employees, this is to the benefit of the company and its stakeholders. If a company does not demonstrate that it especially values its long-term employees, those with an opportunity to leave the company are more likely to do so. Those with the most opportunity to obtain jobs at other companies are often the best employees. A pattern of keeping good employees is much more likely to create the greatest good for the greatest number than a pattern of losing them to competitors.

On an individual case basis, it is hard to argue that long service gives an employee a right to additional consideration when performance becomes and remains unsatisfactory in spite of the steps taken in progressive discipline. In the absence of such a right, the manager does not have a duty to give extra consideration to a poorly performing employee because of length of service. Similarly, an employee has a duty to perform their job in a satisfactory manner regardless of length of service, or to accept the consequences.

As we said above, fairness and justice as an ethical approach requires consideration of a system perspective as well as an individual perspective. If long-term employees whose performance becomes unsatisfactory are similarly situated with other employees whose performance either becomes or remains unsatisfactory, then there is no argument from this view for different treatment. But are long-term employees, in fact, similarly situated with other employees? An argument can be made that this is not the case, especially for long-term employees whose performance has consistently been satisfactory or better.

In economic terms, an employee is an employee. All are interchangeable, and they are viewed primarily as a source of costs and/or productivity. Economics abstracts from individual considerations, in order to provide insights that would otherwise be lost in the details of individual employees, managers, customers, shareholders, etc. However, in the world where a manager must tell an employee, face to face, that he can no longer work for the company, individual managers confront individual employees. Each has a personal history and a history with the company. Each may well approach the interview with uneasiness and may leave the interview with intense feelings of discomfort. To ignore all of this is to take a less-than-accurate view of the situation. This is not to say that feelings change everything or that emotions should rule rational judgment. It is to say that there is more to the situation than meets the economic eye.

From a purely rational point of view, a long-term employee who has consistently performed well is an asset, a known quantity. Human resources professionals sometimes say that the best predictor of what an employee will do is what an employee has done. People change, adults sometimes alter their behavior. More often and more predictably, people remain basically the same. Humans are creatures of habit; resistance to change is a widely documented phenomenon. Selection processes for new employees are designed to identify the candidate who is most likely to perform satisfactorily in the position that is open. Employee evaluation processes are in place partly because selection processes do not always do what they are intended to do. It is necessary to determine whether a new employee, or an employee new to a job, or for that matter an old, long-term employee is in fact performing the tasks of their job in a satisfactory manner. But when an employee has established a record of satisfactory performance over a long period of time, the fact that their performance deteriorates is unusual and worth consideration.

Sometimes the reason for deteriorating performance is clear. If an employee is suffering due to personal circumstances, such as divorce or the serious illness or death of a spouse or child, this fact may well be known to the manager. Under normal circumstances, people who undergo such personal trauma act differently for a time, then gradually return to their "normal" selves. Experience has shown that this is the case, at least sometimes, in terms of work performance. A period of poor performance when the employee is overwhelmed by personal circumstances is sometimes followed by gradual improvement to the former satisfactory level. If the poor performance is not such that it causes serious harm to others, such as fellow employees or customers, keeping the employee on the job might be not only defensible, but the best course of action. We will examine the reasons for this below.

The reasons for deteriorating performance often lie in health problems, either physical or psychological. An employee may or may not volunteer information to his manager about such problems. As we will see in the chapter on privacy and monitoring, there are delicate issues involved in questions relating to an employee's health. It is also important to remember that managers are usually not qualified as counselors and, in the case of alcohol or drug dependency or serious psychological problems, managers are usually not qualified either to diagnose or to treat. To the untrained person, it is not always easy to determine whether changed behavior patterns are the result of physical illness, psychological illness or chemical dependency. Since it is hard to know how to solve a problem when one does not know what the problem is, the simplest approach here is to deal exclusively with the job performance issues.

If a manager employs progressive discipline as described earlier in this chapter, her focus can remain on the employee's performance. If that performance does not improve to a satisfactory level, further warnings and termination follow. Since the manager often does not know what underlies the deterioration of the employee's performance, and is probably not qualified to deal with the causes even if they were known, the best course would appear to be to consider the causes as the employee's concern, and not the manager's. Another possible approach, though, also deserves consideration. The first step in progressive discipline is an interview with the employee to indicate that performance is unsatisfactory and to specify the required level of improvement and the time by which it must be attained.

During this interview, a manager might suggest to the employee that performance that was previously satisfactory has now become unsatisfactory and there must be some reason for this change. If the employee is dealing with a personal problem, professional help might be in order. If the company has an Employee Assistance Program, the employee might be encouraged to use this program to seek help. An Employee Assistance Program is a benefit provided by some companies to employees and their families.[11] The Program provides a limited number of company-paid visits outside the regular medical insurance plan to professionals from a variety of fields. Such plans often provide the assistance of psychologists, substance abuse counselors, debt counselors and others. The company learns only how many visits have occurred, but not the diagnosis or treatment provided.

Whether a company has an Employee Assistance Plan in place or not, the recommendation by the manager to the employee that they seek professional help is a delicate one. Some individuals with substance abuse or other psychological problems are slow to admit that they have a problem. Some do not "believe in" or trust professional counselors. Any implication that the employee is abusing alcohol or drugs or has a serious psychological problem may be resented by the employee, even if it is true. An accusation that is not true could lead to distrust, anger or even litigation. The risks of these negative reactions must be weighed against the possibility of helping a long-term, good employee to regain a performance level that satisfies the manager and allows the employee to keep his job. The individual manager faced with such a situation might well seek advice from a human resources professional. Because the human resources staff see and deal with more of these problems than an individual manager, and because they have greater knowledge of what resources are available to employees, their input can be very helpful in deciding on a course of action.

Whether the source of a long-term employee's deteriorating performance is known, suspected or unknown, there remains a question of whether it is ethical to treat them differently from anyone else in dealing with unsatisfactory job performance. If it is judged to be more important to help and retain long-term employees than others, then the greatest good for the greatest number might be achieved by making some extra effort to correct the situation when a long-term employee's performance deteriorates. Again, behavior that results in immediate termination is not under consideration here. If the employee can be brought back to their previous satisfactory level of performance, the employee benefits by not losing their job, the company benefits by retaining a good employee who is experienced and the only unhappiness caused is to those affected during the employee's period of unsatisfactory performance. Some of this would be true of any employee and the aim of progressive discipline is to improve performance and gain the benefits described here.

It is difficult to argue that an employee has a right to special treatment in a situation where performance has deteriorated, simply because he has been employed by the same company for a long time. If we take the system perspective, managers have a duty to see that their units operate well and that their individual decisions support patterns of decision-making that are favorable to the company. If it is a good thing to encourage good employees to stay with the company by maintaining a pattern of treating long-term employees well, then individual decisions are the only way to create and maintain this pattern. This is a rather vague argument, and it does not seem to create a real duty on the part of managers in individual cases to give extra consideration to long-term employees whose performance has deteriorated. At best, the manager may have a somewhat vague duty to consider additional factors in such a case. Whether or not she acts on such factors is a case-by-case decision.

Fairness and justice would ask first whether long-term employees are similarly situated with other employees. If they are, the conclusion is clear: they are to be treated similarly. We have made a case, though, that long-term employees who have performed well over that long term are, in fact, different from other employees. The company knows more about them and they about the company. Their reliability, at least until the deterioration in performance, is well established. In many jobs, or departments, long-term employees know more than those who have been there a shorter time. Institutional memory is embedded in long-term employees. It is sometimes very useful to know what a department or division or the company did the last time a similar problem arose, whether or not it worked, and why. Long-term employees tend to know these things, even if they are not written down.

A generation ago, it was not terribly unusual for an employee to spend their entire working life, or at least a substantial portion of it, with one company. This is less and less the case, so the meaning of long-term has shifted considerably in the last few decades. So far in this discussion, we have not used the term loyalty. It is a concept that is not in fashion now. However, the writing on corporate culture makes a point that, where many employees do in fact stay in the same organization for a long time, there is a tendency to do favors and act altruistically in ways that help the company. The thought is that, when employees expect to be around for a good while, the old adage that what goes around comes around has real meaning. If I do something extra for you today or this month, the time will come when I need something extra and you will remember and reciprocate. This assumption, when it is part of a company's culture, can facilitate overall company performance in ways that are subtle but significant.[12] If the overall patterns in a company do not in any way encourage long-term employment, some of these intangibles are lost, to the detriment of the organization. An argument can be made, then, that long-term employees are not similarly situated with others and that providing them with extra consideration is not automatically unfair or unjust.

Friendship and Terminations

There is one further consideration before we leave the topic of termination for performance. We have discussed, under rights and duties, the rights that come by position, such as those of a police officer or a chief financial officer. Business theory does not address this subject, but some people at work, including some managers and subordinates, are friends. There are rights that one has because one is in the position of friend. I raise the issue here because it seems most likely to arise in the case of long-term employees. The fact that neither economic theory nor business theory in general addresses friendship at work does not mean that such friendships do not exist or do not influence the actions of individuals in the workplace.

In Aristotle's main work on ethics, *The Nicomachean Ethics*,[13] the bulk of the book describes the various virtues and the faults which come when they are practiced either too little or to excess. The most engaging and moving chapter of this work is his discussion of the virtue of friendship. Friendship is the theme of movies, plays and novels, but does not appear as a central topic in most philosophy. Some managers feel that it is not a good idea to become friends with any subordinate because in the role of manager they will have to evaluate and perhaps discipline the subordinate, and friendship will make this more difficult. The fact is that many people do make friends at work. Sometimes these people are bosses and subordinates.

Friends can call on friends for things that they would not ask of strangers or acquaintances. This is what is involved with the rights by position of friends. We do not normally think or talk of the rights of friends, but in some meaningful sense we do owe duties to our friends that we do not owe to others. How does this play out in the workplace? In a system where merit is the basis for compensation and promotion, friendship can make objective judgment more difficult. If a manager bases evaluations or compensation decisions on friendship in a system that requires that they be based on merit, he is wrong in doing so. Such decisions do not constitute the greatest good for the greatest number. His duty as a manager is to operate within the merit system. For purposes of evaluation and compensation, friendship is not a factor that separates people and makes a special, similarly situated group of those who are the manager's friends. Further, a merit system relies on objective assessments by managers of the performance of their employees. Friendship can cloud objective assessment.

People do become friends with others in the workplace. If this is the situation between manager and subordinate, the manager has a duty to try to achieve objectivity in his decisions about evaluation and compensation as well as terminations and to be aware that friendship is not a factor that should influence these decisions, directly or indirectly. Since friendship can and sometimes does pose a problem in this regard, even more care needs to be taken in situations where kinship or romantic involvement between manager and subordinate occurs. In fact, many companies have explicit policies prohibiting managers from overseeing the work of their own family members. It is harder to specify or enforce a policy against supervising an employee with whom a manager is romantically involved, but the difficulties of objectivity in such situations are so great as to make it a situation to be avoided rather than dealt with. Even if fairness were achieved in such a situation, the perception of fairness is so unlikely to occur that the situation is best avoided.

Layoffs

One large class of terminations remains for analysis: that of layoffs. Whether they are called layoffs, reductions in force or down-sizing, the terminations considered here are triggered not by unsatisfactory performance or by major individual offenses by employees, but by a company's decision to reduce the size of its workforce.[14] The question at issue here is whether it can be moral, and if so, when, to terminate the employment of someone who has not done anything to cause their termination.

After World War II, the economies of many countries grew for an extended period. This was particularly true in the United States. In a dramatic change from the long period of economic depression and high unemployment that extended from 1929 to 1942, the period following the war was one of economic growth and low unemployment. Although guaranteed lifetime employment never did become a formal promise at most American companies (as it did in many large companies in Japan), an unofficial policy of continued employment for those who wanted it was in force at a number of large companies in the United States. It was not uncommon for an individual to work for the same company for twenty years or more, and many people retired from the first company they went to work for.

In the last two decades of the twentieth century, this standard changed dramatically. The mergers and acquisitions that became so popular during this period resulted in thousands of layoffs each time that two large companies merged. As global business competition increased and American companies became more and more conscious of their costs, emphasis on reducing labor costs resulted in layoffs. This was particularly true in some industries where labor unions, over a period of many years, had bargained wages and benefits up to a point where companies could no longer pay them and remain competitive. This was true of steelworkers, auto workers and some parts of the construction and trucking industries. During these two decades, the expectation of lifetime employment with the same company became more and more unrealistic. The acceptability of companies announcing that hundreds or thousands of their employees were being laid off slowly grew (although not among the employees who were laid off). It became common for a company's stock to increase significantly in value on the day that it announced layoffs.

When analyzed from a financial point of view (that of the company, not the employee), layoffs generally appear to be a good thing. Even if the employees who are terminated are given severance pay and their benefits are continued for a period of time, all of these expenses are normally taken in one quarter and usually as extraordinary, non-recurring expenses. After that quarter, the company's expenses are lower by the amount of the salary and benefits that would otherwise have been paid to the workers who were laid off. The assumption, in this kind of financial analysis, is that the work that generates revenue will continue to be done, but by fewer employees. If the amount of revenue is reduced because less work is done, the whole point of the layoffs, at least from a financial perspective, is negated, except in the case of closing an unprofitable factory or store.

In an earlier article, I showed that layoffs from the management point of view can be divided into three types.[15] Layoffs to save the company involve dire situations. In this case, typically, a company has become non-competitive because of excessive labor costs. This means that it costs the company significantly more in terms of labor to produce its goods or services than it costs the company's competitors to produce theirs. Because of this cost differential, the company can no longer sell a sufficient volume of its goods or services at prices that allow for a profit, or sometimes even at moderate but tolerable losses. In such a case, the company (at least in the United States) faces bankruptcy if it does not do something to change the situation. Thus, layoffs intended to alleviate such a problem are classed as layoffs to save the company.

A second broad category of layoffs are those that I have categorized as layoffs to improve the company. In this situation, managers view their competitive situation, especially as it appears in the near future, see that the company is in danger of becoming non-competitive because of labor costs and take action to remedy the situation before the company reaches the point where bankruptcy is imminent. The key point here is that management perceives a serious problem, either present or looming, relating to labor costs and decides to take proactive steps.

The third broad category of layoffs involves layoffs to change the company. The first two categories are also aimed at change, but in this category the company is competing well. However, management in looking to the future decides that it could compete even better and be more profitable if staffing changes were made. Such layoffs often occur as part of a merger or acquisition.[16] In this case, two companies become one, and some employees become redundant and thus unnecessary. When one bank merges with another, they do not need two managers of internal audit or two full payroll departments. Thus total employment is reduced, and some employees are laid off. Another situation that is included in layoffs to change the company occurs when management decides to focus the company's efforts on its core competences and hire other companies to perform functions at which the company has no special skill. For example, a company that employs janitors to clean its buildings may contract out the whole function of cleaning to a firm that specializes in such services. Unless that firm agrees to hire all the janitors the company presently employs, some or all of them will be laid off.

Most managers do not have decision-making power on the question of whether or not there will be layoffs. Ironically, most senior managers who decide this issue do not usually take part directly, in the sense of telling laid-off employees that they no longer have jobs. This unhappy task usually falls to lower-level managers, whose workers are actually being laid off. Because of this involvement, the question of whether layoffs are ethical has some practical concern for most managers. Another factor that involves most managers is that layoffs are not always limited to workers. Managers are also sometimes laid off, and this makes the issue much less abstract and more immediate. A third factor concerning layoffs that affects middle managers and supervisors is the question of which employees will be laid off. Top managers sometimes decide that the workforce will be reduced by some percentage, with the decision as to which individuals are laid off being left to middle managers and supervisors. Thus the ethical issues of whether there should be layoffs, and who specifically should be laid off, are matters of concern for most managers.

The first issue is whether there should be layoffs. A utilitarian analysis would conclude that layoffs to save the company are moral, since they lead to the greatest good for the greatest number. If indeed the options are to lay off some employees now or to go into bankruptcy and possibly go out of business, then more people benefit by laying off some people now. These layoffs cause a great deal of unhappiness for those who lose their jobs and their families. They also cause some degree of unhappiness for the managers who must tell employees that, in spite of their good performance and through no fault of their own, they no longer have jobs. If the result of not conducting layoffs now is bankruptcy, then this result carries greater unhappiness for more people.

Even if the company later emerges from bankruptcy as a going concern, it will probably do so as a smaller company, so some employees will lose their jobs anyway. Bankruptcy also causes major unhappiness for stockholders, whose stock usually becomes worthless. It causes unhappiness for lenders, who usually recover only part of the money loaned to the bankrupt company. It causes unhappiness for customers, suppliers and others who are negatively affected by the uncertainty of bankruptcy filing and proceedings. If the company does not emerge from bankruptcy and instead closes down, all employees suffer the negative consequences of losing their jobs. Lenders, suppliers and customers suffer more harm. The net result is usually not even close to a balance. More harm than good is done.

Layoffs to improve the company, the second category, present a more mixed picture when a utilitarian analysis is carried out. If the situation is closer to bankruptcy than to good health without the layoffs, the analysis given above tends to hold true, although the arguments are not quite as strong. If the company is doing reasonably well, but it appears to management that in the face of competition it will probably not do so well in the future, a utilitarian would weigh the chances of greater harm later against the present limited harm caused by layoffs now. The same sorts of arguments would be used, but with diminishing force as the present condition of the company is seen as stronger, or the present estimate of future competitive pressures is seen as less certain.

Finally, layoffs to change the company, the category that involves making a strong and successful company even better, are difficult if not impossible to justify from a utilitarian perspective. The present harm of layoffs is clear; the future benefits to be gained are not so clear and may even not come to pass.[17] Companies that are performing well are seldom over-staffed, unless their good performance is the result of some temporary competitive advantage that is sufficiently strong to cover up for weak management practices. Companies that are strong and successful sometimes justify layoffs on strictly financial terms, with optimistic assumptions used to justify the expected savings. During the 1990s, at a time when layoffs were becoming accepted practice, Tom Peters published a book which had as its subtitle the memorable phrase "you can't shrink your way to greatness."[18] A utilitarian would insist on considering the unhappiness brought about at the time of layoffs as well as the happiness projected to occur in the future as their result.

The central question in a rights and duties analysis of layoffs is whether employees have a right to keep their jobs. If they do, such a right imposes a duty on managers not to lay them off. A question that is sometimes ignored in discussions of layoffs is whether managers have a duty to save the company from serious harm, such as bankruptcy, and whether that duty might also involve conducting layoffs when necessary. First, the employee's right to keep their job. Most employment contracts and labor-management contracts specify the conditions and circumstances under which an employee can be terminated. These specifications establish contractual rights to keep a job. As we have seen, tenure and civil service provide similar quasi-contractual rights to employment.

Legally, the doctrine of employment at will in its pure form states that employees do not have any right to keep their jobs, since they can be terminated for good reason, bad reason or no reason at all. However, this doctrine has been extensively modified by laws prohibiting employment actions (which include termination) based on such categories as age, gender and race. The tort of wrongful termination has been developed in the American legal system.[19] While the law concerning this tort is evolving, it places further constraints on management's legal freedom to terminate employees. The Sarbanes–Oxley Act, passed in 2002, makes it illegal under some circumstances to fire a whistle-blower. Further, some legal cases have found an implied contractual right to a job in certain situations. All of these limitations on termination seem to point conceptually to some sort of right of employees to keep their jobs, even if there is no contractual basis for such a right.

Some countries, especially Japan and Western European countries, have a much stronger sense of this conceptual right for employees to keep their jobs. This conceptual right is expressed in their employment practices and in their legal protection for workers. Views on this possible right have changed substantially within the last fifty years, particularly in the United States. It is very difficult or impossible to make a clear argument for a right to continued employment as a human right. As we have seen, it is a legal right under some circumstances but not others. If it were a position right, we would have to argue that the position that grants the right is simply that of employee, and this does not seem to be factually true. Finally, continued employment can be a contractual right, if it is agreed to by both parties to the contract.

Without such a clear right, there is no clear duty on employers not to terminate employees. However, just as we argued that there are ethical implications in the employment process when an employer offers a resource (a job) to one applicant and not to others, so there are ethical implications in the termination process when an employer takes away a resource (a job) from one employee and not from others. Fairness and justice in the process are important. When some satisfactory employees are laid off and others are not, there is a problem from the terms of fairness and justice, at least if satisfactory employees are a class or group that is similarly situated. The application of fairness and justice is most illuminating, not in considering whether to conduct layoffs but in deciding who will be laid off. Some satisfactory workers will lose their jobs, while others will not. How this is done can affect the fairness of the outcome.

The most common ways of deciding who gets laid off are reverse seniority, entire groups, percentage distribution and performance. Reverse seniority, or laying employees off by the rule of most recently hired are first laid off, is the usual provision in labor-management contracts. Entire groups means that a store, branch or manufacturing plant is closed down and all those who work there are laid off. Percentage distribution means that top management decides that a certain percentage of employees will be laid off from each unit (store, branch, geographic division) and usually local managers are left to determine which employees will comprise the assigned percentage for the local unit. Layoffs by performance means that the poorest performers will be laid off. While this last is the most reasonable approach from an economic point of view (since the point of the layoffs is to improve performance), it is probably the least frequent.

Reverse seniority can be defended as fair because it uses the same criterion (hire date) for decision-making and applies that criterion to all those subject to possible layoffs. It can have the unintended effect of terminating promising younger employees while keeping mediocre older ones. It can also have the unintended effect of making future hiring more difficult when the company's performance improves because applicants may become aware that job security is lowest for new hires. It is easy to apply because it does not require managers to exercise judgments about individuals and then defend those judgments.

Layoffs by entire groups also has the benefit of apparent ease of decision-making and similar treatment of similarly situated people. It also absolves managers of the need to make and defend decisions about individual employees. It has the disadvantage that it will almost certainly result in the layoff of some very good performers. To avoid this, some companies will offer employment at other locations to some or all of those employees whose branch or plant is closing. When this requires relocating to a different geographic area, it is usually not seen as an attractive or even viable option by most employees of the unit that is closing. From a utilitarian point of view, this approach sometimes causes much more harm and unhappiness than the other approaches. If a plant in a small town closes and all of its employees are laid off, the impact reaches far beyond those employees. The whole town suffers because a significant number of workers suddenly lack incomes. Spending decreases, the need for various forms of welfare assistance increases, the tax base is often diminished greatly by the plant closing and other impacts ripple out into the community. This does not automatically and always make plant closings in small towns wrong, but a utilitarian analysis shows that the greater impact of this approach does have greater moral impact.

Layoffs by percentage are relatively easy from a top management perspective, but very difficult from the perspective of lower managers and workers. From an operational point of view, such layoffs are not the most rational approach because it is rare that all units can or should equally withstand the reduction of a set percentage of their workers. Some units in a medium or large organization will be relatively over-staffed and some relatively under-staffed. The impact of percentage layoffs will be much greater on some units than others. Some units may need to retain or even increase staff. For instance, if the performance problem facing the company is decreasing sales, then staff reductions in the sales units may well be counterproductive. Layoffs by percentage push the decision about who should be laid off down to middle or lower management levels, but the same decisions have to be made. This approach has the initial appearance of fairness because all employees are subject to layoffs and, if all employees or at least all units make up one group, then similar treatment is afforded to all. Actually, the disparate impact of such layoffs on different groups makes this an unfair method of conducting layoffs. This approach spreads the pain of layoffs, but seldom accomplishes the greatest good for the greatest number by helping the whole company in the most effective way.

Layoffs by performance are comparatively rare. From a strictly rational, economic point of view, this is a desirable approach to layoffs. If a company wants to get maximum impact with minimum layoffs, then terminating those employees who are the lowest performers is calculated to do the least harm and thus enhance the benefit of layoffs. To do so across the board, however, would produce other problems. It is very unlikely that all the worst performers will be in the same units that can best sustain layoffs. To use our previous example, if the problem the company faces is reduced sales, then any layoffs in the sales department, even of relatively poor performers, might be counterproductive.

Another practical problem that arises is identifying the worst performers. If this is to be done objectively, then the company's performance appraisal system should play a key role in making decisions. Unfortunately, many companies do not have sufficiently accurate performance appraisal systems, or they do not differentiate sufficiently in their ratings, to serve as a solid basis for determining layoffs by performance. It may well be also that managers are more hesitant to do layoffs on this basis because it is harder to justify their decisions when using performance as a basis than it is when using reverse seniority or laying off all employees in a unit.

In terms of fairness, some combination of performance and current unit staffing would constitute the best basis for layoffs. Not all units are equally able to sustain layoffs and so treating all units as similarly situated is not truly fair. Not all employees are equally deserving of keeping their jobs based on their performance. At the extreme, if a manager had to choose between laying off her best performer and one who was part way through progressive discipline on the way to termination for performance, the choice would be easy and the fair choice would be clear. Most cases are not this clear cut, but the argument for making performance part of the decision on a basis of fairness is clear.

The decision to conduct layoffs is often made rather quickly in the face of severe performance difficulties. Managers do not have time to carefully examine each alternative and project the immediate and secondary consequences of each one. Managers faced with these decisions are also often under a good deal of pressure to improve performance, show results and make clear why they should not be blamed for the poor performance. Under such conditions, it is easy to make decisions for a simple and clear program of layoffs. This probably explains the popularity of layoffs by percentage and the use of reverse seniority. These approaches are the easiest to communicate and to implement. Unfortunately, they have serious problems built in that make them less likely to achieve the longer-term goals that are part of a manager's job.

We have now shown how the three basic approaches to ethics can be used to analyze actual situations faced by managers in the hiring, evaluating and terminating of employees. In the next chapters, we take up specific topics and examples in the areas of privacy and of financial reporting.

ten

Privacy

Applicants and Employees

One of the fundamental responsibilities of a manager is to supervise or oversee the work of employees. The word supervisor comes from two Latin words that literally mean "look over." When the employees who directly report to a manager work in the same physical space as the manager, supervision can be accomplished by looking out over the employees. Managers in the contemporary working world are often physically separated from those employees who report directly to them and, even when they are in the same physical location, the manager has many other things to occupy his time besides literally watching his employees. Advances in technology have made it possible in many cases for a manager to have very detailed records of each employee's actions throughout the work day. Technology has also made it possible for managers to know more about the activities of their employees away from work than ever before.

Overseeing the work of others can mean very different things depending on who those others are and what work they are doing. It is one thing to supervise the work of a group of data entry clerks and quite another thing to oversee the work of a group of field sales people or long-haul truck drivers. Very different approaches are used in overseeing the work of servers and busboys in a restaurant than in overseeing the work of senior executives who report to a CEO. In all cases, the responsibility of the manager includes assigning and coordinating the work of direct subordinates and reviewing the results of that work.

A data entry clerk who is out of the office for a week (assuming the work is done at the office and not from home) presents a different situation than a long-haul truck driver who is not in the office for a week because he is delivering a load, or a Vice President of Sales who is not in the home office for a week because she is visiting regional sales offices. Checking up on the physical whereabouts of the clerk after an hour might be a reasonable supervisory action, whereas checking on the whereabouts of the truck driver or the Vice President of Sales in the same time frame might not. This very general discussion of what constitutes supervision sets the background for our discussion of privacy.

Meanings of Privacy

Employees (and we should remember that managers are also employees who report in turn to their managers) generally agree that they owe their employers an honest day's work for an honest day's pay. Beyond this, however, many employees do not feel that they owe the company they work for, or their manager as its representative, their total and undivided attention for every minute of every work day. Much less do they feel that they owe their private thoughts while at work or their personal lives while not at work. In other words, employees have some expectation of privacy.[1]

When managers ask questions of their employees, they have an expectation that the answers given will be truthful. Realistic managers know that not all employees will tell them all the truth all the time, but the basic expectation is for truth-telling rather than lying. When employees ask questions of their managers, they have a similar expectation that the answers given will be truthful, with similar limitations on this expectation. These expectations do not hold true always and everywhere. Relations between employees and their bosses can become so poisoned that neither expects anything positive, including truth-telling, from the other. Nonetheless, as a general premise, the expectation of truth-telling rather than of lying seems to be founded in reality.

Each individual has information about himself at many levels. Some of this information is freely and generally shared and some of it is shared with no one. Privacy, in its most basic meaning, concerns the levels of information and the sharing of them. Our names are, as a general rule, freely shared. Our annual income is less freely shared, and information about some medical conditions, such as sexually transmitted diseases, is very closely guarded. Different individuals place different levels of importance on the same information. Some people have their home telephone number listed in widely distributed telephone directories; others choose to keep their number unlisted.

An individual's thoughts are also subject to various degrees of sharing and guarding. If a manager asks an employee who is a baseball fan what he thinks of the local team's chance of winning their divisional title, he will probably get an honest answer. If the same manager asks the same employee what he thinks of the manager's leadership style, the chances for an honest answer diminish considerably. The answer that an employee gives to her manager if asked about her greatest hope or greatest fear might differ from the answer to the same question if the inquirer were her husband instead of her boss. Some people feel free to post their personal thoughts and opinions on internet blogs or Facebook, while others find these public expressions of private ideas and feelings to be abhorrent. These are simple facts of everyday life, yet they are often not taken into account when the issue of privacy is discussed.

Finally, an individual's body is at issue in some discussions of privacy. Visual monitors (cameras) might be accepted as a valid method of oversight in a bank's cash vault but not in an employee changing room. Pre-employment or annual physical examinations might reasonably be required of airline pilots, but perhaps not of part-time employees at a fast-food store. Requiring physical samples (hair, blood or urine) to test for drugs might generally be found acceptable for workers at a nuclear power plant, but not for senior executives of a financial services firm. All of these issues, in one way or another, involve privacy of the body.

We said above that the responsibility to supervise takes different forms for managers depending on such circumstances as the physical presence in the same work area of employees. The responsibility to supervise also takes different forms depending on the nature of the work being done.[2] Where there are significant safety risks not only to the workers but also to customers or to the public at large, the responsibility of managers to prevent accidents is greater than where the work presents little or no risk even to the worker.[3] Airline pilots and police officers face different risk profiles at work than do data entry clerks and sales persons. Where the manager's responsibility is greater, it is reasonable to expect that the worker will be subject to more intense oversight. Intense oversight by the manager will, as a general rule, mean less privacy for the employee.

The assumption in our discussion thus far is that the manager has a job to do and that an important part of this job involves supervising those workers who report to the manager. This task of the manager requires interaction with the workers, as well as with the process by which they accomplish their tasks and with the results of that work. A self-employed artist painting in her studio is in a fundamentally different position from the sales person in an art gallery who sells the artist's paintings. A composer working at his piano is in a different position from the symphony musician playing as part of an orchestra performing the composer's work. Most work in developed countries is done in organizations. Individual workers are part of a larger picture, and their individuality is subject to constraints because of this fact. When we examine the moral issues involved in a supervisor's intrusion on her subordinate worker's privacy, this organizational setting is an important component of our analysis.

We saw earlier that the objective of the hiring process is not to be fair but to select the employee who will best help the organization to achieve its goals. It is also true that the point of the supervisory role of managers is not to learn about the employee but to accomplish through workers the tasks for which the manager is responsible. In carrying out this role, information about workers is sometimes needed. Applicants or workers may not recognize or agree with this need, and it is here that issues of privacy and monitoring come to the fore. While this description may make it seem as though the worker is simply a tool at the disposal of the manager, in fact managers and workers often come to know each other on a personal basis and sometimes socialize or become friends. This is a natural outcome since they spend time together in a work setting and often share common interests.

The person who applies for a job is in a somewhat different position than the person who is already employed. Since most people who apply for a job will be rejected, the likelihood in this process is that the individual applicant will not have an ongoing relation with the company to which he is applying. The need for information in order to assess an applicant is also different from the need for information in order to supervise a worker. In each case, though, we have a similar situation, that of an individual sharing or refusing to share information with an organization through its representatives. This is different from sharing information with one's family, friends or doctor. In the introductory paragraphs of this chapter, we discussed information about a person, a person's thoughts and a person's body as three areas of concern in issues of privacy. We will examine each in turn, taking the application and employment situation first. As we have done in previous chapters, we will use the three basic approaches to ethics in our analyses.

Categories of Privacy

Privacy and Information

When an individual applies for a job, he is normally asked to provide information about his identity and his qualifications for that job. Identity includes such items of information as name and address, social security number (in the United States) and not a great deal else. In order to insure against illegal discrimination in the employment process, many items of information that were routine parts of a job application are no longer requested. These exclusions cover such items as an applicant's age, marital status, health history and hobbies. If an applicant is hired, more personal information might be gathered in the process of setting up employee records. This is because the hiring decision has been made and information gathered at this point can no longer be used to discriminate in the hiring process.

In addition to identifying information, applicants for a job are normally expected to provide information about their educational and work history. Because this information is seen as relevant in assessing the applicant's qualifications for the job, more information and more detailed information are normally requested and sometimes verified by the potential employer in the areas of educational attainment and work history. Most applicants routinely provide such information and doing so does not present a privacy issue to most people. One area that sometimes causes problems is information about why the applicant left previous jobs. If the applicant was terminated for cause, or because of such work-related issues as poor attendance or unsatisfactory job performance, the potential employer would typically consider this to be relevant information and the applicant would typically prefer that the potential employer not find out the facts. Many companies now have a policy of refusing to comment on reasons for termination, giving only dates worked and salary information to other companies.[4]

A second area that sometimes causes problems is the accuracy of the information provided by the applicant. Many companies consider the provision of accurate information sufficiently important that they make it grounds for termination if they discover that an employee provided false information on an application. It is not always clear whether an applicant who provides false information considers this a privacy issue (in the sense that the company does not have a right to know, therefore the applicant does not have a duty to provide accurate information) or whether the applicant acknowledges the company's right but chooses to attempt to deceive.

A utilitarian approach to assessing the morality of a company's seeking information about applicants starts by asking whether the gathering of such information provides the greatest good for the greatest number. Again, we return to the point that the goal of the employment process is to select the applicant who will best help the company to achieve its goals. Failure to do so, especially if such failure becomes routine rather than isolated, will result in the company's failure to achieve its goals. This can have a number of negative consequences, including uncompetitive performance and eventually bankruptcy with its attendant loss of jobs for employees and negative effects on investors, lenders, suppliers and others. Thus, a utilitarian would argue that employee selection is important in terms of its results.

If this is the case, then accurate relevant information about applicants is a reasonable goal of the company in its employment process. The key term here is relevant. If there is information that the applicant would rather not reveal, and it is not relevant to the employment process, then the applicant will suffer and no one will gain, with the result that the greatest good for the greatest number is not accomplished. Managers might well feel that information about an applicant's health or hobbies would help in making the hiring decision but, at least in the United States, the law precludes managers from using such information in the hiring process, so most companies do not allow such inquiries. As we saw above, there are differences in what is relevant depending on the work to be done. An applicant for a position as an accountant would normally not be asked about his driving record, whereas an applicant for a position as a bus driver would be required to provide such information. An organization such as the Federal Bureau of Investigation performs very thorough background checks on its applicants.[5] At the other end of the scale, a fast-food restaurant hiring a part-time worker might perform no investigation at all. The time and money invested on background checks for fast-food workers with very limited responsibilities and an average expected time on the job of four months would almost certainly not yield the greatest good for the greatest number.

A rights and duties analysis of employer information gathering concerning work applicants is a bit more involved. The employer has a right to relevant information about applicants in order to do a reasonable job of employee selection and placement. The applicant has a right to privacy. The right to privacy concerning information about oneself is largely a legal right. It has some basis in the human right to dignity, but this right would seem to be limited to particularly private information, such as that concerning some health conditions. Some health conditions would prevent the applicant from performing the job—even the restrictive United States laws against hiring discrimination allow airlines to deny blind applicants who want to be pilots. Laws that prevent the use of specific information (e.g., age, religion, nationality) lead to the logical conclusion that companies that do not have a right to use such information also do not have a right to gather it.

As long as the information gathered by the potential employer from the applicant is relevant to the employment process, the applicant has a duty to provide the information and to provide it honestly. This duty arises because of the applicant's position. If she were not applying for a job, she would have no duty to provide information to the company, but since she is applying for the job, she has a duty to provide relevant information honestly.[6] This may seem obvious, but researchers estimate that between 40 and 70 percent of applicants exaggerate their resumes.[7] In brief, the company's right to know relevant information about the applicant in order to carry out the selection and employment process outweighs the applicant's right to privacy. It not only outweighs the right to privacy, but it imposes a duty on the applicant to provide the information truthfully.

From a fairness and justice perspective, a company is required to treat similarly situated applicants in a similar way. This means that applicants for the same or similar jobs should be treated similarly in terms of what information is requested of them. As we saw above, when the risks or responsibilities of one position differ from those of another, the information needed to assess applicants also differs. Therefore, it is fair and just to seek more information from applicants for positions with higher risks and responsibilities. The two key ideas here are that the information be relevant to the selection and employment process and that the same information is sought from applicants for the same or similar positions.

Privacy and Thoughts

A wise person of my acquaintance once said, "I never get in trouble for what I think; only for what I say." Thoughts, like information, range from those that are commonly and easily shared to those that are shared with no one. The information-gathering stage of the selection and employment process is normally conducted first by collecting written information, in the form of a resume or application. Once candidates are screened based on this written information, those who appear to be best qualified for the position in question are normally invited for interviews. The written information gathered through resumes and applications is normally objective rather than subjective. Applicants are asked for identifying information (name, address, social security number) and for educational and job-history information (schools attended, degrees earned, previous jobs held and dates).

During an interview, it is common for employers to ask applicants for subjective information. Applicants are often asked to identify and discuss their own strengths and weaknesses, to give examples of how they have handled work-related situations well or badly and to discuss what they would do if faced with a specified scenario on the job. Applicants are also often asked to further discuss objective information that has already been provided in writing, such as their responsibilities in a previous job or their reasons for leaving a previous employer. A refusal by an applicant to discuss any of these issues would almost certainly harm his chances of getting the job for which they have applied.

It is worth noting that not every kind of subjective information can properly be sought in a pre-employment interview. All of the questions described above are relevant to the task of selecting the best employee for the open position. An interviewer cannot properly ask which candidates the applicant voted for in the last election, whether he attends church regularly or what he thinks is the best way to discipline children. An interesting and complex set of questions arises surrounding the use by employers of psychological tests or tests designed to measure the honesty of applicants.[8] Psychological tests are commonly used for public safety positions, such as police and fire department officers. They are much less commonly used for white-collar workers and seldom, if ever, for blue-collar workers. Such tests typically ask the subject to respond to true/false or multiple-choice questions concerning what many applicants consider to be very private matters. However, within the range of relevant questions, there are clearly some that the applicant might not want to answer, or to answer truthfully. How, then, do we analyze the ethical issues that arise in such a situation?

From the manager's perspective, we have established that the task at hand is to select the best candidate for the open position. Is it ethical for the interviewing manager to ask the applicants about things the applicants might prefer not to answer? A utilitarian would address this issue by asking whether, in spite of the applicant's discomfort, more good would be done by asking such questions than harm. The manager, all other things being equal, will do a better job of selecting the best candidate if she is aware of how each candidate has performed in the past and is likely to perform when put in the job.[9] It is a commonplace among human resources professionals, and perhaps among managers generally, that the best single predictor of what an employee will do is what an employee has done. This does not deny the possibility that people can change their behavior patterns, but it does assert that such patterns usually remain stable. An applicant who has been fired from his last three jobs for being rude to customers is probably not a good selection for a customer service position.

The utilitarian would say that the good that comes about when a hiring manager makes an informed choice among applicants extends not only to the successful applicant but also to his fellow workers, to customers or others he deals with in his position and to the hiring manager who has gained a good employee. The harm that results from asking applicants to answer questions that they might prefer not to answer is limited to the applicant. Therefore, the utilitarian would conclude that it is moral to seek the applicant's thoughts on job-related matters such as those described above, as long as the tests have been validated for the position in question.[10]

A rights and duties analysis would proceed along the same lines as that which we followed previously concerning the hiring manager's right to seek relevant information from applicants and the applicant's duty to provide such information. The applicant does not have to provide his thoughts on the questions asked in the interview. He can end his status as applicant. The manager, however, does have a duty to make an informed choice among applicants and has a right to ask each applicant for his or her thoughts on such matters as those identified above. Here again, the applicant's right to keep his thoughts private must be weighed against the manager's position. If viewed from the opposite perspective, it is clear that the applicant does not have a right to deny the manager the answers to relevant job-related questions, or to lie in answering such questions, and to maintain his position as applicant.

Is it fair for a manager to ask an applicant for his thoughts on job-related questions and scenarios such as those outlined above? As long as other applicants are treated similarly, then fairness and justice are observed. In the chapter on employment we saw that procedural justice (treating applicants for the same job in a similar manner) is a key means to obtaining distributive justice (awarding the open position to the best-qualified applicant). Power is not equally distributed in an interview between a hiring manager and a job applicant, but the position of each is simply different and, as long as the manager is fair in his treatment of the applicant, there is nothing unethical in this situation.

Physical Privacy

Information about an applicant's physical condition and health may be relevant to the hiring process, depending on the requirements of the job. Some positions, such as fireman, policeman or warehouse worker, require physical strength and agility. When such requirements are clear, applicants are usually required to affirm that they are able to perform the required tasks and, in many cases, they are also required to pass physical tests as part of the application process. Applicants for various positions are also required to take and pass a pre-employment physical exam. This requirement normally applies only to applicants who have been tentatively selected for a position, as a last screening stage. Physical exams can serve several purposes for an employer. They can provide independent professional confirmation that the applicant is capable of meeting the physical requirements of the position. They can also provide a baseline for determining whether subsequent injuries or disabilities are job-related.

Applicants may not want to reveal the existence of physical problems or may not even know of their existence. They may be glad to get a physical exam paid for by their potential employer or they may be angry that a physical exam reveals a condition that makes them ineligible for employment. In any case, employers may legally require pre-employment physical examinations as a condition of employment. Normally pre-employment physical exams are scheduled by human resources representatives and the results of the exams are sent to the same human resources representatives. Thus, the hiring manager (assuming that the position is not in human resources) would only be aware of specific information from such an exam if it is such that it prevents the hiring of the employee. From the applicant's perspective, however, there is still a privacy issue, since someone representing the company will learn specifics of the applicant's physical condition and will use this information in employment decisions.

Ethical analysis of this privacy issue is basically the same as the analysis provided earlier regarding privacy and information, and privacy and personal thoughts. The utilitarian would approve of job-related physical tests and pre-employment physical exams if the information thus discovered is relevant to the selection process. The greater good that comes from hiring individuals who are physically capable of doing the work required outweighs the harm that may come to the individual applicant who feels that a violation of privacy has occurred. The utilitarian would also note that the applicant is not required to apply for any given job or class of jobs. If an individual feels that they will suffer serious personal unhappiness from physical tests or a pre-employment physical exam, he or she can simply refrain from applying. Further, a utilitarian would approve of the practice of limiting pre-employment physical exams to individuals who have otherwise passed all screening and are going to be offered a job if they pass the physical. This limits the number of individuals who might suffer personal unhappiness because of such a requirement, as well as the expense of providing such exams.

A rights and duties analysis would acknowledge that the applicant has a right to privacy, including physical privacy. It would also recognize that the employer has a right to assurance that applicants will be able to perform the duties of a job if they are hired. In a world where truth is not always told, confirming the applicant's ability through physical tests or a pre-employment physical exam is a reasonable step for a potential employer to take. Since information so obtained is confidential, as long as the employer treats it as such and limits its use to employment decisions, the employer's right to know that the applicant can, in fact, do the job outweighs the applicant's right to physical privacy. Such procedures are fair and just as long as they are applied uniformly. That is, all applicants who reach a certain stage in the screening process are similarly tested in order to determine their physical capacity to perform the job in question and the results of these tests are used in the same way for each applicant in determining his fitness for the job.

Drug Testing

A much harder question concerning physical privacy is that of drug testing. Since many of the issues involved here are the same whether we are discussing testing of applicants or testing of employees, we will treat this issue as applying to both kinds of situation.[11] The issue here is not whether an employee is physically capable of lifting seventy-pound packages into a truck, or carrying a heavy coil of fire hose, but whether the employee has recently used illegal drugs. Again, the assumption is that we are operating in a world where truth is not always told (particularly about illegal behavior) so that the employer does not simply rely on the statement of the applicant or employee that they do not use illegal drugs. The testing involved typically requires that the employee provide physical samples (hair, blood, urine) so that medical tests can be performed to determine the presence in the body of illegal drugs. This may or may not be more intrusive than the procedures that are part of a pre-employment physical exam, but there are two differences between drug testing and pre-employment physicals. One is that drug testing involves not just an applicant's or employee's physical ability to perform certain tasks, but her possible use of illegal substances. The other is that many people view their private practices away from work as being more a matter of privacy than their physical ability to lift packages.

From the employer's perspective, it is important that each employee perform his or her job in a satisfactory manner. An employee who is impaired by the physical or mental effects of one or more drugs is likely to fail in her job performance. The effects of that failure can range from minor (an assembly-line worker who is a bit slower than usual in performing a repetitive task) to catastrophic (a nuclear power plant operator who fails to react to a warning signal). According to the American Council for Drug Education, "substance abusers are ten times more likely to miss work, five times more likely to file a workers compensation claim, 3.6 times more likely to be involved in a work-related accident and 33 percent less productive than non-users."[12] Drug-impaired employees can pose a threat of danger to themselves, their fellow workers and to customers and other members of the public who are impacted by their actions. Obviously, an impaired data entry clerk is not as much of a danger to others as an impaired airline pilot. The employer's interest in the employee's drug use turns on two major concerns. One is the employee's ability to perform his or her job satisfactorily; the other is the danger that an impaired employee poses to himself and to others. In addition to the concern that an impaired employee not perform poorly or harm himself or others, the employer also has to be concerned with liability issues. A truck crash caused by a drug-impaired driver not only causes human suffering and property damage, it also presents major legal liability to the driver's employer.

The problems that concern employers arising from drug-impaired employees are equally serious whether the impairment results from legally prescribed medicine or from illegal drugs. For the employer, the issue is not the drug but the impairment. Different drugs have different effects on the body and these effects last for varying amounts of time. Employers are not usually pharmacists and they cannot reasonably be expected to know the timing and effects of the many drugs available to employees, legally or illegally. The effects of drugs diminish with the time that elapses since the last dose was taken. Therefore, drugs taken while at work will presumably have their maximum effect while the employee is working. Drugs taken during the time not at work may or may not have residual effects while the employee is on the job. Some drugs, such as marijuana, leave traces in the system for many days after the last usage, while other drugs, such as alcohol, are metabolized within hours and leave no trace in the system relatively soon after they are taken.

Obviously there are complexities surrounding the issue of drug impairment that make individual cases difficult to judge. At the same time, the dangers of performance by impaired employees are sufficiently serious that employers must take some steps to reasonably assure that employees do not pose a serious danger to those with whom they come in contact. One further consideration in dealing with this issue is the fact that any requirement for drug testing implies at least the possibility that the employee being tested may be drug-impaired and cannot be fully relied on to tell the truth about such impairment. In addition to issues of privacy, there are also issues of trust involved with this subject. This may be one reason why senior executives, whose decisions often have far-reaching consequences, are seldom subject to drug testing.

To further complicate the issue of drug testing and impairment, there are legal requirements in some industries mandating drug tests, both as pre-employment requirements and in the form of prescribed random testing of employees. Some of these rules appear obvious. Bus drivers and train engineers who are involved in on-the-job accidents are automatically drug tested after the accident. Other rules are less obvious and give rise to issues of privacy and trust as discussed above. Nonetheless, companies operating in industries that have such legal requirements must test their employees at least at the level required by the laws or regulations, whatever their executives may think of these rules.

Further, the Drug-Free Workplace Act of 1988 "requires some Federal contractors and all Federal grantees to agree that they will provide drug-free workplaces as a precondition of receiving a contract or grant from a Federal agency."[13] The Act does not mandate drug testing, but does require that covered organizations take the following steps:

1. Publish and give a policy statement to all covered employees;
2. Establish a drug-free awareness program;
3. Notify employees that, as a condition of employment on a Federal contract or grant, the employee must a) abide by the terms of the policy statement and b) notify the employer, within five calendar days, if he or she is convicted of a criminal drug violation in the workplace;
4. Notify the contracting or granting agency within ten days after receiving notice that a covered employee has been convicted of a criminal drug violation in the workplace;
5. Impose a penalty on—or require satisfactory participation in a drug abuse assistance or rehabilitation program by—any employee who is convicted of a reportable workplace drug conviction; and
6. Make an ongoing, good faith effort to maintain a drug-free workplace by meeting the requirement of the Act.[14]

From this preliminary discussion, we can see that there are several major issues in any ethical analysis of drug testing, whether of applicants in the context of the employment process or of employees in the ongoing employment relationship. Among the major issues are the applicant's or employee's physical privacy, the manifested lack of trust on the part of the employer, the possible revealing of criminal activity in the case of illegal drugs, the supervisor's responsibility to oversee the satisfactory work of the employees who report to him and the company's exposure to liability if a drug-impaired employee causes harm to others. Taking all of these concerns into account, we will now examine how each of the three approaches to ethics might help in analyzing the morality of employee drug testing.

A utilitarian analysis begins, as we now know, with the question of whether an action will accomplish the greatest good for the greatest number of people. Drug testing causes concern quite often for the applicant or employee being tested. This concern can vary from very mild to acute. The applicant or employee need not be guilty of using drugs in order to feel concern over the procedure, since the testing does involve invasion of physical privacy in a fairly intrusive way. However, an applicant who is concerned about testing is free to give up the position of applicant. It is harder for an employee to give up her position as employee, as we discussed in the chapter on terminations. The concern of the person to be tested may extend to family or other close acquaintances if they have indeed been using illegal drugs, since the discovery of this fact might lead to serious consequences if the family or acquaintances have previously been unaware that the individual is a drug user. The consequences in terms of employment will also probably be severe. An applicant who is found through testing to have used illegal drugs is very unlikely to be hired, even if they were otherwise the preferred candidate. An employee who tests positive almost certainly faces consequences ranging from required rehabilitation to immediate termination.

The employer who finds that an applicant or employee tests positive for illegal drugs might also suffer harm. If the drug use is limited to time away from work, and does not impair the person's ability to adequately perform their job, the employer must decide what, if any, action to take. While regular drug users are considered likely to be at least occasionally impaired at work because of their habit or addiction, the fact of testing positive does not automatically mean performance impairment at work. Once the employer knows that an applicant or employee has tested positive, it is difficult to ignore this knowledge. In the case of an applicant, the typical response by employers is to refuse or withdraw a job offer. In an individual case, this might lead to harm by causing the company to fail to hire the best qualified applicant whose drug use might not affect his work performance. When viewed as part of a pattern of decisions, the routine refusal to hire those who test positive clearly presents the better choice. It would be an unusual company that would achieve the greater good by routinely hiring applicants that it knows to be drug users!

What good do we put in the scale to weigh against the harms of testing for drugs and refusing to hire applicants or terminating employees who test positive? In our previous discussion of the issues involved, we linked drug use to impaired work performance. The harm that comes from an impaired worker, as we saw, can range from relatively mild to catastrophic. Nonetheless, there is harm. The drug may make the worker feel good, but the unsatisfactory work performed while impaired makes the supervisor, fellow workers, customers and perhaps others feel bad. Since it is not always easy to predict what harm might occur because of an impaired worker, but clearly some harm could be extremely serious (nuclear power plant operators; airline pilots), it seems reasonable to err on the side of caution in calculating harms and benefits in the matter of drug testing.

A utilitarian would caution that the harm created by drug testing should not be taken too lightly and that serious consideration be given to the benefits that are weighed against this harm. If managers are tempted to dismiss the harm from drug testing, they might stop to consider whether they are also subject to testing, and if not, why not. There is some indignity in being asked to go to a rest room and provide a urine sample. There is also implied distrust, for if the one being tested were truly trusted, he would simply be taken at his word concerning drug use. Because testing programs are usually not administered by the hiring manager (for applicants) or by operating supervisors (for employees), it is easy for managers to pass off any negative feelings on the part of those tested and blame someone else for the inconvenience or embarrassment. We must remember that drug testing is a program put in place and kept in place by management, not by employees. While an individual manager may not have any say in the design or operation of a drug-testing program, inasmuch as she is part of management, employees tend to attribute their negative feelings about such programs not to an abstraction, but to their own manager.

A rights and duties analysis of drug testing starts by asking who has rights in this situation and what duties those rights impose on others. As we have previously discussed, managers have a right to know that applicants or employees can or will do their job-related duties in a satisfactory manner. Applicants or employees have rights to privacy and duties to perform their job if selected. Each of these rights imposes duties on others, and it is the weighing of these respective rights and duties that constitutes the heart of this analysis.

To the extent that a hiring manager or a supervisor of current employees is responsible for seeing that applicants can and employees do carry out their job-related duties satisfactorily, they have a right to information that is necessary to do so. This information includes knowledge of whether and how an applicant or employee is so impaired that they will not or do not perform their duties adequately. Thus, the manager has a right to know whether the applicant will be or the employee is impaired by drugs. The manager has this right by position. When he ceases to be a manager, or ceases to have a managerial relationship with the applicant or the employee, then it will literally be none of his business whether or not the individual in question is drug-impaired. But while they are in the managerial relationship, it is his business and his responsibility. The next logical question is whether they can, with reasonable certainty, obtain the information they need by asking rather than by testing. Since asking is less intrusive than testing, and involves less violation of privacy, if asking sufficed they might well not have the right to conduct testing.

We know that applicants and employees sometimes lie, and they are more likely to lie when truth-telling involves significant harm to them. Admitting to drug usage, or to impairment because of drug usage, clearly portends significant harm to the applicant or employee. Thus it is reasonable for the manager to suspect that she may not obtain accurate information about drug usage or impairment simply by asking. We might logically ask, at this point, whether all managers have a right to test all applicants and employees, and if so with what frequency, given the preceding analysis. In fact, even the most rigorous programs do not test every employee every day. Testing of applicants, even for positions that are not safety-related, has become somewhat common.[15] Testing of employees on a random basis is legally mandated for safety-related jobs and is up to the discretion of management otherwise.

In addition to issues of privacy, there are also cost concerns in deciding who should be tested and how often. If the objective of a drug-free workplace is granted as valid, then management has the right (and perhaps the duty) to take reasonable steps to assure that this objective is met. This objective, which includes freedom from impairment due to legal drugs, clearly needs no defense when safety-related positions are involved. When they are not involved, the objective of a drug-free workplace is still defensible. By definition, a workplace is intended for work. Whatever the nature of the work (with the possible exception of some kinds of creative activity), managers have a reasonable expectation that their workers will not be impaired by the use of drugs, and workers whose performance depends partially on the inputs or cooperation of others have a similar reasonable expectation.

Whether and when testing of employees to assure a drug-free workplace is a reasonable step is the question at hand. It is or should be clear to employees in safety-related positions that performance impairment due to drugs is a legitimate concern of management and that managers have a duty to take steps to deal with this issue. The reasonableness of this argument, together with the legal requirements for random testing of such employees and automatic testing after accidents make employee opposition to such testing less likely. In cases where safety-related positions are not involved, employees may resent the intrusion of privacy involved in providing physical specimens, as well as the implied lack of trust in requiring that they do so. The employer has a right to maintain a drug-free workplace and the employees have a right to physical privacy. There does not appear to be a clear and easy answer as to which right trumps the other. Legally, employers may test, but morally, according to a rights and duties analysis, the answer is not clear.

This may seem to be an unsatisfactory answer. The point of ethical analysis is to help managers to make the morally right decision in real-life work situations. The fact of the matter is that, in some situations, the morally right action is clear. This is the case with drug testing and safety-related positions. The duty of management to assure that workers in safety-related positions are not drug-impaired trumps the right of workers to physical privacy, at least to the extent that management can require random drug testing of these workers and automatic testing when accidents occur. For positions that are not safety-related, it is not clear from a rights and duties analysis that management either does or does not have the moral right to require drug testing of employees.

A fairness and justice analysis of this issue focuses on whether similarly situated employees are treated in a similar way regarding both process and outcome. In terms of testing applicants, a company could test all applicants, or all applicants for certain positions, or all applicants who pass an initial screening procedure and become finalists for a position. Any of these rules would meet a fairness test. Analysis of the question of testing current employees would proceed along similar lines. If random testing is used for all employees, or for all employees who hold certain positions, then fairness requires that the selection for testing be truly random. In the case of automatic testing after an employee is involved in an accident, as long as this procedure is followed every time an employee is so involved, the procedure meets a fairness test.

Another issue relating to fairness and justice is the question of action taken as a result of a positive test. The most common form of testing now in use in the United States involves testing for five drugs, all of which are illegal. Some companies automatically terminate an employee who tests positive for use of any of these drugs. Some companies offer an employee the choice between participation in a drug rehabilitation program and termination of employment. Some companies offer this option to a first-time offender, but automatically terminate an employee who tests positive a second time.

Most companies have a standard procedure for acquiring physical samples from employees (blood, hair, urine) and for processing these samples. The procedure often involves dividing the sample in two, testing one of the two, and if the results are positive for drug use, subsequently testing the second sample, using a more rigorous (and more expensive) testing method. Positive results are typically reported by the laboratory analyzing the sample to the employer. At this point, a member of the human resources department (or company medical staff if the company has such) will typically ask the employee if there is any medical reason why the test results would be positive. In other words, standard procedures have been developed, particularly for positive test results, that provide as much protection as is reasonably possible against mistaken test results.

These procedures serve several purposes. They are intended to assure that any employee who tests positive for drug use will be afforded procedural protection against mistakes. This accords with attempts to be fair and just in testing and in subsequent decisions based on test results. The procedures described provide a basis for protecting the company's interests if a terminated employee subsequently sues the company. In the case of post-accident testing, the procedures also provide a basis for deciding how to handle legal claims for liability against the company as a result of the accident. Is it fair and just that an applicant who tests positive for illegal drug use is dismissed from further consideration, but an employee who tests positive is offered the option of entering treatment and keeping his job, subject to certain restrictions? Yes, because an applicant is not in the same situation as an employee. The definition of an ethical act under fairness and justice is the similar treatment of individuals who are similarly situated. Thus fairness does not mean treating everyone in the same way. Fair treatment does not have to be equal treatment if the individuals involved are not similarly situated.

Employee Monitoring

We have now completed our discussion of privacy concerns for applicants and of the issue of drug testing for employees as well. We turn now to the issue of privacy in the area of employee monitoring. Applicants are really not subject to monitoring, so this discussion does not apply to them. Employees have supervisors (even senior executives are supervised in some sense by more senior executives). Supervisors have, among other job responsibilities, the obligation to oversee the work of those who report directly to them. As we saw at the beginning of this chapter, this oversight can take the form of literally watching the employees at work, but it often takes other, less direct forms.

In general, monitoring tends to be more intense for less skilled workers doing jobs that are more routine and less intense as the skill level of the workers rises and discretion in carrying out the work process increases. Thus, fast food workers whose job may be as limited as spreading mayonnaise on buns or cleaning tables have low skill levels and little discretion involved in their work. The executive chef in a fine restaurant or the chief financial officer of an insurance company have jobs that require high levels of skill and considerable discretion is not only allowed but expected in the way they perform their jobs.

Does an employee actually have a reasonable expectation of privacy at work, such that monitoring might be offensive, or is this the kind of question that only a philosopher could love?[16] Assuming that the reader is employed, simply ask yourself this. If your boss pulled up a chair next to yours, or came and stood next to you, and said, "Don't mind me, I'm just going to stay here all day and watch you work," would you be troubled? There clearly is some reasonable expectation of privacy, in the sense that workers at any level do not expect to have one-on-one, full-time monitoring of their work by their manager. On the other hand, if you had no contact whatever with your immediate boss for a period of three months, you might reasonably conclude that something was wrong.

Monitoring can be broken down into two broad categories: monitoring of the work process and monitoring of results. Normally, monitoring of the work process is more intrusive than monitoring of results, although technology has made possible automated monitoring of some work processes. Some types of work, such as manufacturing and data entry, lend themselves to process monitoring. Supervisors are normally located in the same physical space where the work occurs, and customers are not normally involved in the work process. Quantity of work done is best monitored in such jobs by monitoring results. This can take the simple form of counting output, whether the output consists of components assembled at a workbench or medical records transcribed during a shift. When performance issues arise concerning work quantity, there is usually not much room for dispute, since this type of monitoring is objective. Monitoring of quality for such work involves different issues.

In manufacturing work, there are two quite different approaches that companies take to the monitoring of quality. The differences can be clearly seen in automobile assembly. For many years, Japanese auto companies have treated quality as the concern of every worker and have monitored the manufacturing process for quality problems. American auto companies, for the most part, have monitored quality at the end of the assembly process by having inspectors examine finished automobiles for defects. In this view, quality is the business of engineers who design the manufacturing process and inspectors who examine finished products, but it is not a major concern of assembly workers.

Clearly, these differences in approach lead to differences in the responsibility of manufacturing supervisors. If quality is not a major concern of the assembly workers whom they supervise, then quality monitoring is not a significant part of the supervisor's job. This means that monitoring will be limited to whether workers are physically present and to quantity of work produced. In tasks such as data entry, computer programs typically provide quality checks, with edits and audits to assure that the information being processed is valid. Computer programming and similar tasks also have a certain amount of built-in quality monitoring and, in some cases, quality really cannot be ascertained until a program is finished and tested.

Service jobs are different in several respects from manufacturing jobs. Because service jobs frequently involve interaction with customers as part of the work process, there is more variation in the process than with manufacturing jobs. Further, it is much harder to define just what constitutes a quality performance without reference to the final result. Selling, teaching and healing all involve more individual discretion on the part of the worker than do manufacturing jobs. Often the supervisor is not in the same physical place as the worker in service industries and, even if a sales supervisor is present in the same store as the salesperson, it is difficult to directly monitor the interaction between salesperson and customer. Monitoring of results rather than of process is more the norm for service jobs than it is for manufacturing jobs.

Continuous one-on-one monitoring of an employee's work is both intrusive and expensive. A total lack of any form of monitoring means that the manager is not doing at least one part of her job. Where, then, is the middle ground, and what ethical issues arise in this area? A utilitarian analysis focuses on results. If enough monitoring is performed so that the supervisor is reasonably sure that the work of his people is being performed in a satisfactory manner, the good that follows is a well-run operation, with benefits for workers in the form of continued employment, for customers, investors and others with a stake in the good performance of the company. Insufficient monitoring can easily lead to unsatisfactory work performance, with the opposite results. This situation, in total, creates more harm than good and does not meet the utilitarian standard.

Supervisors, by their position, have a right and also a duty to monitor the work of their employees. Because the managers, owners of the company and others have a right to good performance, supervisors also have a duty to take those actions required, including monitoring, to reasonably assure such good performance. Workers have a duty to perform their jobs in a satisfactory manner. As we saw above, workers do not forfeit all rights to privacy, in thought or in action, when they accept a job. Therefore, they have a right to be treated as adults, and as humans rather than machines. These rights impose some duty on supervisors to limit their monitoring activities to what is reasonably necessary to assure adequate performance. A supervisor who insists on monitoring every movement of a worker violates that worker's right, just as much as a worker who resists any monitoring at all violates the supervisor's right to do his job.

Fairness and justice call our attention to similar treatment of similarly situated individuals. Trainees who are brand new to a job are not similarly situated with thoroughly experienced workers, and the monitoring of trainees would normally be more intense than that for experienced workers.

Workers would normally be monitored more closely by their foreman than the foreman would be by the shift manager. Workers who have not performed satisfactorily would normally be subject to closer monitoring than others in the same position who have performed up to expectations. Thus, fairness and justice allow for, and in fact require, a nuanced approach to monitoring.

The preceding analysis applies both to monitoring the work process and to monitoring results. Monitoring of the work process can sometimes be unobtrusive but is often known to the worker as it happens. Monitoring of results is less obtrusive and is often not known to the worker until feedback is provided by the supervisor. Since performance appraisal, salary increases and promotion opportunities often depend on monitoring of results, this type of monitoring is often a matter of concern to employees. The same ethical analysis applies to results monitoring. One further element that enters in is that the supervisor has additional responsibilities when salary increases or promotions, as a result of good performance, or discipline and termination, as a result of bad performance, are at stake. From this perspective, the purpose of monitoring is not only to assure the generally satisfactory operation of the work unit, but to determine who will benefit and who will suffer as a result of performance differentials. The ethical analyses that are provided in the chapters on performance appraisal and compensation and on termination are also relevant here.

Email and Internet Monitoring

One final issue that comes under the general topic of monitoring and employee privacy is the monitoring of email and internet usage. Many workers in many industries now have computers as work tools, and access to email systems and the internet are commonplace. In some ways, these technologies are similar to telephone systems, and in some ways they are different. As with workplace telephones, workplace computers and their connections to email systems and to the internet are typically the property of the employer rather than the employee. Since the company owns the equipment, it seems reasonable that the company may set standards for its use. A company that prohibits personal use of the telephone at work or of company-provided cell phones can logically extend this policy to a prohibition of personal use of company computers, whether for sending and receiving email or for personal use of the internet. A company that has such a policy could logically expect to conduct monitoring to assure that its policy is being followed. This is where things get interesting.

We will first consider whether and when it is ethical for a company to prohibit personal use of company computer systems, and then what ethical problems arise in monitoring to assure that such a policy is being followed. In the early days of personal computers, when equipment was more expensive and less common, companies sometimes defended their prohibitions of personal use of company computers on the basis of allocating scarce resources. What computing power was available was needed to conduct company business, and the expense of providing this power, as well as its relative scarcity, served as a reason for limiting its use to company business. As computers and network access have become more common in the workplace, and the cost of providing them has dropped, prohibition of personal use because of resource scarcity has become a less convincing argument.

A moment's thought will show that total prohibition of personal use of company computers is not a reasonable policy. If an employee who is unexpectedly asked to work overtime were to use the company phone to call his childcare provider, a manager would hardly be able to object to this personal use of company equipment. If, instead, the employee were to use the company computer to send an email message to the same childcare provider under the same circumstances, it would be equally difficult to object to this violation of the personal use policy. At the extreme, then, a total prohibition of personal use of company telephones or computers does not seem defensible.

Suppose that a worker spent four hours of each work day using the company phone system to gossip with friends and to conduct personal business. The worker's manager would have a reasonable concern and a cause to intervene and change the worker's behavior. The same would hold true if the worker were using the company's computer to send email messages to friends and to conduct personal stock trades for four hours a day. Indeed, if the worker used his own laptop computer, during work time, for the same length of time and the same purposes, the manager would have an equally reasonable cause for concern. The real issue is not so much which equipment is being used, or even who owns the equipment, but the fact that the worker is not giving a day's work for a day's pay. If the worker were a manager, the same concerns would apply.

Other types of harm can occur through employee misuse of company computer systems, whether advertent or inadvertent. Companies that are in a "quiet period" before stock issuance are not allowed to communicate certain kinds of information. An employee sending an email could easily violate this prohibition, causing a company violation of Securities and Exchange Commission rules. An email message from an employee concerning pricing plans could violate anti-trust laws. A message concerning union organizing activities, sent to other employees within the company, could violate laws regarding permissible and impermissible tactics during an organizing campaign. An employee forwarding an email that is in bad taste or is sexually explicit could contribute to issues of hostile environment. All of these and more create potentially serious issues for a company.[17]

Once we have established the fact that a manager has a legitimate concern about the extent of her workers' personal use of company computers, it logically follows that the manager may, and indeed should, conduct some degree of monitoring to satisfy this legitimate concern. The issue then becomes how to identify personal versus company use of email and internet access. One way is to ask the worker but, as we saw earlier in this chapter, while truth-telling is normally expected between employee and manager, it cannot always be assumed. Therefore, the prudent manager will verify by some means that abuses are not occurring.

What makes this issue particularly interesting is that software is available that can allow managers to review any or all email addresses contacted, and the content of all email messages, both sent and received. It is also rather easy for managers or systems administrators to review what internet sites have been visited from a specific terminal. The review can list all sites or can identify sites with certain names or characteristics.[18] There is a further complicating issue in that, in the United States, it is illegal to create a hostile work environment. For gender-related cases, a hostile work environment can be created if management allows the display of sexually explicit images where workers or the public can see them. A worker, looking at a pornographic web site even briefly, could trigger a hostile environment charge if his computer monitor can be observed by others and if someone is offended by images on the screen. Although a single instance would not normally result in legal damages, management has an obligation to prevent such occurrences.

Many employees consider the content of their email messages to be private. In terms of accessibility, email is in fact more like a postcard than a sealed letter. Perhaps it should not be, but in fact a postcard can be read by a postal delivery person or a sorter in the post office. A sealed letter cannot be read unless someone opens the envelope and removes the letter, an act which is illegal. Further, an email message is retained on the computer system, accessible to a systems administrator, even if the sender or recipient has deleted it.[19] A letter (or even a postcard) can be physically destroyed by its recipient. The fact that a manager, alone or with the help of a systems administrator, can read the addresses and content of employee email does not necessarily mean that she should, or that it would be ethical to do so. Like the telephone, email can be used for activities as innocent as wishing someone a happy birthday or as sinister as sending trade secrets to a competitor.

Internet access provided through company computers opens a very wide door, through which one can reach many destinations. For some workers, such as a purchasing agent using business-to-business software, internet access is an essential tool of their job. For others, it is occasionally useful, but not as essential. For many workers, some internet sites provide information that might satisfy their professional or personal curiosity, but that has no real relevance to their present job. Internet access can also provide employees with the means to do personal shopping from their desk, to check up on the latest news or sports scores and stories, or to view pornographic images. At the extreme, internet access can provide employees with the ability to read or download bomb-making instructions at their desks.

The varied content available through the door that is internet access raises several distinct issues for managers. One issue, discussed above, is that of extended internet use for any personal purpose during working hours. The issue here is not so much what the employee is doing (personal internet use) as what the employee is not doing (the work for which they are being paid). A second issue involves internet use for personal activities that may be legitimate on an individual level, but that management does not want to have occurring in the workplace. This could include such activities as viewing pornographic images or online gambling. A third issue involves activities that are personal but should not be occurring under any circumstances, due to their violation of legal or ethical principles. The example of downloading bomb-making instructions fits here.

In terms of privacy expectations, the internet is perhaps most like the telephone. A manager might overhear a telephone conversation at an employee's desk. However, except for certain limited situations (stock brokers, 911 operators) where calls are routinely recorded, there is an expectation of privacy when one is speaking on the telephone. There are legal requirements that must be met before telephone messages can be recorded without the party's knowledge. Even records of numbers called are normally private. Internet sites visited are recorded within a company's system, but workers do not generally expect these records to be made publicly available. However, many workers know that there are such records and that they can be accessed under limited conditions. A key element in any monitoring program is that employees be notified of its existence.

In our ethical analysis of a manager's possible actions in the areas of email and internet monitoring, we will address three questions. The first is this: is it ever ethical for a manager to monitor an employee's use of email or the internet at work? The second, at the opposite end of the spectrum and assuming an affirmative answer to the first, is this: are there any ethical limits on managerial monitoring of email or the internet at work? The third question, which assumes affirmative answers to the first two, is this: how can we go about defining or describing these limits?

Can it ever be ethical for a manager to monitor an employee's use of email or the internet at work? A utilitarian would surely answer this in the affirmative, using much the same argument we presented above. The company has provided workers with computers for their use and the computers are typically connected both with an email program and with the internet. We can assume that these computers have been provided so that the workers can use them in performing their jobs and not merely for the workers' entertainment. As we have argued previously, the greatest good is accomplished by having the company's various operations performed well rather than poorly. This requires that workers spend at least most of their work time performing their assigned tasks, rather than pursuing personal business or interests. If there were no monitoring at all, some workers would most probably abuse their freedom to use their computers for personal business or interests, and managers would have no way of knowing who was doing this or how often. The most serious offenders would probably produce little enough work that managers could tell something was amiss. Managers could also spend their time leaning over workers and observing their computer screens. The first of these solutions may be effective only for very serious offenders, and the second is both impractical and intrusive, yet it would still constitute monitoring.

As we saw earlier in this chapter, privacy issues at work require a balancing of employee concerns with management needs. In the case of monitoring computer use, the greatest good for the greatest number will occur if some monitoring is allowed. With regards to the second question, whether there are any ethical limits on managerial monitoring of computer use, a utilitarian would again answer in the affirmative. It would be theoretically possible, although impractically expensive and offensive, for management to monitor both the address and content of every email sent or received, and to identify and examine every internet site visited by every employee. The costs of such an extensive monitoring regime, in terms of both money and morale, would be such that they would cause more harm than good. Thus, unlimited monitoring would not create the greatest good for the greatest number. We will discuss what the ethical limits might be and how we might arrive at them after examining the first two questions from the perspectives of rights and duties, and fairness and justice.

Under a rights and duties analysis, can any management monitoring of email and internet usage be morally justified? Managers, by their position, have a right and a duty to oversee their workers in such a way that the various tasks that make up the business are completed in a satisfactory way. Workers, by their position, have a duty to give a day's work for a day's pay and to perform their work in a satisfactory manner. However, workers are employed, not owned, by managers. Therefore, they retain some rights to privacy and individuality, even at work. If managers had no right whatsoever to monitor how workers spend their time during work hours, they could not carry out their duty to oversee the satisfactory functioning of the business. The right of the workers to privacy and individuality does not extend to the point that managers must remain in the dark as to what their workers are doing during work hours. The duty of managers to run the business, then, permits them to conduct at least some monitoring of the activities of employees during the work day. There is nothing intrinsic about monitoring computer usage that makes it so private that managers' right to monitor is completely trumped in this area by workers' right to privacy.

Since monitoring of email and internet usage at work is not totally precluded by a rights and duties analysis, we turn now to the second question of whether such an analysis sets any limits at all on the monitoring activities of managers. As we saw above, workers do not give up all rights to privacy or individuality at work—they are employed, not owned. Just as a utilitarian analysis does not justify complete monitoring of every email message and every internet site visited, so also the rights of workers to be treated reasonably limit the rights of managers to conduct monitoring of computer usage. The ultimate in monitoring would be for a supervisor to sit with each worker all day every day and observe or monitor everything that the worker did. Such an extreme of monitoring activity would display total lack of trust in the worker. It would also probably drive the supervisor to distraction, since there are few less appealing activities than watching someone else work all day. Although this extreme of monitoring is not practical, it would also not be ethical, according to the rights and duties perspective. The rights of employees to some reasonable degree of privacy and individuality in the workplace would be violated. Hence supervisors have a duty not to conduct unlimited monitoring.

Is it fair and just for managers to monitor the work of their employees and, if so, are there any limits to such monitoring? As long as similarly situated individuals are treated in a similar manner, regarding both process and outcome, there should be no problem from this perspective. In regards to monitoring the work process, for some kinds of workers, such as field sales representatives or those involved in research and development, there might be no monitoring of the work process at all for extended periods of time. Other workers, such as those on assembly lines, might be subject to daily monitoring. Although all are workers, all are not similarly situated. The nature of the work dictates, to some extent, the type and extent of monitoring. The higher one goes in management, the less monitoring of the work process occurs, as a general rule. Again, managers at different levels are situated differently, so the levels of monitoring can differ and fairness and justice can still prevail.

The analysis for monitoring of results is similar. Different types of work and different levels of management call for different types and levels of results monitoring. Total items processed or total dollars of sales are easily monitored. Because companies want and need such information on a regular basis, this kind of results monitoring may be performed as frequently as daily. Attempts by a board of directors to monitor the results of a CEO's work on a daily basis would make no sense. It sometimes happens that the work of an employee whose performance has not been satisfactory is monitored more closely or more often than that of other workers doing the same job. Is this fair? In the chapter on performance appraisal and compensation, we discussed progressive discipline as an ethical way of dealing with employees whose performance is unsatisfactory. Progressive discipline typically involves monitoring of performance that is beyond the routine for employees performing a given task. The fact that the employee whose performance is unsatisfactory is treated differently from his fellow workers does not mean that fairness and justice have been violated. The employee in question is not similarly situated because his performance is not satisfactory. Other employees performing at similarly low levels would also be subject to closer monitoring, if progressive discipline is followed as a standard practice.

It sometimes happens that employees who are specially favored because of personal relations with their supervisor or for other reasons are not monitored as closely as their fellow workers or, if they are so monitored, evidence of unsatisfactory performance is not acted on as it would be for most workers. This situation does not meet the criteria for fairness and justice, and by these standards should be judged to be unethical. Not only is this unethical, it is also poor management practice because employees are quick to sense unfair treatment of management favorites, and this practice builds resentment of management very rapidly. As we indicated in the chapters on employment and on performance appraisal and compensation, both the fact and the perception of fairness are very important for managers to succeed.

Are there any limits to the monitoring of employees from the fairness and justice perspective? It might seem that, if a company or a manager decided to take monitoring to an extreme, they could conduct constant one-on-one monitoring even if it were extremely intrusive and burdensome, as long as they did so for (or perhaps to) all similarly situated employees. However, there is one other element to the definition of fairness and justice as a moral perspective, and that is proportionality. In the legal system, this is sometimes stated as a maxim: the punishment should fit the crime. Monitoring that was extremely intrusive and burdensome would not be fair or just unless there was some clear and compelling reason for doing it. When there is good reason to suspect an individual of a particularly serious crime, police agencies will sometimes put that individual under constant direct surveillance, watching his every move. It is hard to think of a circumstance where such an extreme of monitoring in a business setting would be justified. Fairness and justice, then, argues against too much monitoring.

We have now established that all three basic approaches to ethics provide bases for approving of at least minimal monitoring of employees by managers and that all three agree that an extreme degree of monitoring would not be ethical. Where, then, is the middle ground? As with many things that are measured on a continuum, it is easy to see the issues at either end and, as we move toward the middle, the issues become more difficult. What we have established is that monitoring, to be ethical, must involve some work-related need and be balanced with concerns for individual privacy. Managers tend to be more aware of work-related needs than their employees. It is helpful when considering this issue for managers to remember that they are also employees and they are subject to some degree of monitoring by their bosses.[20]

As we have seen throughout our discussion, the more intrusive a monitoring procedure seems to those who are subject to it, the more justification is needed for the monitoring to be ethical. This kind of balancing test is often applied in law; it also makes sense in ethical analysis. If there were simple, all-inclusive rules or checklists that could be easily applied and that yielded clear answers in given situations, this topic would not be of major concern. It is because there are no easy answers (except at the extremes, which are seldom encountered in the real world of work) that analysis is needed, and that balance between management needs and employee privacy must be sought in individual cases.

Since the goal of managers is a workplace that works, in the sense that the goals of the business are accomplished through the efforts of employees, this goal is a good one for beginning an ethical analysis of workplace monitoring. Since the employees, including managers, who do the work are humans and not machines it is also important to be aware of their rights and their desire to be treated fairly. Using these two starting points, individual situations can be evaluated in terms of whether managerial monitoring of employees, either in type or in degree, can be morally justified.

eleven
Accounting and Financial Reporting

No area of business practice has resulted in as much negative publicity over the years as that of accounting and financial reporting. Even the subprime mortgage lending crisis involved a large element of accounting and financial reporting.[1] Judging from press coverage of recent scandals and political reaction to these scandals, it appears that no area of business practice is less understood.[2] Yet, without the advanced knowledge of a CPA or a chief financial officer, some true things can be usefully said about the areas of accounting and financial reporting. In this chapter, we will explore some of the basic functions involved and some of the rules of the game, and perform an ethical analysis of some of the key issues.

The accounting function within a business is intended to present a picture, in numbers, of the state of the business at a single point in time (summarized typically in the balance sheet) or a summary of activity over a period of time (summarized typically in the statement of earnings and the cash flow statement).[3] A good deal of detailed activity underlies these summary statements. In a large organization, separate units carry out various phases of the accounting function: accounts payable, accounts receivable, cost accounting, budgeting, payroll accounting and others. It is important, though, to bear in mind the overall purpose of the accounting function from the point of view of the total organization, since each of the specialized units contributes to the final product.

The Importance of Financial Reporting

Financial reporting is the face of accounting that many managers and most outsiders see. In the United States, quarterly results are very closely watched by executives, financial analysts and others. Annual results are perhaps subject to less scrutiny and in many ways are simply viewed as an adjunct to fourth-quarter results. Many companies prepare, but do not publicly release, results on a monthly basis or even more frequently. As has been widely reported in recent years, the performance and future prospects of a company are measured not only by quarterly results, but by the relation of these results to the expectations of financial analysts. Certainly growth in revenues and in profits are important, but there have been numerous instances of companies that reported both growth in revenues and in profits compared to the same quarter of the previous year, yet failed to meet analysts' expectations for earnings per share and had their stock price decrease dramatically as a result.

Financial reporting, then, not only provides management and others with a summary of the company's performance over a period of time or a statement of its financial condition at a point in time. It also plays a role in determining whether investors will bid the stock price up or down and whether the top managers will be judged to have succeeded or failed in their management of the company.[4] Since stock ownership, through options or through direct ownership, has become a major factor, if not the key component, in the personal wealth of many top managers, the stock price has also become a more and more important criterion for judging personal success as well as corporate performance. In the government sector, accounting has the same basic purpose that it does in the private sector, but many of the rules and procedures are different. Further, the impact of financial reports on the top manager's personal financial position is much less direct than in the corporate sector.

In this chapter, we will view accounting and financial reporting from two perspectives. The first is that of financial reporting, as embodied mostly in the three key financial statements: the balance sheet, the income statement and the cash flow statement. The second is the broader perspective of the accounting process, which involves the work of many individuals throughout an organization. This second perspective in many ways feeds the financial reporting function. The summary numbers presented on the three major statements are constructed from accounting for detailed transactions in many areas of the company. For instance, WalMart's revenue for fiscal 2010 was $422 billion. This appears as a single line on the income statement. However, to arrive at that number the company must record and summarize all the sales at all the checkout stands in all the stores that WalMart operates, in addition to the charges made for online purchases. Further, it must adjust the total amount of sales to reflect returns to the stores and credited amounts for these returns. The number of individual transactions that comprise the total revenue number is staggering.[5] Yet, each of them is a part of the accounting and financial reporting process.

According to the Sarbanes–Oxley Act, which became law in 2002, the chief executive officer and the chief financial officer of publicly traded companies must sign their company's financial statements, attesting to their accuracy. At least these two officers, and perhaps other senior executives, have legal responsibility for the accuracy of their company's financial reports. In this chapter, we will explore the moral responsibility of these two officers, and of others, for a company's accurate financial reporting. The Sarbanes–Oxley Act also placed additional emphasis on the responsibility of boards of directors, and particularly on their audit committees, to assure that company financial reporting is accurate. Publicly traded firms in the United States are legally required to have an outside firm audit their annual financial statements and issue a formal statement attesting that they have done so and describing the results of the audit.

It would appear, then, that we now have no shortage of individuals who are responsible for accurate financial reporting, at least in a legal sense. If we can establish that at least some individuals have moral responsibility as well for accurate financial reporting on a broad basis, we can use this fact to consider the moral involvement of the many people throughout an organization whose recording and summarizing of transactions contribute to the final reports. In order to identify ethical issues in this area, we will start with a consideration of the purposes of company financial reports.[6]

The three major financial statements issued by companies (balance sheet, income statement and cash flow statement) are used by a variety of different audiences. Top management of a company, including its board of directors, uses them to measure company performance relative to goals and to competitors. If a company is judged to have performed well, rewards are bestowed on executives and perhaps on other employees. If a company has earned profits, executives determine how to use these profits—whether to distribute them to stockholders as dividends, to invest them in internal growth or growth by acquisition, to retain them as a cushion against harder times ahead or to put them to some other use. If a company has done poorly, executives may face stable or decreasing compensation or even the loss of their jobs. They must determine how to improve performance and perhaps how to raise the funds necessary to do so.

These decisions can have far-reaching consequences. If poor performance results in layoffs and other forms of cost-cutting, some or all of the company's employees will suffer negative consequences. Following a year (or even a quarter) of poor performance, all employees are likely to feel increased pressure for harder work and better results. Following a period of good performance, opportunities for new projects, new spending and the promotions that often come with growth will be present. Thus, although top executives and directors most closely scrutinize financial results, their impact often reaches to all employees.

Financial reporting is also used by investors. Both individual and institutional investors determine whether to buy, hold or sell a company's stock based at least in part on the company's reported financial results. During the period in 2001 and 2002 when WorldCom was fraudulently listing hundreds of millions of dollars of current expenses as capital expenditures each quarter, their CEO was intent on keeping the stock price up. He owned hundreds of millions of dollars in stock and had borrowed almost $400 million from the company.[7]

Financial reporting is not the only reason for the actions of investors. During the technology bubble of the late 1990s, some stocks were purchased at prices that could not be justified by any financial theory, except possibly the "greater fool" theory. This theory states that it does not matter what a company's assets, earnings or cash flow have been or will be when choosing to buy a stock: it only matters that a greater fool will subsequently buy the stock from me at a price higher than I paid for it. However, a company's financial reports do constitute one of the bases on which investors make their decisions.

Another group that makes use of financial reporting consists of banks and other lenders. Just as individual borrowers must show evidence of their ability to repay when seeking loans, companies must also give indication of the ability to repay, whether borrowing from banks or issuing bonds. This is a very complicated subject, but in essence, the more heavily a company is already in debt, and the weaker its cash flow, the more difficult it is for that company to obtain funds from lenders. Companies that reorganize through the bankruptcy process typically repay less than half of their debt, which means that lenders that intended to provide the company with loans actually provided gifts. This is a situation that lenders, of course, strive to avoid.

In addition to lenders, other companies who have financial contracts with a company have a significant interest in its financial condition. Derivative contracts, particularly credit default swaps,[8] between AIG and many other financial institutions had reached such a volume by late 2008 that the federal government provided over $150 billion to AIG rather than see it go bankrupt and endanger the solvency of many other financial institutions. The volume and complexity of financial derivatives, as well as the lack of clear financial reporting for these derivatives, played a major role in the financial crisis of 2008 and the accompanying Great Recession.[9]

Governments are also concerned users of a company's financial reporting. Corporate income taxes, sales taxes, excise taxes and others all form a significant part of the revenue flow that allows governments to provide services and pay for them. The amount of revenue that a corporation reports, the amount of tax deductions that it takes and the amount of taxable income that results are of very considerable interest to governments. Not surprisingly, corporations wish to minimize the taxes that they pay, while governments wish to maximize their tax revenues from corporations. In addition to tax agencies, government regulatory agencies rely on corporate financial reports.

In total, a considerable number of individuals and groups use corporate financial reports and rely in various ways on their timeliness and honesty. Timeliness means not only the date on which quarterly or annual reports are issued, but also refers to the fact that reports are supposed to provide up-to-date information about the company. In this sense, there is an issue of timeliness (it could be subsumed under the broader category of accuracy) when a company recognizes all the revenue from an extended contract in the first period when in fact it will be received over several quarters or even years. Similarly, there is an issue of timeliness when a company delays write-downs for unrecoverable expenses or fails to set aside reasonable reserves for litigation or other contingent costs.

It is impossible to have a rule or a law for every possible accounting event. Generally Accepted Accounting Principles (GAAP) are an accepted body of guidelines for dealing with accounting events. They quite properly allow managers discretion in deciding how and when to report some accounting events that do not match up with clear rules. The accepted guidelines for many other countries are known as the International Financial Reporting Standards (IFRS). While GAAP constitutes a rules-based approach to accounting, IFRS is, on the whole, a principles-based approach. Studies have been under way for a number of years in the United States concerning the possibility of adopting IFRS as the accepted standard for financial reporting. Since this system is principles based, one of its perceived advantages is that it would limit the ways that some companies use the rules embodied in GAAP to distort rather than clarify financial reporting.[10]

The United States Internal Revenue Code (IRC) is an immensely complex set of laws, regulations and interpretations governing federal taxation. Despite frequent cries for its simplification, the IRC grows more complex each year, as more laws are passed and more regulations are issued. Disputes over tax issues involving millions of dollars for individual corporations are not unusual. If the government prevails, taxes are increased and profits are diminished. If the company prevails, the reverse occurs. The impact on financial reporting and the determination of corporate profits is often significant.

While there can be legitimate disputes about how to treat an accounting item under GAAP or under the IRC, some determination must be made. Management, with the advice of internal specialists, external auditors and financial consultants, must make these determinations and issue a quarterly or annual statement that includes the impact of their decisions. In such cases, management typically means the chief financial officer and the chief executive officer. These titles are held by individuals who also have many other responsibilities by reason of their corporate positions. Nonetheless, they do make decisions, financial reports are issued reasonably soon after the end of the quarter or fiscal year and all of the parties enumerated above do rely on these financial statements. Since the senior officers who attest to the accuracy of the financial reports cannot possibly be familiar with every transaction in even a medium-sized corporation, they must rely on the accounting systems and people who operate them.

One of the issues that we will analyze from an ethics standpoint is the creation and maintenance of accounting systems. Some individual transactions do come under the direct command or scrutiny of senior executives. The creation of special purpose entities at Enron, the misclassification of expenses at WorldCom and the very large personal loans at Adelphia are examples of transactions that were almost certainly known in some detail by the most senior officers of the respective companies. We will analyze the moral responsibility of senior management regarding such transactions and also examine the situation of other managers who are encouraged or required to execute such transactions. Since employees in many departments execute transactions that ultimately aggregate to the major financial statements, we will also examine the moral concerns of managers and supervisors who oversee the many employees engaged in such transactions.

Senior Managers and Financial Reporting

Senior managers are responsible both for establishing and maintaining accounting systems and for personally initiating or approving major financial transactions. These are issues that most managers either do not deal with at all or only deal with on orders from senior management. The ethical issues here are relatively clear-cut. As we saw at the beginning of this chapter, there are many individuals and groups who use financial reports in order to make significant decisions. Obviously there is a social or interpersonal aspect not only to the financial reports but also to the processes leading to the information embodied in these reports. The basic issue involved is truth-telling. This is, then, a subject with moral implications.

A utilitarian analysis indicates that accurate financial reporting creates the greatest good for the greatest number of people. If a company's basic financial statements are consistently accurate, they can be relied on for decisions by the many groups that we described above (senior management, investors, lenders, government, etc.). If they are not consistently accurate, then all of these groups will be forced to make decisions based on bad information. It is reasonable to conclude that decisions based on consistently accurate information and financial reports will be better decisions, all else equal, than decisions based on inconsistent or inaccurate information. It is in the best interests (meaning the greatest good for the greatest number) of a number of individuals and groups if financial reporting is consistently accurate.

It appears from descriptions of financial wrong-doing at various companies that individual executives or management teams saw the greatest good for the greatest number in avoiding bankruptcy. Once false financial reporting had become entrenched, it became necessary in their eyes to continue to report lies in order to avoid the harm that would come to them and others from accurate reporting. A moment's reflection shows the flaws in this thinking. The likelihood of false reporting being detected increases over time. The severity of judgment both by government officials and by employees, customers, investors and lenders becomes worse as the extent of the false reporting grows. The possibility of setting things right financially and continuing the company as a growing concern diminishes as the true financial problems worsen. One of the longest-running false reporting schemes ever was conducted by Bernie Madoff. It ended not with greater good for anyone, but with huge financial losses to many individuals and with Madoff serving what amounts to a life term in prison.

Since top management has ultimate responsibility for the accounting systems that gather and summarize financial information and for major individual decisions about financial reporting, it follows that top management has a moral obligation according to this analysis to provide consistently accurate reporting. The chief executive and chief financial officer have a legal obligation under Sarbanes–Oxley, but they also have a moral obligation under utilitarianism. This moral obligation extends to other top officers as well. If accurate sales numbers are required to meet the sort of standards we are discussing, it is hard to see how the chief sales or marketing officer could remain totally disconnected from the sales reporting.

Analysis in the light of rights and duties reaches similar conclusions. The various individuals and groups that use financial reports have a right to expect that these reports will be accurate. They have this right under the rubric of truth-telling as a human right, under the rubric of legal rights since false financial reporting is, at least under some circumstances, against the law and under the rubric of position rights as investors, lenders or regulators. The rights of these individuals and groups to consistently accurate reporting impose a moral duty on those responsible for the financial reports. As we have seen, consistently accurate financial reporting requires both the establishment and maintenance of accounting systems that feed into these reports and individual decisions on major items that affect financial reports. Both of these are the responsibility of top managers; hence their moral duties regarding consistently accurate financial reporting.

In order to analyze the role of top managers in the areas of accounting and financial reporting from the perspective of fairness and justice, we must consider the various users of the financial reports. Inaccurate reports can have differential effects on different users. If a company's performance is made to appear better than it actually was, the stock price may rise and lenders may be happy to provide the company with more money. Suppliers and customers may be anxious to do more business with the company. Executives of the company may benefit from higher compensation and the rising price of their company stock. The unfairness of these consequences is easiest to see in an extreme case, where the truth about performance leads to bankruptcy, as happened with WorldCom, Enron and others. In these cases, executives of the companies sold at least some of their stock before the truth about performance became known. Executives received substantial severance packages when they left the company, but other stockholders found their stock to be worthless at bankruptcy, lenders and suppliers recovered only a small portion of the money that was due to them and employees lost their jobs and sometimes all of their retirement savings when the stock became worthless.[11]

In such situations, it is clear that executive investors profited while employee investors and outsiders lost. Lenders, suppliers and others who were unpaid prior to the declaration of bankruptcy of the company lost heavily, while others who were paid before the true condition became known came out whole. Similarly situated individuals and groups were certainly not treated in similar ways. When we switch our focus to those responsible for the inaccurate reporting, it is clear that their behavior has caused unfair and unjust results. In other words, moral wrong has been done.

In other cases, where inaccurate financial reporting leads lenders, investors and others to take actions they would not otherwise have taken, although bankruptcy does not occur, the consequences are still unfair. These consequences, when they result from decisions that are based on a company's financial reports, have a direct connection to the actions of the executives responsible for the reports. They are not, in a strict sense, caused by the reports, since the decision-makers were free not to invest in or lend to the company in question. Nonetheless, such decisions are often made with some degree of reliance on the financial reports and might have been made differently if the results reported had been different. Since it is ethical to be fair, it is unethical to provide false or inaccurate financial reports because of the unfair results that follow from such reporting.

One category of unethical financial reporting results from individual decisions made by top executives regarding major items. Examples of such decisions might include listing large amounts of current expenses as capital expenses in order to reduce their impact on reported profits (WorldCom) and carrying large amounts of corporate debt off the books in order to make debt ratios appear more favorable (Enron, Citibank). Most managers have no input into such decisions, or perhaps even any awareness that they have been made and carried out. Sometimes the execution of such decisions does involve a number of managers besides those who actually make them (Enron, HealthSouth). To the extent that many managers are involved in the execution of such decisions, we will discuss them in the next section.

A second category of unethical financial reporting results from carelessness in establishing and maintaining accounting systems. As we have already seen, it is the accounting systems that capture details that ultimately aggregate to the reported financial figures in quarterly and annual reports. If these systems do not gather data accurately and categorize it correctly, then the reports that summarize this data will not be accurate. If top executives do not concern themselves with the establishment or monitoring of accounting systems, they cannot realistically certify the financial reports that draw information from these systems.

Many managers who are not accountants tend to dismiss the importance of any accounting that takes place within their departments or units as peripheral to the real purpose of their operation. It is easy to focus on the importance of customer service and the goal of satisfied customers and not pay attention to the correct accounting for handling returns. Manufacturing operations usually focus on the number of units produced or the number of defects turned up in quality checks. They often spend little time or effort on accounting correctly for the costs of producing finished goods and may try to minimize the reported costs of scrap or re-work in order to measure up to standards. While it is true that the primary responsibility of sales, manufacturing or purchasing is not accounting, if the data gathering systems are not well designed and used correctly, inaccurate financial reporting is the likely result. We turn now to considerations of ethical issues that affect all managers in the area of accounting and financial reporting.

Non-Accounting Managers and Financial Reporting

Some accounting systems are pervasive. Payroll accounting involves every unit of an organization that has at least one paid employee, and this is by definition every unit. It is hard to think of a unit that does not use supplies and equipment of one kind or another, no matter what the basic function of the unit. Supplies and equipment constitute costs that need to be properly accounted for. While most organizations have a person or unit in charge of purchasing supplies or equipment, accounting for existing inventory involves many non-accounting departments and units. In large offices, equipment inventory is typically considered a bother at best and a waste of time at worst by most departments. Yet, if it is not done with some accuracy on a periodic basis, the amount shown on the balance sheet for property, plant and equipment can be inaccurate and theft can go undetected.

Although senior managers may approve the creation or alteration of major accounting systems, the normal functioning of these systems involves many lower-level managers and the employees who work for them. Senior managers establish criteria for authorized spending by employees. Accounts payable clerks may be authorized to disburse up to $5,000 without further approval, and the chief financial officer may be authorized to disburse up to $5 million. Individual managers are often authorized to order equipment purchases for their units as long as the amounts are included in the current year's budget. Many non-accounting managers play some part in authorizing transactions that ultimately affect financial reporting.

Lower and mid-level managers also have responsibility for some part of the daily operation of systems that record routine transactions. The front-end manager in a supermarket oversees checkers who record the individual transactions involving every head of lettuce and can of tuna fish purchased in the store. The teller supervisor at a bank branch oversees tellers who process thousands of individual financial transactions a day, all of which are entered in accounting systems that ultimately aggregate to financial reports. Managers of all sorts oversee individuals who clock in and clock out, take vacation days or sick days and otherwise take part in the many events that are the beginning of payroll accounting. Supervisors of billing clerks at doctors' offices and hospitals oversee the processing of individual transactions that aggregate through accounting systems to financial reports. Managers of Internal Revenue Service offices oversee clerks processing individual tax payments and refunds that aggregate to government reports of revenue receipts.

Almost every manager, at whatever level, has as part of their responsibility some accounting or book-keeping transactions. To the extent that this basic accounting is done accurately, financial reports can be accurate. To the extent that it is done inaccurately, financial reports will be necessarily inaccurate. One can show statistically that if errors in accounting throughout a company are truly random, there should be about as many instances of over-reporting as under-reporting. However, on close examination, the assumption of truly random errors is unlikely to bear out. We will explore this point in some detail later in the chapter. Even if the assumption of random errors did hold true, acceptance of accounting and financial reporting systems that reflect widespread errors in the hope that they will balance out does not seem to meet the obligation of managers to provide accurate financial reports.

Since many users of the reports generated from accounting systems depend on their accuracy, it follows that accurate reporting results in the greatest good for the greatest number. Since accurate reporting requires that each manager involved with any of the accounting systems pay some attention to the way their employees provide input to these systems, we can see that there is an ethical issue involved. Some of the most widespread accounting abuses in recent years occurred at Enron. Over twenty individuals filed guilty pleas or were convicted of criminal charges for Enron-related matters,[12] and the accounting firm Arthur Andersen was found guilty of one criminal charge (later overturned) and ceased to exist within a matter of months of the conviction. When one reads about the business practices at that company and sees how many managers were either actively or passively involved in deceptive accounting, it becomes clear that real harm can be caused by negligent or malicious use of accounting systems.

We saw earlier in the chapter that various users of accounting systems, such as investors, lenders, regulators and others have a right to honest reporting. This right implies a duty for those who prepare financial reports to see to their honesty and accuracy. For this to happen, it is not enough that managers refrain from lying in their financial reporting. There is also a duty to take positive steps to assure that the input to accounting systems is both accurate and timely. Without such input, the output of such systems cannot satisfy the rights of users to honest reporting. What this means is that managers have an ethical duty to be proactive and observant in assuring that those who report to them provide accurate and timely input. This might take the form of assuring accuracy in payroll reporting, the completion of expense reports or proper accounting for returns or spoilage. Whatever form it takes, this duty to oversee accounting is very seldom mentioned in the job descriptions of managers outside the accounting areas, yet it clearly is required if the organization as a whole is to provide honest reporting.

The fairness and justice perspective requires that accurate financial reports be provided to all users of these reports. This means that managers must see to it that the input from the area they manage is accurate. The old saying "garbage in, garbage out" is true of accounting systems. It does not satisfy the demands of fairness and justice if sloppy and inaccurate accounting results in poor quality financial reports that are then made available to all users. Many managers who do not have final responsibility for the production of financial reports are unaware of the contribution to the final numbers that their employees make. It is also not a sufficient excuse to avoid concern with accounting systems to say that, statistically, random errors should cancel each other out, and the final results should be sufficiently accurate in spite of errors. While this is true of random errors, not all errors in entries to accounting systems are random.

If a system allows input from clerks in a given department to be coded in a number of different ways, and the clerks find the system too complicated to master, or to allow for rapid input, the results are predictable. Most clerks will adopt a few codes as the preferred ones and in case of doubt will make an entry into one of these few codes. Over time, this approach will result in systematic errors charging too many expenses or crediting too much income to the favored codes, and not enough to the others. The resulting summary accounting reports will be inaccurate, with a consistent over-reporting in some areas and under-reporting in others. Overall totals may be correct, but the breakdown within categories will be consistently inaccurate.

Consider errors made by checkout clerks in supermarkets or retail stores. Under normal conditions, one would expect that there would be about as many overcharges as undercharges. However, customers are much more apt to protest (and hence correct) overcharges than undercharges. Thus, the errors are not random and cannot be expected to balance each other out. The same phenomenon holds true for payroll accounting. Employees who are underpaid are much more apt to question the payment (and hence generate a correction) than employees who are overpaid. Again, in the area of accounts payable, vendors are more apt to question underpayments than overpayments.

Managers in all areas must, then, tend to the accuracy of whatever accounting transactions occur in their area. To the extent that this is not done, the accuracy of the financial reports that represent aggregations of individual transactions will suffer.

Most managers do not make policy decisions about financial reporting. The Sarbanes–Oxley Act requires only that the CEO and chief financial officer certify the accuracy of financial reports. However, in a number of large companies, the managers or officers in charge of divisions of the company are being required by the CEO and CFO to internally certify the accuracy of the numbers from their divisions that make up the company totals. This requirement means that some non-accounting managers are being made specifically and formally responsible for the accuracy of the accounting that goes on within their areas of responsibility. Such a requirement is very much compatible with the explanation we have given above that accurate financial reporting for the company is impossible without attention to the accounting for individual transactions that are summarized in the company financial reports.

Non-Accounting Managers and Fraudulent Financial Reporting

All of this assumes that the members of management are making good faith efforts to provide accurate financial reports. However, this assumption is not always valid. What is the ethical responsibility of managers who are not responsible for major policy decisions that affect financial reporting when they become involved in the creation of false financial records? While deliberate falsifying of financial reports is probably not a common occurrence, it does take place. We will use the events that occurred at Enron as examples, since that case is particularly well documented.

When members of senior management decide to falsify the company's financial reporting, other members of management will often be involved in recording specific fraudulent transactions. Since these other members of management are not responsible for determining company policy, there is a strong temptation for them to simply do as instructed and record the transactions as directed from above. It is clear that a number of managers at Enron who were not responsible for making policy knew or strongly suspected for an extended period of time that the company was falsifying its accounting records. Sherron Watkins, a vice president at Enron, was chosen by *Time Magazine* as one of three individuals who were together the "Person of the Year" for 2002. All three of those chosen were whistle-blowers.[13] Ms. Watkins was sufficiently concerned about the false accounting at Enron that she wrote an anonymous memorandum to Kenneth Lay, who was CEO at the time, about her concerns. She subsequently identified herself as the writer and met with Mr. Lay. In a phrase made famous after Enron's bankruptcy, she said that she was "incredibly nervous that we will implode in a wave of accounting scandals."[14]

Executives at Enron, particularly the chief financial officer, made policy decisions to create subsidiaries known as special purpose entities and use these entities to purchase Enron assets that had lost much of their value. These entities were also used to keep a large amount of debt off the Enron books and hidden in such a way that even a careful study of Enron's financial statements would not reveal this debt. By the time Enron declared bankruptcy, its financial statements showed approximately $13 billion in debt. After the bankruptcy declaration, a special committee of the board was formed to investigate the company's financial reporting. This committee concluded that the actual Enron debt at the time of bankruptcy was not $13 billion but $38 billion! The accounting for various transactions was so complex that it appears doubtful that anyone at Enron, including the chief financial officer, knew the full extent of the company's debt.[15]

In order to reach this level of inaccurate reporting, many individual transactions over a considerable period of time had to be recorded. Senior executives, division managers, traders and others at Enron received large numbers of stock options, the value of which depended on Enron's stock price continuing to rise. Enron, because of the nature of its business, needed to borrow large amounts of money on a regular basis. Its lenders had to be assured that income was increasing and debt was reasonable. In the last weeks before the company declared bankruptcy, many outside parties, including lenders and traders from other companies, came to doubt the validity of Enron's financial statements. Credit was essentially cut off both by lenders and traders and, with the stock price sinking rapidly as investors began to doubt the company's value and future prospects, Enron had no source for the cash it needed to continue operating.

Many Enron managers and accountants who recorded individual transactions that were at best inaccurate and more likely fraudulent had at least some suspicion of the nature of these transactions. Nonetheless they did record them, and the deceit and misdirection continued. It is not clear that any individual manager or accountant could have intervened effectively and stopped the practice of inaccurate reporting. The efforts of Sherron Watkins (who was a corporate vice president at the time) in her communication with the CEO did lead him to request an outside investigation of some accounting transactions. However, despite her recommendation to the contrary, he assigned this review to the same outside law firm that had previously helped to structure and approve many of the transactions in question, and directed them to conduct only a narrow inquiry. Not surprisingly, they did not find problems with the transactions they reviewed.

The normal recommended action when an employee, including a manager, judges that an action is wrong and will be harmful to others is to discuss the situation with the employee's immediate supervisor. Some companies have appointed an ethics officer or ombudsman to whom employees can make such reports, but this channel is not available in many companies. If the immediate supervisor advises or orders the employee to continue with the action in question, the employee can decide to accept this decision, go to someone else within the company (other than their immediate supervisor) or go to someone outside the company, such as a regulator or news reporter. This last step is commonly referred to as whistle-blowing. Several studies have shown that whistle-blowers frequently lose their jobs and suffer other serious personal consequences as a result of their actions, so this is a step that should not be taken lightly or without consideration of the likely consequences.[16]

When false financial reporting becomes as widespread, frequent and embedded as it was at Enron, it is very unlikely that any non-accounting manager below the most senior level could do anything within the company that would change the practice. Three courses of action are open to a manager caught up in a situation such as the one we are describing. One is to make the entries as ordered and remain silent; another is to quit her job; and the third is to report what is going on to someone or some group outside the company that has the power to take effective action.[17] Any of these actions may have serious consequences for the individual and perhaps for others. Since a number of managers and mid-level staff accountants from Enron and other companies involved in recent corporate scandals were in fact indicted and faced criminal prosecution, this is not a decision to be treated as an interesting theoretical puzzle. To the extent that the issue is legal, an attorney is the correct source of advice, and not a book on ethics. Since there are also ethical considerations involved, we will now consider each of these two solutions.

A manager or other employee who quits because he is faced with being required to perform unethical acts may be leaving a job that he otherwise finds quite satisfactory. Enron richly rewarded its employees, with high salaries, stock options and other forms of reimbursement. Managers leaving

Enron were unlikely to find comparable compensation at their next employer, which means that they would suffer real-world consequences by quitting. Further, employers generally ask applicants why they left their previous position. An applicant who says that he left because he was being required to perform unethical (and perhaps illegal) acts as part of his job might well be perceived as excessively sensitive or scrupulous rather than as a person of high moral character. Until very near the end, Enron was perceived by most outsiders as an admirable company. It was ranked as the most innovative company in *Fortune*'s annual Most Admired Companies survey several times in a row. It is possible to finesse the issue by saying that the resignation was due to personality differences (also a warning sign to prospective employers) or to seek greater opportunities (suspicious if resigning from a high-paying, innovative company). The point is that resignation is not always an easy step or one without significant risks.

A utilitarian analysis of this situation would have to examine several factors. The employee who terminates will no longer be involved in deceptive accounting or financial reporting. It is likely, though, that someone else will take his position and will continue the deception. Thus, in terms of impeding false financial reporting, no good is likely to be done. As we have discussed, the employee who terminates may well suffer harm in terms of compensation and even employment. The false financial reporting, as we showed earlier in the chapter, does not result in the greatest good for the greatest number and is in fact unethical. However, the termination of the individual who objects to the unethical behavior required of him but cannot stop it does not appear to produce the greatest good for the greatest number. Against this analysis must be weighed the fact that an employee who is later indicted and perhaps convicted of criminal wrong-doing suffers very great personal harm, and that this harm extends at least to his family. In weighing this practical legal consequence, we should note that employees who have been indicted in the past scandals have been almost exclusively involved in either accounting or auditing functions. The practical legal threat to non-accounting managers appears to be small. However, the consequences of indictment are so great that even a small threat must be carefully considered.

Rights and duties shows the same situation in a different light. A manager or accountant has a duty to perform his job in a satisfactory manner, but does not have a duty to commit unethical or illegal acts in the course of performing his job. In fact, legally, the employee has a duty to his employer not to commit illegal acts. Conversely, the employer has a right to a reasonable day's work, competently performed, by the employee. However, the employer clearly does not have a right to require that the employee perform illegal or unethical acts as part of his job.

What, then, are the rights and duties of an employee who is expected to perform illegal or unethical acts as part of his employment? An employee has both a legal and a moral duty not to break the law. The fact that he did so at the direction or with the permission of his employer does not relieve him of this duty, either legally or morally. Thus an employer does not have the right, either legally or morally, to require the employee to perform illegal actions. A more difficult case is the situation where accounting practices are being followed that are not illegal, but that are unethical in that they clearly promote false financial reporting. An example of such transactions would be the continued and widespread use of special purpose entities by Enron to hide the actual debt status of the company.

As long as such accounting is done within the letter of the law, it is technically legal. As we indicated above, Generally Accepted Accounting Principles leave considerable room for managerial discretion in recording transactions. Some of the transactions recorded by Enron, WorldCom, Tyco, Health South and other companies involved in widely reported scandals were legal, although misleading. When an accountant or manager is expected to record or approve such transactions, she has a duty to do so, or to resign her position. Obviously if every employee involved in any way in accounting could decide to record or not to record each transaction based on his own interpretation of its appropriateness, a company could not attain consistent reporting of financial activities. Someone has to set policy, and others have to follow policy.

Normally a non-accounting manager will not have the same degree of technical knowledge as those who determine a company's accounting policies. Non-accounting managers do not need to be knowledgeable about Generally Accepted Accounting Principles or the provisions of income tax law that relate to corporate reporting. Thus they do not have the same duty as an accounting manager to assure that the company's financial reporting and the accounting that supports it are legal and not deceptive. As we discussed earlier, non-accounting managers do have a duty by their positions as managers to assure that the accounting systems within their area of responsibility are being used accurately as designed.

In terms of fairness and justice, as we have just discussed, not all managers are similarly situated with respect to their knowledge or their obligations related to the company's accurate financial reporting. Thus it is fair not to place the same requirements on accounting and non-accounting managers. The obligations of accounting managers (including auditors) in situations such as the one we are discussing are more complex. Since this book is concerned with ethical behavior in those areas that are of concern to all managers, we will not deal here with these more complex obligations and considerations. We could also consider, under fairness and justice, the fact that non-accounting managers are not similarly situated with accounting managers, and thus should be more hesitant to make judgments about the morality of accounting practices. This does not mean that they should be totally accepting of any practices, no matter how deceptive, but they should also not be too quick to judge that serious wrong-doing is taking place and that they have a moral obligation to do whatever is necessary to stop it.

This analysis provides an example of how a manager concerned about ethics can use the three basic approaches to philosophy to think through a difficult situation and come to an answer that may not at first seem to be intuitive. Some people, reading about the financial scandals that have occurred at various companies, quickly reach the conclusion that everyone in any way involved must be guilty, if not of criminal activity, at least of serious ethical wrong-doing. Undoubtedly some non-accounting managers from the companies involved felt at least a twinge of guilt at their involvement, however peripheral. Nonetheless, a careful ethical analysis shows that, at least when dishonest accounting practices were widespread and either initiated or sanctioned by top management, the morally correct decision for at least some non-accounting managers is to continue in their jobs and to follow the directives of senior management, at least until a satisfactory alternative position could be found.

Conversely, top managers and accounting managers who justified their dishonest reporting by seeking only to comply with the letter of the law might find through an ethical analysis that they were doing things that were simply morally wrong. As we saw in earlier sections of this book, there are ethical obligations that sometimes go beyond the letter of the law. Financial transactions designed solely or principally to present a dishonest picture of a company's financial position, even if they can perhaps be justified by attorneys or accountants, remain deceptive and hence morally wrong. They do not pass muster with any of the three basic approaches to ethics.

In our consideration of the ethical obligations of non-accounting managers with regard to accounting and financial reporting, there is one category of decisions that we have not yet considered. This involves individual decisions that appear to be deceptive or illegal but do not appear to be part of a widespread and deeply embedded practice. In our previous discussion, we saw that at a company like Enron, where accounting abuses were common and appeared to have top management approval, an individual non-accounting manager (or even a lower or mid-level accounting manager) is unlikely to be able to achieve any real change in the pattern of abuses. Assuming that most companies do not manifest such patterns of widespread abuse, we need to consider the case of the non-accounting manager faced with a deceptive or illegal entry or practice in his area of responsibility.

In order to put some bounds on this discussion, we will assume that the manager in question has at least a basic knowledge of accounting. We will also assume that the entry or practice in question is one that is not excessively complex or technical. Examples of such entries or practices might include things like the following. A manager may be asked to assign hours worked on one project to a different project. An employee may try to claim sick leave when the manager knows that the employee is actually taking a vacation. Expenses that belong under one account may be charged to a different expense account. Expenses may be increased to include a kick-back or bribe for a vendor or regulatory official. Such issues arise at least occasionally in almost any organization. To the extent that the manager is responsible for accounting entries or practices within his area, once he becomes aware of such issues, he must either take action to prevent the improper entry or practice, or refrain from taking such action. The moral issue is substantially the same whether the manager makes the entry himself or knowingly allows a subordinate employee to make it.

At first blush, a utilitarian argument might maintain that, at least in some cases, greater good can be obtained by making or allowing such entries than by stopping them. Allowing a good employee to claim a few days' sick leave when the employee is actually on vacation might keep that employee from leaving and going to work for a competitor. Increasing an expense amount to allow for a relatively small bribe or kick-back might assure that an important customer or vendor remains with the company and continues to provide an overall profitable relationship. If a greater good results, and only a lesser evil is allowed, then it appears that utilitarianism would bless such transactions. However, if we consider the impact on accounting systems overall when random false entries are condoned, the conclusion seems somewhat different. Just as we saw in the discussion of random lies in performance appraisal systems, it does not require a great frequency of such lies to diminish significantly the usefulness of the whole system, so also with accounting systems a relatively small number of false entries can diminish the accuracy and credibility of the whole system.

When the entries or practices in question are illegal, there is a further problem from the utilitarian approach. As we have already seen, the greatest good for the greatest number occurs when laws are followed by all to whom they apply. If each individual or organization subject to a law were free to decide whether to follow the law or not, the force of laws would be greatly diminished. Much more good comes from the following of laws than from the breaking of them, on a society-wide basis. While an individual manager or even a company may derive some good from illegal entries or practices, the harm that can come to the company if discovery occurs is much greater. Although there were a number of major settlements made by Arthur Andersen in its last few years for failure to detect major fraud, the criminal conviction that brought the company to an end was for one memo by one employee that the jury saw as encouraging destruction of evidence.

As we have maintained throughout this chapter, many stakeholders have a right to accurate financial reporting, and managers have a duty to do what they can to assure that financial reports are accurate. Deliberate falsification of even a minor item in the overall scheme of things still violates this duty to provide accurate financial reports. The likely defense to be raised against this duty is that the item or practice involved is too minor to have a material impact on a company's financial reports. While this may be true in a given case, it does not provide moral justification for false entries or misleading practices. Many individual small actions can sum to large totals. From the pattern perspective, we may not be able to identify any one of these small items that was material to the company's overall reports, but the total of the items may well be material. Because of this, each individual item must be viewed not only in itself but also as part of a pattern. If the pattern violates the duty to provide accurate financial reporting, either no one is responsible or each manager involved in an individually small part of the pattern must share responsibility.

Fairness and justice suggests that one manager not be allowed to benefit from false entries or practices while another manager is not allowed to benefit in a similar way. If all managers are free to benefit from false entries or practices when it suits them, it is clear that no accounting system can have credibility. An additional argument lies in the fact that the users of financial reporting should have equal access to accurate reports. If individual managers know part of the truth, but their false reports or practices keep this part of the truth from others, it is quite possible that no one, including the chief financial officer or other senior company officials, can know the truth about the company's financial activities and condition. If many individual managers are making false entries independent of each other, it seems clear that no one, either on the individual manager level or on a more senior level, can in principle know what true accounting would reveal about the company's financial activity and condition. If no one within the company can know, it is certain that no one outside the company can know. A system which keeps everyone ignorant of the true financial condition of the company can hardly be characterized as fair and just.

We have seen, then, that individual non-accounting managers do have a moral obligation regarding financial accounting. Although they do not set up accounting systems, and are not responsible for consolidating results from different operational areas and different accounting systems, they are the first line of defense against false entries and misleading practices within their limited areas of authority. Not only do these managers have an obligation to see that such systems are used with reasonable care and accuracy, as we discussed earlier in this chapter, but they also face specific decisions about ordering or allowing false entries or practices that lead to inaccurate accounting. Many managers might prefer to leave both of these functions to auditors, on the grounds that the manager has been hired to oversee a purchasing, or customer service, or sales department, and not to be an accountant. In spite of this preference, our analysis shows that there is a moral obligation on the part of every manager to take care of the accounting systems that are used by his department or to which members of his department provide input.

twelve

Ethical Managers and Ethical Organizations

Throughout this book, the emphasis has been on defining the ethical act. Our context has been the individual manager making a decision or taking an action that impacts others. If we shift the unit of analysis from an individual act to an individual person and ask what it is that lets us describe a person as ethical or unethical, can we simply say that the ethical person is the one who takes ethical actions, as defined in earlier chapters of this book? One immediate problem with this approach is that of frequency. Must the ethical person *always* make ethical decisions, or nearly always, or more often than not?

Aristotle, in his *Nicomachean Ethics*, provided a well-reasoned answer to this question.[1] He maintains that the ethical individual is the one who usually or normally performs ethical acts. He does not quantify "usually" or "normally" but the picture that he provides is of a principled individual who consistently follows his principles. Both psychology and common sense tell us that no one attains perfect consistency in a lifetime of actions and decisions. Aristotle's view on this issue is often referred to as virtue ethics because he characterizes ethical acts as virtuous acts and he explains at considerable length his views on what constitutes virtue.

For Aristotle, the virtuous person is the one who avoids extremes. He defines courage as the mean between cowardice (too little bravery) and foolhardiness (too much bravery). Similarly, generosity is the mean between stinginess and profligacy. One becomes virtuous by repeatedly making individual virtuous decisions; in other words, by practicing the virtues. He places strong emphasis on experience. One does not become virtuous by thinking about or studying virtues, or by wishing to be virtuous. It is only in the real world of everyday decisions and actions that one achieves consistency in virtue by the accumulated experience of individual virtuous (ethical) acts.

At the beginning of this book, we defined ethics as the study of social or interpersonal values and the rules of conduct that follow from these values. Aristotle might take this definition one step further and add that it includes actions consistent with these rules of conduct. As indicated earlier in the discussion of ethics in Chapter 3, virtue ethics as a system is difficult to use in defining the ethical act and, for this reason, we did not treat it as a basic approach to ethics throughout the book. However, it does offer useful guidance in thinking about what it means to say that an individual is ethical. We have talked briefly in various places throughout the book about ethical actions and ethical patterns. In this chapter, we formally address this issue at some length.

Ethical Managers

Managers, by the nature of their jobs, make many decisions and take many actions. In trying to decide whether a manager is ethical, we will examine the patterns that these decisions and actions exhibit. This is not the only possible way to answer the question. We could ask about a manager's principles or beliefs regarding the task of managing, or regarding the way decisions should be made. We could ask about a manager's life outside of work and ask whether she is an ethical parent, sibling, friend, neighbor, etc. We could ask others for their opinions about whether a manager is ethical or not. We could devise a survey or checklist and ask the manager to respond, then judge whether she is ethical based on her responses. However, none of these approaches provides as sure a measure of how ethical a manager is as does an examination of what a manager does.

It would be strange, but not impossible, if a manager expressed ethical views, chose ethical answers on survey instruments or checklists, was thought to be ethical by others and in spite of all of this acted unethically on a regular basis. Since ethics, as we have defined it, is about both values and the rules of conduct or action that follow from these values, using actions as the basis for judgment provides the most solid basis for conclusions about an individual's ethics or morality. Thus we can say (with Aristotle) that an ethical manager is one who consistently acts ethically. This definition allows for an ethical manager to be human and to slip occasionally but not for one who regularly acts unethically to be judged as ethical by any other standard.

As we have discussed at various points in this book, some decisions of managers are constrained by the rules, practices and culture of an organization. A negotiated labor-management contract constrains the ability of a manager to decide who is similarly situated with regard to salary increases.

Rules promulgated by the human resources department may constrain managers in their decisions about promoting or terminating employees. In general, it is ethical for managers to follow such contract provisions or company rules, and it is unethical for managers to violate them. In an organization, someone or some group must be responsible for setting rules and establishing guidelines. Otherwise, the organization could not act coherently over a large number of decisions because individual managers will inevitably differ on at least some occasions about the right thing to do.[2]

However, if all that a manager had to do was to search out the specified decision for any given situation and then to execute that decision, managing would not be the challenging and interesting job that it is. In order to make ethical decisions, a manager must first know whether the situation already has a prescribed decision. Managers usually may not fire an employee who is two minutes tardy for the first time they have been late. Managers usually must fire an employee who physically assaults a fellow employee. Within the extremes, there are many cases where a manager must make a judgment, and it is these judgments that provide the possibility of ethical or unethical decisions. As we have seen in the applied chapters of this book, part of every manager's job is to make decisions that affect others in significant ways. Another way of saying this is that many managerial decisions have ethical impacts.

As we have also seen earlier in this book, it is almost always ethical for managers to obey relevant law in their decisions, and unethical to disobey it. This still leaves a broad area of decisions where the law either is silent or allows for a variety of decisions. The ethical manager, then, consistently recognizes the ethical impacts of her decisions and makes individual decisions that are ethical rather than unethical. Although most managers do not have decision-making authority (or sometimes even input) for the general rules that constrain some managerial decision-making, they do make choices to follow or not to follow these rules. They also make choices in areas where there are no constraining rules or where multiple choices are possible within the constraints set down by rules.

It is within this area of allowed choices that an individual manager can be described as ethical or unethical based on her pattern of decisions. Rosabeth Moss Kanter has described supervisors as lacking in power because they are at the lowest level of authority.[3] All levels of management above supervisors contribute to the making of policies and rules that supervisors must enforce, but the responsibility for seeing that workers follow these policies and rules rests primarily with the supervisor. Since most organizations are structured like pyramids, with workers at the bottom, it stands to reason that if we simply count employees, we find the largest number are workers and the next largest number (the largest of all management ranks) are supervisors.

In spite of this lack of power, supervisors are the ones that most employees see as the face of management. Even supervisors have genuine choices to make in implementing rules and policies, and in addressing issues where there is no explicit rule or policy. Generally speaking, as one ascends the management ladder, at each step more authority is embodied in management positions. This means that at each ascending step, more choices and more important choices are authorized and are expected of managers. Directly or indirectly, managers at each higher level deal with more and more individuals, both within and outside of the organization. Thus their scope for exercising interpersonal values increases.

Ethical Organizations

We have discussed what it means to say that a manager is ethical; now we must turn to the issue of what it means to say that an organization is ethical. Two points immediately arise. One is the relative newness of the organization, especially the corporation, as a major actor in society. The other is the fact that many judgments made about whether an organization, and again especially a business organization, is ethical relate to areas of decision-making and action that are outside the scope of this book. We will take up each point in turn.

As we saw in the chapters on philosophy and ethics, much of the foundational thinking and writing on ethics occurred before large business organizations existed. Throughout much of known history, and even today in some parts of the world, the only large organizations are governments (including armies) and churches.[4] The body of thought and writing on ethical organizations is neither as wide nor as deep as that on ethical individuals. Thus we cannot turn to Aristotle, or Plato, or Aquinas, or Kant for insight on this topic, except by analogy.[5]

In the introduction to this book, we made clear that the scope of the book does not encompass all of business ethics, but is limited to the analysis of situations that all managers face, such as hiring, firing and privacy issues. When companies are judged to be ethical or unethical, especially by the popular press, the issues under consideration often entail the actions or inactions of companies with regard to stakeholders other than their employees. Many of the major corporate scandals of the first years of the twenty-first century centered on financial fraud and deceptive accounting. In several cases, the individual actions of CEOs and other top officers were the object of very negative reporting, and the companies were judged to be unethical based on the actions of one or a few individuals. Even at Hewlett-Packard, where the scandal involved invasion of privacy, it was board members rather than employees whose privacy was violated.[6]

In order to discuss this issue sensibly, we start with a discussion of how an organization is and is not similar to a person. Legally, a corporation is treated as a person. It has certain legal rights and certain legal duties. A corporation can sue and be sued, accessing and being held to account by the legal system as an individual person. At the same time, organization theory provides several differing views of just what an organization is. For our purposes, we will treat organizations and corporations in the same way, although there are many organizations that are not incorporated.

In a widely used textbook, Gareth Morgan provides and discusses eight different images of organizations, which he also refers to as metaphors.[7] Among these images are those of machines, organisms, brains, cultures and political systems. In another important book on organizations, W. Richard Scott[8] identifies three perspectives on organizations: those of rational, natural and open systems. While individual humans are complicated, organizations are also complex, but in different ways. One of the broadly accepted tenets of organizational theory is that humans form or join organizations in order to accomplish things that they cannot accomplish as individuals. Organizations range in size and complexity from two-person businesses to such giants as General Electric, Walmart and the United States Department of Defense. What they have in common are such features as groups of individuals, structure, purpose and rules.

One of the features of organizations, structure, is especially relevant to understanding what organizations are, and how they act. To varying degrees, structure is defined by rules, but rules also apply to other facets of organizations. Structure, which includes but is not limited to hierarchy, is a major determinant of both authority and responsibility within organizations. In business corporations, the stockholders or owners have ultimate authority, but limited responsibility for the actions of the organization. Because they are the owners, stockholders choose, evaluate and sometimes terminate the individual with the most authority, namely the chief executive officer. Since stockholders are often widely dispersed and not particularly knowledgeable about the affairs of the corporation, they elect a board of directors to perform oversight functions on their behalf. This board of directors has both the authority and the responsibility to choose and oversee the CEO and to review and approve or disapprove major corporate decisions such as mergers and acquisitions.

The chief executive officer has both the authority and the responsibility to select other officers and managers, to make and enforce rules regarding the corporation's operations and to delegate authority and responsibility to individuals and committees. In Chapter 5 on Rights and Duties, we saw that one of the four sources of rights, as well as duties, is position. The chief executive officer has the right to make decisions and take actions for the corporation because of his position. Many other officers and managers also have rights to act in limited ways for the corporation because of their positions. Thus the kinds of decisions to be made on behalf of the company (hiring, terminating, disbursing funds, etc.) are ultimately made by individuals. Even the decisions that are reserved to groups, such as the board of directors, are ultimately made because more individuals in the group voted for than against the decision.

This is an extremely important point in deciding what it means for an organization to be ethical or unethical: the decisions of the organization are made by individuals. When we say that Enron defrauded customers and investors, or that WorldCom loaned its CEO $400 million with his stock in the company as collateral, we mean that individuals did these things. Not everyone at Enron engaged in fraudulent activity; not everyone at World-Com approved of the CEO loan, but some individuals, acting on the part of the corporation, did these things. Structure allows or requires certain individuals and not others to make certain decisions. Structure determines and indicates not only who may make certain decisions (authority) but also who is answerable for decisions made by others (responsibility).

An organization is not unitary in the sense that all of its members agree on a set of values or on which actions best embody those values. We sometimes say that Catholics believe this or Muslims believe that. However, these religions each have millions of members and, within each one, there is considerable diversity of belief. There are official church positions on certain value judgments and which actions are prescribed or prohibited to advance these values. Not every member agrees with these positions. Several Protestant denominations have been dealing with very strong internal disagreements over such issues as the ordaining of gay and lesbian clergy and the right of individual congregations to secede from the main body of the church and maintain ownership of church property. Similarly, managers within a corporation may disagree strongly about an action or a policy of that corporation.

In Chapter 11 on Accounting and Financial Reporting, we saw that the Sarbanes–Oxley Act, legislation passed in 2002, requires among other things that the chief executive officer and chief financial officer both attest under oath that a company's financial statements are true and accurate. This law places legal responsibility for the very important function of financial reporting squarely with these two corporate officers. Prior to the passage of this law, one could have reasonably argued that these two officers already had responsibility for the accurate reporting of the company's financial results. By their positions, they have the moral duty to see that this function is fulfilled correctly.

Except in a small company, neither of these individuals (the CEO and CFO) would normally do the actual preparation of reports, but the systems that produce the reports, the people who operate these systems and the reports themselves are ultimately their responsibility. When we say that a company has the duty to report its financial results accurately and honestly, it is these two individuals in whom this duty resides. However, as we saw in Chapter 11, many more individuals besides these two officers have input to and impact on the final financial reports. Both Bernie Ebbers of WorldCom and Richard Scrushy of HealthSouth, when on trial for massive corporate financial fraud, stated under oath that, although they were CEOs at the time the frauds took place, they did not know that their companies' financial statements were false.[9]

In 2008, Bank of America decided to purchase Merrill Lynch. This decision was made very quickly under extreme duress during the worst month of the financial crisis (September 2008). This decision was reached by Bank of America's CEO with very limited input from other executives and approved very quickly by the board of directors.[10] When Bank of America decides on policies that it will follow in dealing with foreclosures and short sales on home mortgages, senior executives in one part of the bank make recommendations and these recommendations are ultimately approved by the CEO. When an individual home is being sold through either foreclosure or a short sale, individual managers at a much lower level decide on acceptable terms for that sale. If a senior executive of a large bank is arrested for drunk driving or embezzlement, the arrest will probably be national news. If a branch manager is arrested on similar charges, it will probably be local news and, if a teller is arrested on the same charges, it will probably not make the news at all, unless the branch is in a small town. All are members of the organization, but the degree to which they are seen as representing the organization varies substantially.

Organizational Culture

The culture of a company is hard to define, but it can be both influential on the actions of individuals within the company and defining of the company's ethical stance. One definition of organizational culture is "the deeper level of basic assumptions and beliefs that are shared by members of an organization, that operate unconsciously, and that define in a basic 'taken-for-granted' fashion an organization's view of itself and its environment."[11] Schein explains that the term "culture" is sometimes used to describe practices or artifacts that show how an organization does things, but that those are really ways of reading or understanding the underlying assumptions or beliefs. Some organizations have strong cultures (the United States Marine Corps, Nordstrom, many small family businesses). When this is the case, the shared assumptions and beliefs can be more effective in shaping the behavior of individuals within the organizations than written codes of conduct or long lists of rules and procedures.

It is hard for an individual manager to be ethical in a culture that emphasizes and rewards unethical behavior. The reverse is also true: a strongly ethical culture encourages ethical behavior on the part of individuals and makes unethical behavior more difficult. A pacifist who abhorred combat would have a very difficult time either joining or succeeding in the Marine Corps, as would someone with no sense of customer service at Nordstrom, or a rebellious son or daughter who disagreed fundamentally with the way their parents ran the family business. An organization with a strong culture can and does influence the behavior of individuals within the organization.

As with many issues, it is easier to see differences and to define them at the extremes than near the middle. Companies with cultures that are either very ethical or very unethical are easier to tell apart than are companies with cultures that differ only slightly in the degree to which they are ethical. Enron, at least in the years just before its bankruptcy, clearly had an unethical culture. Nearly twenty former managers and executives of Enron were either convicted or have pled guilty to charges relating to their activities while employed by the company. Further evidence of the Enron culture can be found in books published since the company's collapse detailing both individual and corporate actions over the last years before bankruptcy. As several books and articles make clear, Enron had a culture that encouraged and rewarded not just innovation but the breaking of rules and standards when the result was profitable. It also regularly employed accounting practices that obscured rather than clarified the results of its various financial innovations.[12]

When we say that a company is ethical or unethical, one plausible meaning is that it has an ethical or unethical culture. In other words, the basic assumptions and beliefs shared by most if not all members of the company include interpersonal values and rules of conduct that could properly be judged ethical or unethical. This approach to defining an ethical company is obviously non-quantitative. Researchers who study corporate ethics often comment on the difficulty of getting reliable answers, either in interviews or by using questionnaires, when the subject matter is such that people prefer not to cast themselves in an unfavorable light. This is sometimes referred to as the social response bias. The approach we are discussing here in determining whether an organization is ethical is similar in concept to that used above in determining whether an individual is ethical. If an ethical person is one who typically or consistently makes ethical decisions, then by analogy an ethical organization is one whose members typically or consistently make ethical decisions in their organizational roles.

Much of the research on ethical decision-making identifies perception as the first step.[13] In other words, before an individual can bring any kind of ethical reasoning to bear, she must recognize that the issue at hand has an ethical component or ethical implications. Organizations where ethical concerns are part of the culture should logically make it easier for managers to perceive the ethical implications of decisions with which they are confronted. For example, in an organization where hiring practices and policies emphasize fairness, and where managers are exposed to some sort of training on issues such as diversity and sexual harassment, we would expect that there would be more perception on the part of more managers that their hiring actions and their handling of sexual harassment complaints involve ethical as well as legal considerations. This does not assure that managers in the organization will act more ethically than in organizations where such awareness is harder to come by, but it does at least provide one necessary component for such ethical action.

The United States Sentencing Commission is an independent agency in the judicial branch of the federal government. It was created in 1984 by Congress to provide guidelines for federal sentencing and perform related tasks.[14] These guidelines contain a section on the mitigation of sentences for corporations convicted of violations. If a company has in place "an effective program to prevent and detect violations of the law … [and] self-reporting, cooperation and acceptance of responsibility"[15] it will be treated differently than one that does not, if both are found guilty and appear for sentencing. Such policies and programs as described are thought to make the organization more ethical, or at least more prone to be legal.

The descriptions of Enron's culture during the last years before its collapse depict a company where cleverness, complicated transactions and accounting, and breaking of rules were widely perceived to be desirable and fairness to customers and honesty in reporting were perceived to be less desirable or even undesirable. When the unspoken rules promote unethical behavior and discourage ethical behavior, the perception that ethical issues are important tends to be lost. Very few individuals openly and enthusiastically embrace unethical behavior as such. One way to pursue what the culture encourages (unethical behavior) without frankly embracing it is to avoid consideration of ethical issues in business decision-making. Such a culture dulls the perception of ethical implications and tends to view decisions in other terms, such as cleverness, complexity or originality. If a decision is not perceived as having ethical implications, then judgments about the morality of the decision can be avoided. This may be one reason why bribes are often discussed as gifts.

Changing or Impacting a Company's Culture

We have discussed how an organization's culture can impact an individual manager's behavior; we now turn to the issue of how senior managers can impact an organization's culture. Most writers on corporate culture agree that it is very difficult to change an organization's culture and that such change, if it is substantial, requires several years to accomplish. Edgar Schein, in his book on organizational culture and leadership, identifies five mechanisms by which an organization's leader or leaders can impact a culture. These are attention, reaction to crises, role modeling, allocation of rewards and criteria for selecting and dismissing employees.[16] We will consider each of these methods or mechanisms in turn.

Attention

CEOs especially, and all managers to some extent, signal to their employees what values are important and what sorts of actions embody those values by the things they pay attention to or ignore. This is especially true in the case of a new boss and his or her actions in the first days and weeks in office. IBM nearly went bankrupt in the early 1990s. The company which had, for many years, been considered one of the best-run companies in the world had become extremely bureaucratic and lost its emphasis on customer service. When the board of directors fired the company's CEO, their choice for a replacement was Louis Gerstner, an experienced executive with no background in the computer industry. During his first weeks in office, Gerstner spent much of his time away from headquarters visiting and listening to customers. This puzzled many of his subordinates, but they gradually understood from his subsequent actions that he considered paying attention to customers as central to the company's turnaround.[17]

Zappos.com is a very unusual company, recently purchased by Amazon.com. Zappos.com sells shoes and other clothing items online. They place great emphasis on customer service. Among their practices is free shipping of products and free return shipping if the customer is dissatisfied for any reason. All new employees at Zappos.com, as part of their orientation, spend one week as customer service representatives handling phone calls from customers. This includes employees in such distinctly non-customer related positions as computer programmers. By paying such attention to the customer service function in its employee orientation program, the company strengthens the culture of customer service.

When Stan O'Neal became CEO of Merrill Lynch, he emphasized profits from trading. At the same time, he de-emphasized risk management. He reduced the importance of risk management by having the function report at a lower level, by paying risk managers less and by removing risk managers who objected to profitable trading practices that carried a high risk of failure. O'Neal also made a practice of firing or demoting individuals who brought him bad news about the company's various businesses—the classic syndrome known as killing the messenger. Once word of this practice became widespread, his subordinates stopped delivering bad news to him. When he was finally told of the extent of his company's exposure to toxic collateralized mortgage obligations based on subprime mortgages, "O'Neal looked like he was about to vomit."[18]

Codes of ethics can be seen as one way for a company or a CEO to draw attention to ethical issues. The presence of a code of ethics by itself does not increase ethical perception in an organization. Enron had a sixty-four page code of ethics that was quite admirable in its substance. However, the actions of many employees over a long period of time and the criteria used by management to determine promotions, salary increases and bonuses were greatly at variance with the values and guidelines espoused in their code of ethics. A good code of ethics that is widely disseminated among employees and is regularly referred to by managers can help to increase ethical perception. It is one thing to declare zero tolerance for sexual harassment; it is quite another thing to expose all managers, from supervisor on up, to training in this area, to have a clear policy that is made known to all employees, to have designated individuals to whom such complaints can be brought and to quickly and vigorously investigate any complaints that are filed.

Reaction to Crises

When Louis Gerstner became CEO of IBM in the early 1990s, the company was in a serious crisis, facing possible bankruptcy. Many executives within the company and analysts outside the company thought the only answer was to break up the company so that each piece of the former giant would be more nimble and competitively responsive. Gerstner went on his now-famous listening tour of customers and concluded that IBM had a unique advantage. It was the only company that could provide complete data processing services to large clients and, by breaking itself up, it would lose that advantage. He then proceeded to use the other leadership mechanisms, such as allocation of rewards and criteria for selecting and dismissing employees, to reshape the IBM culture.[19]

Executives at Enron both illustrated and reinforced the culture there by their reactions to the terminal crisis that preceded the company's bankruptcy. When evidence began to mount that Enron's financial results were not as strong as reported, Ken Lay, the CEO, told his employees that all was well and that they should be investing in the company's stock. At the same time, he was selling tens of millions of dollars of his own stock. Many of Enron's employees lost their entire retirement savings when Enron's stock became worthless in bankruptcy. Managers at Enron, in conjunction with managers of their accounting firm, Arthur Andersen, shredded a great many relevant documents as it became increasingly likely that government investigators would find evidence of wrong-doing. In contrast, executives at Dynegy, another Houston power company, considered buying Enron in the midst of its crisis, but after examining available information about the company's true financial status, rejected the purchase and saved their own company. There is a clear difference in the cultures of the two companies in terms of how they approached truthful information and facts.

The famous Tylenol poisoning case from the 1980s did a great deal to establish Johnson & Johnson as an ethical company in the minds of many people. Johnson & Johnson has long had a code of ethics that states that its first obligation is to those who use its products. When it became known that poisoned Tylenol had caused consumer deaths in Chicago, the company's top management decided to recall all Tylenol nationwide and to refund the purchase price to all claimants. This decision was made before it was known whether or not the poisoned Tylenol products had been tampered with locally in one store or somehow had resulted from a production problem on the part of Johnson & Johnson. It subsequently became known that the poisoning was the result of a single individual tampering with a few containers in one store. The recall was estimated to have cost the company $100 million. Nonetheless, the perception of the company and its actions was so favorable that, when Johnson & Johnson re-introduced Tylenol in tamper-proof containers, the product regained full acceptance in the marketplace.

Role Modeling

As noted above, Enron had an extensive code of ethics. On two occasions, the board of directors granted exceptions to this code of ethics so that Andrew Fastow, the chief financial officer, could serve in a management capacity for special purpose vehicles. These were semi-autonomous funds set up to remove certain weak assets and dubious liabilities from the company's books. Fastow made many millions of dollars from his role in managing these funds. At times, he made decisions that, by their nature, either benefited Enron and hurt the funds, or vice versa. Such conflicts were prohibited by the code of ethics, but allowed by the exemptions granted by the board of directors.

Hard work is generally expected of managers in organizations. Jimmy Cayne, who was CEO for many years of Bear Stearns, the large investment bank, was a championship-level bridge player. At least twice a year, he spent seven to ten days at bridge tournaments, largely out of touch with his company. He was also widely known to leave work on Thursday afternoons during the summer months and play golf late Thursday and again on Friday. He was also typically out of touch while on the golf course. Finally, it was reported in the *Wall Street Journal* that he was a regular marijuana user and once invited a woman attending a large meeting with him to join him in a men's room for marijuana use. On the day that Bear Stearns' board of directors voted to file for bankruptcy, Cayne was attending a bridge tournament and had to vote by phone.[20]

When Jack Welch was CEO of General Electric, he made it part of his routine to spend at least part of a day with each class of GE managers at their corporate training center. He also spent several days each quarter with his senior vice president for human resources, reviewing the performance and career progress of the top several hundred managers in the company. His actions were entirely consistent with the fact that GE has long had a reputation as one of the most effective companies in the United States at management development. When Welch retired, there were three internal candidates to replace him. Within three weeks of the announcement that Jeff Immelt was the next CEO, the other two candidates had both been hired as CEOs of major U.S. corporations.

Allocation of Rewards

Rewards in an organization certainly include monetary compensation, but can also include a range of other things, from titles to employee-of-the-month parking spaces. Salary is the most basic form of monetary reward. For upper-level managers, cash bonuses, stock options, deferred compensation, severance agreements and a variety of other forms of monetary rewards are also used. When these rewards are tied to performance, as is usually the case, they naturally tend to encourage the behaviors that are rewarded and discourage other behaviors. Of the thousands of academic articles that I have read in my career, perhaps my very favorite is called "On the folly of rewarding A while hoping for B."[21] The point of the article is contained in its title. Rewards are one powerful means of impacting a culture, but if they are to have their intended impact, they must be designed carefully.

Merrill Lynch was an investment bank with a long history of success advising individuals and investing their money. During 2008, the company suffered, as did many other investment and commercial banks. In September 2008, Merrill Lynch agreed to be purchased by Bank of America and at the end of the year ceased to exist as an independent entity. It was a sudden end for one of the long-time giants of Wall Street. Just before the end of 2008, the year that Merrill Lynch lost $27.6 billion and its independence, the company announced bonuses for the year. According to the *Wall Street Journal*, Andrea Orcel, the firm's top investment banker, was paid $33.8 million in cash and stock for 2008.

One individual's pay, however, is only a small part of the story. Eleven top executives were each paid more than $10 million in cash and stock, and 149 additional executives and traders received more than $3 million each for the year. Much of this compensation was in stock, and the value of the stock fell substantially after the payments were made.[22] While Merrill Lynch's 2008 payments are a particularly outstanding example of the allocation of rewards on Wall Street, they are typical of the culture of investment banks. In the crisis atmosphere of late 2008, such rewards did not go unnoticed. John Thain was CEO of Merrill Lynch when the bonuses were paid in late

2008, instead of early 2009, which would have been customary. At that point, Merrill Lynch was still independent since the purchase by Bank of America was not completed until year-end. Less than a month after the bonuses were announced, and the full extent of Merrill Lynch's 2008 loss was revealed, Thain was fired by Bank of America's CEO.

Goldman Sachs, the most successful investment bank, allocated 40 percent of revenues for salaries and bonuses in 2010. Some employees earn millions of dollars, some substantially less. However, the average pay (total compensation divided by number of employees) was over $400,000. Such compensation practices are fairly typical for investment banks. By contrast, the average president of a major university in the United States earns substantially less than $1 million a year in total compensation. Whatever one thinks about cross-industry comparisons, the use of rewards to encourage certain behaviors and discourage others can be an effective tool for shaping culture. It seems safe to say that many bright, young, aspiring executives desire to work for investment banks rather than universities because of the financial rewards.

Policies and procedures can be used to encourage either ethical or unethical behavior by individuals in organizations. Compensation systems help to determine what individual members of an organization will do and how they will do it. If financial advisers are compensated at a much higher rate for selling the company's mutual funds than other funds, then whether it is good for the clients or not, they are likely to sell the company's funds. If sales and service are both expected from the same employee, but the compensation system is based only on sales, it should not be a surprise that customers receive poor service from that employee. If bosses chastise and demean employees who bring them bad news, then employees will stop reporting bad news, even if the bosses need to hear it in order to deal with reality.

Criteria for Selection and Dismissal of Employees

As we saw in the chapter on ethics and the employment process, the awarding of a job to one applicant and denial of the job to others is a decision with ethical implications. In that chapter, we emphasized the careful definition of requirements for success in the job (minimum job qualifications) and the objective evaluation of applicants for their likelihood of success in the job. Leaders, whether CEOs or human resource vice presidents, who set up systems based on this approach to hiring and who then set up procedures to assure that the approach is followed are creating or reinforcing a culture that favors objectivity and fairness. Similarly, a company that follows the procedures described in the chapters on performance appraisal and terminations creates or reinforces a culture of objectivity and fairness.

Companies where selection and retention of employees depends more on whom you know than what you know embody a culture in which personal influence and favoritism are more important than performance. In such cultures, knowing the decision-maker can be more important than having the qualifications in obtaining a job or a promotion, and being well-connected can be more important than performing satisfactorily in one's job. It is also possible for loyalty to employees to assume such a key position in an organization's culture that failures in performance are not treated with the seriousness that they merit. A number of years ago in an Executive MBA class, a student who was an executive in a small community bank proudly proclaimed that a manager who had been caught embezzling funds was reassigned but kept on as an employee because the bank was loyal to its long-term employees. My reaction, which was typical of most students in the class, was that I would not want to deposit any funds for any purpose with a bank that followed such policies. The student in question was taken aback by this reaction, apparently because his peers at the bank thought as he did—their culture placed loyalty above honesty.

Whistle-blowers are individuals who attempt to change an organization's practice by reporting the problem issue to those outside their chain of command—typically to media representatives or to regulators. They are sometimes misguided or ill informed, but sometimes perform an important service by preventing injury or financial harm to others. Very often, whistle-blowers end up being terminated from their organization because their management superiors consider them disloyal. There are a number of legal statutes that protect whistle-blowers in specific situations, but their termination is still common. Such a reason for dismissal sends a strong signal and reinforces a culture that values loyalty even to harmful practices above organizational responsibility.[23]

We discussed layoffs in the chapter on terminations. This involves terminating employees not because of any performance-related issue but because the company cannot afford to keep all of its staff. The method by which those to be laid off are chosen both reflects and reinforces a company's culture. Although it is not a common practice, laying off employees based on performance sends a signal about doing one's job well. In this situation, the employees laid off have not performed badly enough to be terminated, but have performed less well relative to other satisfactory performers. Layoffs based on seniority (last hired, first fired) send a different signal about which values are important. While this is a common practice, and has the appearance of objectivity because dates of hire are not usually in dispute, the underlying message of this approach is that staying around for a long time is more important than performing well. When layoffs are determined by function, such as laying off all members of the training department, the message that is sent about that function's lack of importance is clear.

Policy-Making and Culture

At various points in this book, we have seen that many decisions of managers are at least partially constrained by company policies and rules. Hiring, promoting, evaluating, rewarding and terminating employees are all important parts of a manager's job. In each of these functions, medium and large companies typically have rules or procedures that all managers are required to observe. Minimum qualifications for jobs constrain hiring, maximum allowable salary increases constrain rewards, performance appraisal systems often require that an employee's work for an entire year be ultimately reduced to a single number for purposes of comparison with other employees and for determining raises and bonuses. If these policies and rules result in unethical decisions, it is the makers of the rules rather than the managers who implement them that bear the blame. If the policies and rules encourage fairness and the observance of employee rights, then the makers of the policies and rules have contributed to ethical decision-making on the part of the organization. While some of these issues have been treated in previous sections of this chapter, it seems good to focus specifically here on the policy-making function in considering the relation between ethical managers and ethical organizations.

Many times when policies and rules are being made or revised, the main concern is for efficiency or uniformity rather than for morality. However, the impact of policies and rules often entails consequences with ethical dimensions. Just as individual managers need to be aware of the ethical impacts of their decisions, those managers who design or approve policies and rules need to be aware of the ethical impacts of decisions shaped or mandated by these policies and rules. In the chapter defining ethics, we saw that awareness of ethical impacts is the first step to making ethical decisions. Similarly, if a company is to be ethical, its rules and policies must foster rather than impede ethical decisions by the managers applying these rules and policies. Whether managers, staff employees or consultants draft and design such rules and policies, it is ultimately the decision of one or more company managers to adopt them and to determine the scope of their application, as well as procedures for considering exemptions.

To take one example, Walmart has been rather widely chastised for its low pay and allegedly inadequate employee benefits.[24] Walmart was, in 2010, one of the largest private employers in the United States, with about 2.1 million employees worldwide, including 1.4 million in the United States. Its salary and benefit policies are set at corporate headquarters and enforced uniformly throughout its several thousand stores. If these policies are ethical, the few executives at headquarters who set them are to be praised. If, as some allege, they are unethical, then those same few executives are to be blamed. Individual store managers, who carry out these policies, do not have any real role in the process of policy-making but, to the extent that the policies are deemed ethical or unethical, the manager who sets the starting salary for a new employee or enforces the waiting period before an employee is eligible for health insurance may well be praised or blamed.

While it is difficult at best for an individual manager at Walmart to deviate from company policy on salary and benefits, there are other policies that are applied differently by different managers. Walmart (or any other company) can have an official policy of non-discrimination in hiring and promotion. Nevertheless, an individual manager can discriminate on the basis of gender or age and, as long as the discrimination is not too obvious, might get away with it for some time before anyone higher up in the organization notices. While this discrimination is going on, applicants for employment or promotion may suffer real harm from the unethical actions of this manager. Rules and policies are not always constraining of all actions by managers, and a company with ethical rules and policies may still act, through an individual manager, in an unethical way.

As we have said repeatedly, ethics is about values in action. One of the most basic human values is that of truth-telling. In an ethical organization, truth-telling will be the norm. Not only will the company's policies favor truth-telling, but the company's managers will be seen to be truthful. This value is embodied in many kinds of decisions and actions made within a company. We have discussed, in an earlier chapter, the importance of truth-telling in performance appraisals. A company might require annual performance appraisals for all employees. However, if the standard practice is for supervisors or managers to obtain employee signatures on the forms on the last day, and not to hold discussions between manager and employee, then the practice minimizes the value of truth-telling by bosses to subordinates. Similarly, a company might have an official policy of being truthful with customers, while at the same time using marketing practices that border on deceptive advertising. If truth-telling is an important value in dealing with others, then what employees actually do in this regard is the real test of whether the company is ethical.

Fairness is another basic ethical value. For a company to be fair, its basic operating policies must be fair, and most of the decisions made by individuals within the company must also be fair. Many critics of business, and many employees of businesses as well, find it unfair that a chief executive officer makes more in compensation in a day than an average worker makes in a year. Arguments have been put forth both for and against high executive compensation, but many people find this policy to be unfair. Whatever a company's official policies might be regarding promotions, if the practice is that friendship or family relations count more than merit in individual promotion choices, the company is acting in ways that do not support the value of fairness. If individual employees take advantage of customers in disputes over product returns or warranties, and nothing bad happens to these employees as a result, the company (through these employees and their tolerant bosses) is acting unfairly.

Sometimes an individual action is so symbolic that it can have a dispro-portionate impact in establishing a company's reputation as ethical or unethical. Sears Roebuck, a trusted retailer for generations, added limited auto service shops to many of its stores in the 1980s. Some time afterward, Sears management decided to increase the sales of parts and services in these stores by compensating the staff on a commission basis. When this practice, and the predictable over-selling of some unneeded parts and services, came to light in state consumer agency investigations and in press reports, Sears' reputation for trustworthiness suffered a serious blow. This was true in spite of the fact that auto repair was only a small part of Sears' total business.

While it is true that a company's reputation for ethical or unethical behavior can sometimes be strongly affected by a single incident or decision, it is more often the case that a company's reputation is built up from a pattern of decisions and actions on the part of many employees and managers who work for that company. In business strategy, it is widely recognized that a company's positive reputation can be a valuable asset in dealings with present and potential employees, with customers, suppliers, investors and other stakeholders. In addition to the reasons given in the first part of this book for the importance of behaving ethically, there are also important busi-ness reasons for doing so.

The two major components of an ethical company are ethical rules, pol-icies and procedures that determine the parameters within which individual employees, particularly managers, may act in making decisions, and ethical employees. As we have seen, a company can have ethical official policies (for example, Enron's sixty-four page code of ethics) and still be an unethical company. A limited number of managers make the rules, at least in medium and large companies. However, all managers make decisions within the context of the rules and the total pattern created by the decisions of man-agers throughout the company is a key factor in determining whether a company is ethical. It is possible to have rules and policies, at least unoffi-cially, that encourage unethical actions. Such was the case at Enron, and to some degree at some of the other companies where famous scandals occurred. Most companies, though, will have rules and policies that mandate or at least facilitate ethical decisions by managers.

In ethical companies, managers, from supervisors through senior execu-tives, will consistently make ethical decisions. This means that managers at all levels will recognize decisions that have an ethical component and try to act ethically in making these decisions. Policies that guide or determine individual decisions will embody values that are ethical rather than unethi-cal. Moreover, these policies will be enforced, with those who follow them in their decisions praised and rewarded and those who ignore or act counter to ethical policies admonished or punished. By a variety of means, ethical companies call the attention of their employees to the importance of ethical behavior on a regular basis.

Ethics programs, whatever form they take, must be multi-faceted to be effective.[25] Some writers have distinguished between coercive and value-centered programs. What our discussion has suggested is that both elements will be present in organizations with strong ethical cultures. Values that are especially important to the organization will be clear and clearly and regularly communicated by a variety of means. Enforcement of these values will sometimes involve an element of coercion, in that clearly unethical behavior will not be tolerated and will sometimes result in negative consequences up to and including termination. Such actions can be labeled coercive, but they can also be seen as symbolic. If a company truly stands for some values and against others, the enforcement of this position will sometimes result in negative results for some individuals. While this is not the only or the principal means of impacting a company's culture with respect to ethics, it is one part of the total effort.

The title of this chapter is "Ethical Managers and Ethical Organizations." We have seen from our discussion that culture is a concept which helps to understand what it means to say that a company is ethical. We have also seen that the relation between an ethical manager and an ethical company runs both ways. It is easier to be an ethical manager in a company whose culture embodies, encourages and enforces ethical values. At the same time, a company's culture is impacted by its managers, particularly its senior managers. These are the policy-makers who design and enforce or fail to enforce policies that direct and constrain the behavior of all managers in the company. However, every manager, from supervisor to CEO, has an impact on the way that such policies are carried out through the many decisions that each manager makes. It is difficult to be an ethical manager in an unethical company; it is more difficult to be an ethical company without ethical managers.

Notes

1 Introduction

1 Perhaps the most lucid thinker and writer about management is the late Peter Drucker. A review of his theories and their impact can be found in Zahra, S. (2003). The practice of management: Reflections on Peter F. Drucker's landmark book. *Academy of Management Executive*, 17:3, 16–22. Drucker wrote thirty-four books, which have been translated into more than twenty languages. One of his earliest books, *The practice of management* (New York: Harper & Row, 1954) is still regarded as a classic worth reading by contemporary managers. For a more current view of the same basic subject, readers might consider Joan Magretta's book *What management is* (New York: Free Press, 2002).

2 For a well-researched and readable history of organizations and management, see Chandler A., Jr. (1977). *The visible hand: The managerial revolution in American business*. Cambridge MA: The Belknap Press of Harvard University Press, and Micklethwait, J. and Wooldridge, A. (1993). *The company: A short history of a revolutionary idea*. New York: Modern Library.

3 Some authors distinguish between the terms "ethical" and "moral" in various ways. Others use them interchangeably. I have chosen the latter course because I cannot discern a clear and explainable difference in their meanings.

4 Many writers distinguish between normative and descriptive ethics. Normative ethics has as its goal a list of moral dos and don'ts. Descriptive ethics aims to describe accurately the kinds of moral judgments that people actually make and the moral principles underlying these judgments. For a thorough discussion of different views concerning the teaching of both normative and descriptive ethics, see Sims, R. (2002). *Teaching business ethics for effective learning*. Westport CN: Quorum Books.

5 Professionals of various types, including consultants, attorneys, accountants and others who deal with managers, even though they are not managers themselves, might benefit from this book.

6 The issue of the morality of layoffs is taken up at some length in Chapter 9.

7 There are many books on business ethics in general, some of them quite good and

well worth the time and attention of readers interested in a broader range of topics than this book presents. Among these are Donaldson, T., Werhane, P. and Cording, M. (2007). *Ethical issues in business: A philosophical approach*, 8th edition. Upper Saddle River NJ: Prentice Hall; Velasquez, M. (2006). *Business ethics, concepts and cases*. Upper Saddle River NJ: Prentice Hall; and Beauchamp, T. and Bowie, N. (eds.). (2008). *Ethical theory and business*, 8th edition. Upper Saddle River NJ: Prentice Hall.

8 See, for example, Farrell, G. (2010). *Crash of the titans*. New York: Crown Business; Cohan, W. (2009). *House of cards*. New York: Doubleday; Hudson, M. (2010). *The monster*. New York: Times Books.

9 It has been my experience in teaching MBA students that those from professions such as accounting, engineering and programming are more troubled by the ambiguity often present in ethical analysis than those whose background is in other disciplines.

2 What is Philosophy?

1 It is a fascinating fact of history that Plato and Aristotle, generally recognized as "two of the greatest philosophers the world has seen" (Copleston, F. (1993). *A history of philosophy: Volume 1*. New York: Doubleday, p. 372) were respectively teacher and pupil. Plato founded his famous school, known as The Academy, in Athens in 388 B.C. Aristotle became his student at the Academy in 367 at the age of seventeen and remained there until Plato's death in 348 B.C.

2 Philosophers recognize Saint Thomas Aquinas as the greatest philosopher of the Middle Ages (roughly A.D. 500 to A.D. 1450). He is also recognized as one of the greatest theologians of the Catholic church. In his writings, he wrestled (not always successfully) with the distinction between philosophy and religion. Aristotle's work was lost to Western civilization for hundreds of years, but was preserved by Arab philosophers. For an account of Aquinas's role in re-introducing Aristotle to Western thought, see Rubinstein, R. (2003). *Aristotle's children*. Orlando FL: Harcourt.

3 John Rawls, one of the most important philosophers of the twentieth century, deals with this issue at some length. His work is discussed in Chapter 6, on Fairness and Justice. Rawls states that one of the assumptions of his discussion of justice in national systems is that the people living in the sort of country he considers have different sources for their sense of values. Some of these sources are religious, but different people derive different values from their different religions. Other people in the sort of country he describes do not have any religion, and so do not derive their sense of values from this source. Somehow, he says, the basic laws and institutions must be agreed upon by all of these people, with their diverse sources of values. (Rawls, J. (2001). *Justice as fairness: A restatement*. Cambridge MA: The Belknap Press of Harvard University Press.) His discussion illustrates well the difference between religious sources of values and philosophical sources.

4 This issue is also true, to a large extent, of philosophy. Many of the great philosophers wrote their works before the first large business organizations arose in eighteenth-century England. Many of the major philosophers, including both Plato and Aristotle, thought and wrote extensively about the purposes and organization of government, but not about business organizations.

5 Behavioral economics is a relatively recent approach to micro-economics which

tries to account for behavior that seems to contradict theories of utility maximization. This approach studies, through experiments, how people actually make choices in various settings and provides explanations that fit the facts revealed by these experiments. A quite readable presentation of behavioral economics is Dan Ariely's book *Predictably irrational, Revised and expanded edition* (New York: HarperCollins, 2009). A more recent review and discussion of the many studies that underlie this approach by a Nobel prize-winning psychologist can be found in Kahneman, D. (2011). *Thinking, fast and slow*. New York: Farrar, Straus and Giroux.

6 In accounting terms, there is a very real difference. If my company sells you a car for $20,000, it records that amount as revenue, even though it promptly mails you a rebate check for $2,000. If, on the other hand, my company sells you the car for $18,000, it records only that amount as revenue. In other words, we can sell the same number of cars for the same amount of money but increase our revenue by 10 percent (or more) simply by sending automatic rebates. Note that this is not true when mail-in rebates or other coupons are used because many customers do not take the necessary step to actually receive the rebate.

7 The Hawthorne experiments were begun in 1924 at the Hawthorne plant of Western Electric. As lighting conditions in an assembly room were first increased and then decreased, researchers were puzzled to find that productivity went up in both cases. Further experiments of various types followed. As researchers pondered the data they had gathered, they came to realize that social interactions as well as physical conditions have to be taken into account in order to explain the performance of workers, even in routine tasks. A discussion of the experiments and their results by one of the social scientists involved in the study, Fritz Roethlisberger, can be found in Shafritz, J. and Ott, J. (2001). *Classics of organization theory*, 5th edition. Orlando FL: Harcourt, pp. 158–166.

8 Readers interested in a more extensive discussion of the major branches of philosophy would do well to read sections of Volume 1 of Frederick Copleston's *History of philosophy* (New York: Doubleday, 1993). In this volume, Copleston provides discussions of both Plato's and Aristotle's views of the major divisions or branches of philosophy. His style is such that those without a background in philosophy can follow his discussion. In the 1993 paperback edition, the relevant sections on Plato are Chapter 19 (pp. 142–162) and Chapters 21–25 (pp. 207–262). Chapter 20 on The Doctrine of Forms is apt to prove too advanced for those without some background in philosophy. On Aristotle, see Chapters 29–33 (pp. 287–371). Also of interest is Chapter 34 (pp. 374–378), containing a comparison of Plato's and Aristotle's views.

9 One of the central issues in political philosophy relates to how much liberty individuals in a society can or should have, and what constraints society, through government and its agencies, should impose. As discussed in the next section of the chapter, ethics concerns itself with interpersonal values. It is not hard to see why Plato and Aristotle both saw political philosophy as an extension of ethics. It is a bit harder to see why this connection tends to be missed by more recent philosophers. Given the degree to which laws and regulations made by government both help and restrain business managers, as we will see throughout this book, the connection between political philosophy and ethics is important for our topic.

10 Isaiah Berlin said that:

Ethical thought consists of the systematic examination of the relations of human beings to each other, the conceptions, interests and ideals from which human ways of treating one another spring, and the systems of values on which such ends of life are based.

(Berlin, I. (2001). The pursuit of the ideal, in Hardy, H. and Hausher, R. (eds.), *The proper study of mankind: An anthology of essays.* New York: Farrar, Strauss and Giroux, p. 1)

11 Recent scientific advances in the study of genetics and of the structure and functioning of the brain have led some people to take a fresh look at issues of human freedom and determinism. For those interested in these issues, two books by well-respected scientists provide reasonably up-to-date information on what scientists now know and agree on in these areas and what topics remain to be explored. The books are: Wilson, E.O. (1998). *Consilience: The unity of knowledge.* New York: Alfred Knopf; and Pinker, S. (2002). *The blank slate.* New York: Penguin Books. As is often the case with such books by scientists, some basic issues, such as the degree to which humans are truly free to choose, receive much less attention than the factual issues that are the everyday concern of science. For instance, both books discuss at some length the influence of genes on human behavior and the way the brain processes signals from the outside world and forms memories. Neither book, in my opinion, gives a really satisfactory treatment of free choice by humans. However, these and similar books are worth reading because scientists have established many facts beyond reasonable doubt that uninformed people misjudge and, because of their misjudgments, make choices harmful to themselves and others.

12 Much has been written in recent years on the topic of CEO compensation. Many of the articles on this subject either assume or declare that CEO compensation is too high relative to that of other employees. At large U.S. corporations, the compensation committee of the board of directors recommends CEO compensation and typically the full board approves what this committee recommends. A small number of consulting firms provide information and recommendations to the compensation committees of many companies. Thus, the consultants at these firms have an important role in determining compensation at the CEO level, and their concern or lack of concern for fairness impacts American business. For an interesting commentary on charismatic CEOs and their compensation, see Khurana, R. (2002). *Searching for a corporate savior: The irrational quest for charismatic CEOs.* Princeton NJ: Princeton University Press.

3 What is Ethics?

1

If ... I tell you that to let no day pass without discussing goodness and all the other subjects about which you hear me talking and examining both myself and others is really the very best thing that a man can do, and that life without this sort of examination is not worth living, you will be even less inclined to believe me.

(Plato, The apology, in Hamilton, E. and Cairns, H. (eds.) (1963). *Plato: The collected dialogues.* New York: Pantheon Books, p. 23)

2 Aristotle's answer to this question, which provides a good example of his approach in understandable language, comprises Book I of the *Nicomachean ethics.* This work is currently available in a number of versions; the one I have used is

Aristotle, *The Nicomachean ethics* (translated by H. Rackham) (1990). Cambridge MA: Harvard University Press.

3 There is an approach to ethics known as egoism which maintains that the moral act is the one that satisfies my own individual desires. Even this approach, though, becomes somewhat complicated because it must deal with instrumental goals as well as direct goals. For instance, I choose to pay money and allocate time and energy to obtain an MBA because accomplishing this personally costly goal will help me attain something that I want badly enough to sacrifice for it. For a good basic description of egoism and challenges made to it, see Sober, E. (2000). Psychological egoism, in LaFollette, H. (ed.), *The Blackwell guide to ethical theory*. Malden MA: Blackwell Publishers, pp. 129–148.

4 As noted in the first chapter, the words "ethical" and "moral" are used interchangeably in this book.

5 For discussions of virtue ethics, see McGuire, S. (1997). Business ethics: A compromise between politics and virtue. *Journal of Business Ethics*, 16, 1411–1418 and McIntyre, A. (1981). *After virtue*. Notre Dame IN: University of Notre Dame Press.

6 Weaver, G. & Trevino, L. (1994). Normative and empirical business ethics. *Business Ethics Quarterly*, 4, 129–144.

7 Wilson, J.Q. (1993). *The moral sense*. New York: The Free Press.

8 Pinker, S. (2002). *The blank slate: The modern denial of human nature*. New York: Penguin Books.

9 Brooks, D. (2011). *The social animal: The hidden sources of love, character and achievement*. New York: Random House.

10 Hauser, M. (2006). *Moral minds: The nature of right and wrong*. New York: HarperCollins.

11 The ideas of moral development, or the influence of people and experiences on an individual's sense of ethics, and of early roots of adult traits have been explored widely. Wilson, in his previously cited book, *The moral sense*, considers these ideas at length. Among classic works on these subjects are Kohlberg, L. (1981). *The philosophy of moral development*. San Francisco: Harper & Row and Rest, J. (1986). *Moral development: Advances in research and theory*. New York: Praeger. Biographers have also had perceptive things to say about the development of an ethical or moral sense in individuals. Robert Caro, in the first volume of his extraordinary biography of Lyndon Johnson, has this to say about Johnson's drive for power:

> ...the more one learns—from his family, his childhood playmates, his college classmates, his first assistants, his congressional colleagues—about Lyndon Johnson, the more it becomes apparent not only that this hunger was a constant throughout his life but that it was a hunger so fierce and consuming that no consideration of morality or ethics, no cost to himself—or to anyone else—could stand before it.
>
> (Caro, R. (1982). *The path to power*. New York: Knopf, p. xix)

12 As Caro discusses extensively in his previously cited biography of Lyndon Johnson, the failures of Lyndon's father late in his life seem to have resulted in a strong drive on the part of the son to control the kind of circumstances that so hurt his father. Children (and adults) are sometimes strongly motivated to be unlike their parents.

13 McLean, B. and Elkind, P. (2003). *The smartest guys in the room: The amazing rise*

and scandalous fall of Enron. New York: Penguin Group, and Swartz, M. with Watkins, S. (2003). *Power failure: The inside story of the collapse of Enron.* New York: Doubleday.

14 Halberstam, D. (2001/1969). *The best and the brightest.* New York: Modern Library.

15 See, for example, Bookstaber, R. (2007). *A demon of our own design: Markets, hedge funds, and the perils of financial innovation.* Hoboken, NJ: John Wiley & Sons; Hudson, M. (2010). *The monster.* New York: Times Books; Kelly, K. (2009). *Street fighters.* New York: Penguin Group; Muolo, P. and Padilla, M. (2008). *Chain of blame.* Hoboken, NJ: John Wiley & Sons.

16 Attorneys wishing to be admitted to the bar in any state in the United States must pass a professional responsibility exam, and accountants wishing to become Certified Public Accountants must pass an ethics component of the CPA exam in order to attain the designation.

17 Piper, T., Gentile, M. and Parks, S. (1993). *Can ethics be taught?: Perspectives, challenges, and approaches at the Harvard Business School.* Cambridge MA: Harvard Business School Press.

18 Schein, E. (1992). *Organizational culture and leadership,* 2nd edition. San Francisco: Jossey Bass.

19 Enron, by all accounts, had a dysfunctional culture in its last years before bankruptcy. The books cited in note 13 above and other sources identify numerous instances of unethical behavior either practiced by or approved by senior management. Yet this company had a sixty-four-page Code of Ethics, which prescribed exemplary behavior in both general and particular terms. The culture (largely unspoken but widely recognized) seemed to prevail over the written word.

20 The Boston Red Sox were the last major league baseball team to hire a black player. Their recalcitrance in this area was not only morally repugnant (although accepted by the team's owner and executives at the time); it also probably cost them success on the field and in pennant races. See Finkelstein, S. (2003). *Why smart executives fail.* New York: Penguin Group, especially pp. 119–125.

21 For a thought-provoking treatment of this subject, see Donaldson, T. (1992). *The ethics of international business.* New York: Oxford University Press.

22 For an informed and thoughtful perspective on the major world religions and their views on morality, see Smith, H. (1991/1958). *The world's religions.* New York: HarperCollins. Some of the most striking moral views in the history of religion have come from so-called fundamentalists. For an informed perspective on this element of religion, see Armstrong, K. (2000). *The battle for God: A history of fundamentalism.* New York: Ballentine Books.

23 For a series of essays by one of the twentieth century's foremost students of culture, and the author of a number of influential books on this subject, see Geertz, C. (2001). *Available light: Anthropological reflections on philosophical topics.* Princeton NJ: Princeton University Press.

24 There is a continuing, lively debate among those who study the law as to just what it is. To vastly over-summarize, one group maintains that the law is the sum total of statutes passed by legislators and the accumulation of judicial decisions interpreting those statutes. Another group maintains that the law, in a given case, is whatever the judge involved says it is. For a discussion of this issue by a widely cited author who is himself a judge and clearly espouses one point of view, see Posner, R. (1990). *The problems of jurisprudence.* Cambridge MA:

Harvard University Press. For a quite different viewpoint, see Dworkin, R. (1986). *Law's empire*. Cambridge MA: The Belknap Press of Harvard University Press.

25 I.F. Stone notes that:

> Homer gives us a rudimentary lesson in sociology and political science. He shows us what in his own time were already considered the hallmarks of civilization. Odysseus fears that he will meet a creature of great strength, "a savage man who knows nothing of justice or of law", the primary elements that characterize a civilized man.
>
> (Stone, I.F. (1988). *The trial of Socrates*. Boston: Little, Brown & Co., p. 24)

The Odyssey, to which Stone refers, was written more than 2,700 years ago.

26 Article 1, the longest article in the United States Constitution, describes legislative powers of the federal government and of local governments.

27 There are many examples in literature of the tension that can exist when law and morality do not coincide. In the classic Greek tragedy *Antigone*, the playwright Sophocles has Creon, the king, decree that the body of one of two brothers killed in battle shall be left unburied. Antigone, the sister of the two slain brothers, defies the king's decree (law) and suffers consequences that also bring ruin to the king. In Shakespeare's *Merchant of Venice*, Shylock forms a legally binding contract specifying that he will be awarded a pound of flesh from his debtor if the debtor defaults on a loan from Shylock. Much of the play is taken up with vivid discussion of the legality and morality of this arrangement and Shylock's insistence on collecting his legal due. Martin Luther King's "Letter from Birmingham Jail" is an eloquent and learned discussion of the moral obligation to violate segregationist laws.

28 For a thoughtful, extended discussion of the relationship between law and ethics, see Lyons, D. (1984). *Ethics and the rule of law*. Cambridge UK: Cambridge University Press.

29 How the executive makes that money is a different question. Andrew Fastow, the former chief financial officer of Enron, agreed to plead guilty to several criminal charges. As part of his punishment, he agreed to pay back almost $30 million in money that he made as a result of his illegal activities (as well as serving ten years in prison). This is a legal settlement, but moral sentiment does not seem to condone his keeping money that he made illegally. Interestingly enough, various reports have placed his total gains from illegal transactions at amounts from $40 million to $60 million.

30 See Carson, T., Wokutch, R. and Cox, J. (1985). An ethical analysis of deception in advertising. *Journal of Business Ethics*, 4, 93–104.

31 Perhaps the most thoughtful, accessible work on this topic is Martin Luther King's "Letter from Birmingham Jail". Written while King was being held in jail by the racist sheriff of Birmingham, Alabama during Civil Rights demonstrations in 1963, King cites (from memory, since he had no reference material available to him in jail) sources as varied as Thomas Aquinas and Thomas Jefferson in his discussion. He argues that it is incumbent on thoughtful people (his letter addresses fellow ministers who objected to his tactics of protest and wanted him to go slowly in advocating integration) to consider whether some laws are moral and to take action if they are not.

32 In a letter from the publisher to readers, Karen House, the publisher of the *Wall*

Street Journal, spelled out very clearly the paper's dual goals of objective reporting in the news sections and strong, clear advocacy in the editorial pages. In her words, "While our news pages are committed to informing our readers, our editorial pages are dedicated to advocating a consistent philosophy and positions that emanate from it." *Wall Street Journal*, January 8, 2004, p. A23.

33 Sun Tzu (1971). *The art of war* (Griffith, S., translator). New York: Oxford Press.

34 Welch, J. with Byrne, J. (2001). *Jack: Straight from the gut*. New York: Warner Books.

35 Machiavelli, N. (1992). *The prince*. New York: Knopf.

36 Friedman, M. (1970). The social responsibility of business is to increase its profits. *New York Times Magazine*, September 13. Reprinted in Donaldson, T., Werhane, P. and Cording, M. (2002). *Ethical issues in business: A philosophical approach*, 7th edition. Upper Saddle River NJ: Prentice Hall, pp. 33–38.

37 Freeman, R.E. (2002). Stakeholder theory of the modern corporation, in Donaldson, T., Werhane, P. and Cording, M. (eds.), *Ethical issues in business: A philosophical approach*, 7th edition. Upper Saddle River NJ: Prentice Hall, p. 42.

38 Ibid.

39 In his biography of Steve Jobs, Walter Isaacson makes it clear that Jobs was a highly motivated manager—one might say driven—long after his financial situation was such that he did not need to work at all. See Isaacson, W. (2011). *Steve Jobs*. New York: Simon & Schuster.

40 Cohen, W.D. (2009). *House of cards*. New York: Doubleday, p. 60.

41 Aristotle (1990/1926). *The Nicomachean ethics* (Rackham, H., translator). Cambridge MA: Harvard University Press.

4 Utilitarianism

1 Both Plato and Aristotle, two of the earliest and most influential philosophers in Western history, wrote extensively about ethics. Many of Plato's dialogues have ethics as either their main theme or as a major subject. *The Republic*, a long dialogue in which Plato suggested that we can best understand justice for individuals by examining it "writ large" in the state, is still widely read and cited in college courses and in writings on ethics. Aristotle's *Nicomachean ethics*, his major work on this topic, is also widely read and cited.

2 Aristotle (1990/1926). *The Nicomachean ethics* (Rackham, H., translator), Cambridge MA: Harvard University Press. It should be noted that Aristotle's basic approach to ethics was not utilitarian. He espoused an approach since known as virtue ethics.

3 "Happiness, therefore, being found to be something final and self-sufficient, is the End at which all actions aim." Op. cit., p. 31.

4 In his translation of *The Nicomachean ethics*, Rackham notes in a footnote that:

> This translation [happiness] of eudaimonia can hardly be avoided, but it would perhaps be more accurately rendered by "Well-being" or "Prosperity"; and it will be found that the writer does not interpret it as a state of feeling but as a kind of activity.
>
> (op. cit., p. 10, footnote a)

5 Bentham, J. (1996/1789). *An introduction to the principles of morals and legislation*. New York: Oxford University Press.

6 Mill, J.S. and Bentham, J. (1987). *Utilitarianism and other essays*. New York: Penguin Books, p. 65.

7 Ibid., p. 65. While this statement refers to "the party in question," it is clear throughout Bentham's writings that he is concerned not just with an individual's happiness or good, but with that of the greatest number.

8 Ibid., p. 278.

9 This may seem like a rather childish approach for a manager to take. Nonetheless, one is struck in reading about the various companies that went bankrupt because of managerial irresponsibility (including numerous criminal acts) in the early years of the twenty-first century how many managers simply refused to face consequences. Parmalat, the Italian dairy company, falsified a bank account said to contain just under $5 billion in company assets. Managers simply made up the account. How they could think there would be no consequences is hard to fathom, but apparently they simply did not consider consequences. Enron managers constructed such a convoluted tangle of special purpose entities and internal accounting transfers that it appears even the company's top management did not know the full extent of its debt at the time it fell. HealthSouth's top managers met every quarter to decide what accounts to falsify and in what amounts in order to report the earnings expected by financial analysts. The consequences of such repeated lies did not deter them from continuing such practices. Many a manager in real life has refused to face the waves. Bad things often followed.

10 For a more detailed analysis of this issue, see Gilbert, J. (2000). Sorrow and guilt: An ethical analysis of layoffs. *SAM Advanced Management Journal*, 65:2, 4–13.

11 An excellent, book-length treatment in plain English of how such decisions actually work in large companies is Bower, J. (1986). *Managing the resource allocation process: A study of corporate planning and investment*, revised edition. Cambridge MA: Harvard Business School Press.

12 Mill & Bentham, op. cit., pp. 86–98.

13 Mill & Bentham, op. cit., pp. 279–282.

14 Amartya Sen discusses the importance of recognizing ethical intuitions as well as using reason and objectivity in his book *The idea of justice* (Cambridge MA: Belknap Press of Harvard University Press, 2009, Chapter 1).

15 See Frey, E. Act-utilitarianism (pp. 165–182) and Hooker, B. Rule-consequentialism (pp. 183–204), both in LaFollette, H. (ed.). (2000). *The Blackwell Guide to Ethical Theory*. Malden MA: Blackwell.

16 Mill, J.S. (1974/1859). *On Liberty*. London: Penguin Books.

17 Many philosophers, beginning with Plato and Aristotle, have taken the view that political theory is simply ethics writ large. They have seen, as did Mill, the issue of law as being very much intertwined with the issue of individual behavior and morality. In this sense, Mill is in line with the history of philosophy on the relation of ethical and legal issues. Mill also discusses why it is necessary to have a law prohibiting murder, even if the victim causes more harm than good to the world. Mill, J.S. Dr. Whewell on moral philosophy, in Schneewind, J.B. (ed.). (1965). *Mill's ethical writings*. New York: Macmillan, p. 189.

18 Freeman, R.E. (1984). *Strategic management: A stakeholder approach*. Englewood Cliffs NJ: Prentice-Hall. See also Donaldson, T. & Preston, L. (1995). The stakeholder theory of the corporation: Concepts, evidence, implications. *Academy of Management Review*, 20, 65–91.

19 Management by Objectives has been considered by some to be a passing fad. For an interesting perspective on whether this is true, on management fads in general and on the ways that Management by Objectives continues to be operative in current

management practice, see Gibson, J. and Tesone, D. (2001). Management fads: Emergence, evolution, and implications for managers. *Academy of Management Executive*, 15:4, 122–133.

5 Rights and Duties

1 Berlin, I. (1997/1958). Two concepts of liberty, in Hardy, H. and Hausheer, R. (eds.), *The proper study of mankind: An anthology of essays*. New York: Farrar, Straus and Giroux, p. 194.
2 For a book-length treatment of this approach, see Thomson, J. (1990). *The realm of rights*. Cambridge MA: Harvard University Press.
3 Gutmann, A. (ed.). (2001). *Human rights as politics and idolatry*. Princeton NJ: Princeton University Press.
4 Declaration of Independence. http://earlyamerica.com/earlyamerica/freedom/doi/text.html.
5 http://showcase.netins.net/web/creative/lincoln/speeches/gettysburg.htm.
6 www.usconstitution.net/dream.html.
7 For a good introduction to the major issues of natural law ethics, see Murphy, M., The natural law tradition in ethics, *The Stanford Encyclopedia of Philosophy (Winter 2011 Edition)*, Zalta, E.N. (ed.). http://plato.stanford.edu/archives/win2011/entries/natural-law-ethics.
8 For a very brief view of the ethical issues in the capital punishment debate, see *The internet encyclopedia of philosophy: Capital punishment*. www.iep.utm.edu/punishme/#H5. For more extended views, see Acker, J., Bohm, R. and Lanier, C. (eds.). (2003). *America's experiment with capital punishment: Reflections on the past, present and future of the ultimate penal sanction*, 2nd edition. Durham NC: Carolina Academic Press.
9 As noted in Chapter 1, two good sources for the views of major world religions are Smith, H. (1991). *The world's religions: Our great wisdom traditions*. New York: HarperCollins; and Armstrong, K. (2000). *The battle for God: A history of fundamentalism*. New York: Ballentine Books.
10 For an informed discussion about the pervasiveness of some ethical judgments in wonderfully plain English, see Wilson, J.Q. (1993). *The moral sense*. New York: The Free Press.
11 Appiah, K. (2001). Grounding human rights, in Guttman, A. (ed.), *Human rights as politics and idolatry*. Princeton NJ: Princeton University Press, p. 106.
12 Several authors in the book cited in the previous note, including Amy Gutman and Michael Ignatieff, cite this plurality of arguments as a strength in support of human rights, rather than a problem of theory that must be resolved.
13 An excellent analysis, with practical examples, is Bok, S. (1999). *Lying: Moral choice in public and private life*, 2nd edition. New York: Vintage. For a quite different view of truth and lying, somewhat more dense but definitely thought-provoking, see Campbell, J. (2001). *The liar's tale: A history of falsehood*. New York: W.W. Norton & Co.
14 Two good starting points for understanding philosophical views on liberty are Berlin, I. (1997/1958). Two concepts of liberty, in Hardy, H. and Hausheer, R. (eds.), *Isaiah Berlin: The proper study of mankind*. New York: Farrar, Straus and Giroux; and Mill, J.S. (1974/1859). *On liberty*. London: Penguin Books.
15 Hobbes, T. (1985/1651). *Leviathan* (edited with an Introduction by MacPherson, C.B.). London: Penguin Books.

16 Marx, K. (1875). *Critique of the Gotha program*. www.marxists.org/archive/marx/works/1875/gotha.

17 Critics of business sometimes maintain that workers in poor countries are held in what amounts to slavery because they are required to work very long hours for low pay and sometimes live in company-provided housing and eat at company cafeterias. The issue is complex and much of what is written about it has a heavy overlay of rhetoric that makes fact-based evaluation difficult. Since most managers will not directly confront this issue in their working lives, I have chosen to leave its analysis to books with more general coverage of business ethics.

18 What we are calling legal rights are not the same as contract rights, yet both are enforceable under legal systems. All citizens are the beneficiaries of legal rights (subject to some exceptions, such as age limits for voting) but only those who form legally binding contracts are the beneficiaries of contract rights. For this reason, we use more precise terminology and identify two explicitly different classes of rights that are legally enforceable.

19 Article I of the United States Constitution deals with legislative (law-making) powers. It is the longest and most detailed of the seven articles that make up the Constitution.

20 One of the most famous works of political theory is Aristotle's *Politics* (Oxford: Oxford University Press, 1995). In this work, Aristotle surveyed the existing kinds of government of his time and comments on the relative advantages and disadvantages of each. It is interesting that Aristotle was deeply opposed to pure democracy (all citizens vote directly and are equally eligible for service in various government positions without regard to special skill or expertise). We must remember that it was by a vote of what we would call an Athenian jury of his peers that Socrates, whose life and teachings are central to the Dialogues of Socrates' teacher and mentor, Plato, was put to death for his teachings. Aristotle argued that there is no one form of government that is best for all groups, but that the make-up of a state and its needs influence the choice of ideal government form.

21 See Sayre-McCord, G. (2000). Contractarianism, in LaFollette, H. (ed.), *The Blackwell guide to ethical theory*. Malden MA: Blackwell, pp. 247–267. In Chapter 6, we will discuss the political philosophy of John Rawls, perhaps the most important political philosopher of the twentieth century. Rawls also is squarely in the tradition of social contract theory, although his version of this theory differs somewhat from those of other philosophers cited here. His most influential book is *A theory of justice* (Cambridge MA: Harvard University Press, 1971).

22 Locke, J. (2002/1960). *Two treatises of government* (edited with an Introduction by Laslett, P.). Cambridge, UK: Cambridge University Press.

23 Very generally, there have only been a few answers given through history to the question of where government gets the right to do what it does. Some have said that this right comes from God (the Divine right of kings); some from heredity (the next heir in line from the royal family); some from military power; and some from the people governed.

24 With the passage of the Sarbanes–Oxley Act in 2002, certain executives in the United States have legal duties that are position duties. The certification of a company's annual financial statements, for example, is a legal duty under this act for the chief executive officer and chief financial officer of major, publicly traded companies.

25 Barnett, R. (2008). *Contracts: Cases in context*. New York: Aspen Law and

Business is a typical textbook for the introductory contract law course taught in law schools. The book is 1,408 pages long.

26 Kant, I. (1999/1781). *Critique of pure reason* (Guyer, P. and Wood, A., eds.). Cambridge, UK: Cambridge University Press.

27 Kant, I. (1996/1788). *Critique of practical reason* (Abbott, T.K., translator). Amherst NY: Prometheus Books.

28 Kant, I. (1993/1785). *Groundwork of the metaphysic of morals*, 3rd edition (Ellington, J., translator). Indianapolis IN: Hackett Publishing.

29 Ibid., p. 30.

30 Ibid., p. 36.

31 Ibid., p. 43.s

6 Fairness and Justice

1 DeGeorge, R. (1995). *Business ethics*, 4th edition. Englewood Cliffs, NJ: Prentice Hall, p. 105.

2 This is not a new idea. Adam Smith, often called the father of economics, writing in 1776, has this to say:

> …man has almost constant occasion for the help of his brethren, and it is vain for him to expect it from their benevolence only. He will be more likely to prevail if he can interest their self-love in his favor, and show them that it is for their own advantage to do for him what he requires of them.
>
> (Smith, A. (1994/1776). *The wealth of nations*. New York: Random House, p. 15)

3 There is a whole discipline known as organization theory. For an excellent collection of articles, both classic and contemporary, on the workings and impact of organizations, see Shafritz, J., Ott, J. and Jang, Y.S. (2010). *Classics of organization theory*, 7th edition. Orlando FL: Harcourt.

4 Sen, A. (2009). *The idea of justice*. Cambridge MA: The Belknap Press of Harvard University Press, pp. 12–13.

5 *Webster's new twentieth century dictionary of the English language, unabridged*, 2nd edition. (1983). New York: Prentice Hall.

6 An interesting view on fairness from a different discipline is found in Brams, S. and Taylor, A. (1996). *Fair division: From cake-cutting to dispute resolution*. Cambridge, UK: Cambridge University Press. Using a wide knowledge of game theory, the authors discuss ways to achieve fairness in the sense that distributions are envy-free. In their words, "Roughly speaking, an envy-free division is one in which every person thinks he or she received the largest or most valuable portion of something—based on his or her own valuation—and hence does not envy anyone else" (p. 2).

7 Intuition or feeling as a determinant of moral judgments is an important element in the philosophy of David Hume, one of the most influential philosophers in the eighteenth century. His work is still widely cited. For an introduction to his ethical theory, see Copleston, F. (1994) *A history of philosophy*, volume 5. New York: Doubleday, pp. 318–341. There is also a school of ethical thought known broadly as intuitionism, proposed by a number of twentieth-century philosophers. This theory is discussed in McNaughton, D. (2000) Intuitionism, in LaFollette, H (ed.), *The Blackwell guide to ethical theory*. Malden MA: Blackwell Publishing, pp. 268–287. Because neither Hume's theory nor that of the twenti-

eth-century intuitionists has attained the same status as the three approaches to ethics discussed throughout this book, they will not be pursued further here.

8 We should note, however, that in a government that employs representative democracy (voters choose representatives, such as senators or county commissioners), the representatives have one vote that substitutes for those of their many constituents. Since the constituents have many different opinions, the elected representative cannot possibly represent the views of each and every one of them when he or she casts a vote in the senate or the county commission.

9 For a thorough discussion of Jefferson's views and practices, see Mapp, A. (1987). *Thomas Jefferson: A strange case of mistaken identity*. Lanham MD: Madison Books.

10 In 1863, during the Civil War, Louis Agassiz was a professor of science at Harvard University. President Lincoln appointed Samuel Gridley Howe to head a commission whose task was to investigate policies for dealing with freed slaves. Howe asked Agassiz's opinion as a scientist on related questions and Agassiz argued strongly against the mixing of the races. Menand, L. (2001). *The metaphysical club: A story of ideas in America*. New York: Farrar, Straus and Giroux, p. 114.

11 The United States Supreme Court overturned the long-standing "separate but equal" standard in the case known as *Brown vs. Board of Education* in 1954. For a discussion of the attitudes at the time and the events surrounding this decision, see Halberstam, D. (1993). *The fifties*. New York: Villard Books.

12 One of the very best discussions of the attitudes and social forces leading up to what is broadly called civil rights legislation can be found in Caro, R. (2002). *The years of Lyndon Johnson: Master of the Senate*. New York: Alfred Knopf.

13 Rawls, J. (1999/1971). *A theory of justice*, revised edition. Cambridge MA: Harvard University Press.

14 Rawls, J. (2001). *Justice as fairness: A restatement* (Kelly, E., ed.). Cambridge MA: The Belknap Press of Harvard University Press.

15 Op. cit., p. 15.

16 For a summary of and commentary on Rawls' main arguments, see Freeman, S. (2003) John Rawls—An overview, in Freeman, S. (ed.), *The Cambridge companion to Rawls*. Cambridge, UK: Cambridge University Press, pp. 1–61.

17 John Rawls, as discussed in the last section, was one of the most influential American philosophers of the twentieth century. Broadly speaking, Rawls was concerned with procedural justice or fairness and the kinds of laws and institutions that would most contribute to procedural fairness. Another important American philosopher, Amartya Sen (originally from India but a colleague of Rawls for many years at Harvard), placed major emphasis on individual situations and distributive justice rather than procedural justice. Each recognized the importance of both procedural and distributive justice, but they differed considerably in their emphasis.

18 A manager (and for that matter, the employee also) might feel that a decision is unfair, although it is the only allowable decision under a given system. For instance, the manager of an employee who has done outstanding work might feel strongly that the employee in question deserves an above-average pay increase. The employee may whole-heartedly agree. However, if they are working under a negotiated labor-management agreement that specifies equal pay increases for all members of the job class, they are legally and morally required to follow that agreement and to limit the employee's pay increase to the same amount received by other employees in that job class.

19 We should note, however, that while procedural justice is concerned with results, the fairness and justice approach differs significantly from the utilitarian approach. Utilitarianism defines the moral act by the accomplishment of one kind of result, namely the greatest good for the greatest number. Rawls argues from a different view. He maintains that there are some individual rights that cannot be sacrificed in the name of the common good. His position, in fact, is based on views of the individual espoused by Kant, who is most definitely not a utilitarian. This difference is explained in Freeman's essay cited in note 16 and at more length in Scheffler, S. (2003) Rawls and utilitarianism, in Freeman, S. (ed.), *The Cambridge companion to Rawls*. Cambridge, UK: Cambridge University Press, pp. 426–459.

20 Rattner, S. (2010). *Overhaul*. Boston: Houghton Mifflin Harcourt.

21 This law, passed in 2002 by the United States House and Senate, was designed to correct at least some of the abuses by such companies as Enron and World-Com that had recently come to light. It is discussed further in the chapter on accounting and financial reporting.

22 However, in the case of negotiated labor-management contracts discussed above, many of the general rules are also specific. Thus, a rule that every employee in a certain job class shall receive a specific salary increase on a specific date is both general and specific. This type of rule leaves no discretion for the individual manager in compensation decisions.

23 This assertion might well be contested by some individuals. However, even strong feminists usually acknowledge that, in discussing specific cases and decisions, different women are, in fact, differently situated. For a discussion of this issue, see Littleton, C. (2003) Reconstructing sexual equality, in Donohue, J. (ed.), *Foundations of employment discrimination law*, 2nd edition. New York: Foundation Press, pp. 346–353.

24 A policy discussion of this issue between two top executives at Goldman Sachs is described in Cohen, W. (2011). *Money and power*. New York: Doubleday pp. 283–284.

7 Ethical Analysis of Employment Issues

1 For a more detailed description of the human resource function and the ways it is usually practiced, see Dessler, G. (2011). *Human resource management*, 12th edition. Upper Saddle River NJ: Prentice Hall.

2 For example, the Civil Rights Act of 1964, as amended by the Equal Employment Opportunity Act of 1972 and the Civil Rights Act of 1991, applies to all private employers in interstate commerce who employ fifteen or more employees for twenty or more weeks a year and to labor unions having fifteen or more members or employees. Dessler, op. cit., p. 32.

3 For a discussion of the issues involved in job design, see Dessler, op. cit., Chapter 4. A classic article on this topic, written almost thirty years ago and still widely cited, is Hackman, J. and Oldham, G. (1976). Motivation through the design of work: Test of a theory. *Organizational Behavior and Human Performance*, 16:2, 250–279.

4 Although the hiring manager usually gets to decide among qualified candidates which is the most qualified, it is worth remembering that this decision may be reviewed with suspicion in the hostile setting of a lawsuit if one of the candidates who is turned down subsequently sues. While this is a relatively rare

occurrence, there is no way to predict in advance when a rejected applicant might sue. Managers cannot take the time, in the real world, to make every hiring decision with full consideration of how it would be defended in court, but it is worth taking some care to think through the justification for hiring one qualified candidate rather than another.

5 We will examine the issue of decision patterns in more detail in the last chapter of this book.

6 The evaluation of companies by the Federal Equal Employment Opportunity Commission, as well as by courts in the case of litigation, is based on this same approach. Allegations of discrimination in hiring are often inferred from patterns of employment. If a company has far fewer women or ethnic minorities or members of some other protected class than the population from which it hires, this statistical deviance is considered as possible evidence of discriminatory hiring practices.

7 A brief summary of the major U.S. Federal laws relating to civil rights and employment can be found in Dessler, op. cit., Chapter 2. A somewhat longer treatment of this topic, with many specific case examples, can be found in White, R. (1998). *Employment law and employment discrimination: Essential terms and concepts*. New York: Aspen Law and Business. For a still longer treatment of these topics, featuring many articles on specific topics in the area of employment discrimination, see Donohue, J. (ed.) (2003). *Foundations of employment discrimination law*, 2nd edition. New York: Foundation Press.

8 Affirmative action in the sense of giving preference to certain individuals because of their membership in some group is not limited to efforts to attain racial equality in employment. Many public sector employers give extra credit on civil service exams to military veterans. Selective universities often have admission policies that give extra credit to "legacies," i.e., the children of alumni and alumnae. Private religious universities sometimes require that faculty members and/or students adhere to the practices of a given religion.

9 For a discussion of the various meanings of affirmative action that uses slightly different categories, see Van Alstyne, W. (2003). Affirmative action and racial discrimination under law: A preliminary review, in Donohue, op. cit., pp. 59–66.

10 A number of essays discussing various topics relating to diversity and discrimination can be found in Donohue, J. (ed.). (2003). *Foundations of employment discrimination law*. New York: Foundation Press. See also Sandel, M. (2009). *Justice: What's the right thing to do?* New York: Farrar, Straus and Giroux, especially Chapter 7.

11 S.W. Gilliland has done a considerable amount of research in this area. See especially Gilliland, S. (1995). Fairness from the applicant's perspective: Reactions to employee selection procedures. *International Journal of Selection and Assessment*, 3, 11–19.

12 There have not been as many as twenty female CEOs in the 500 largest companies as compiled by *Fortune* in any one year.

13 Some argue that women have only recently attained senior executive positions in corporations and that, given time, more women will be eligible and chosen to be CEOs of major corporations. However, women are currently presidents (the equivalent of CEOs in the academic world) at some of the largest and most complex universities in the United States. Women have been governors of states for some time. Women have been cabinet secretaries in the Federal government,

as well as holding such key positions as National Security Adviser. Any of these positions is at least equal in scope, complexity and skill requirements to the position of CEO of a major corporation. Thus the argument that few if any women are yet prepared by their career experiences to assume such positions seems weak at best.

14 In spite of the best intentions of employers, in some situations the achievement of a diverse workforce, at least in some respects, proves to be impossible. For a variety of reasons, there are very few females with degrees in engineering, at least in the United States. Similarly, the number of individuals obtaining doctorates in business administration each year who are members of ethnic minorities is far smaller than the number that universities and colleges need to hire in order to reach reasonable levels of diversity. In some respects, this actually works in favor of the groups in question, since companies will make higher salary offers to female engineers, and universities to those who are both members of an ethnic minority and have doctorates in business administration.

15 For a full discussion of the position rights and duties of applicants, see Gilbert, J., Alder, G.S. and McAllister, D. (2010). Rights and duties of employers and applicants. *Advances in Business Research*, 1:1, 73–81.

16 Much of the discussion of minimum qualifications as they relate to employment discrimination comes under the general headings of adverse impact or disparate treatment. For a brief discussion of some of the key issues involved, see Dessler, op. cit., pp. 139–141.

17 Alder, G.S. and Gilbert, J. (2006). Achieving ethics and fairness in hiring: Going beyond the law. *Journal of Business Ethics*, 68, 449–464.

18 There are several ethical issues involved in the process of gathering facts about candidates, mostly involving privacy. These issues are discussed at some length in Chapter 10.

19 Rakesh Khurana, in his book *Searching for a corporate savior* (Princeton NJ: Princeton University Press, 2002) makes the interesting argument that, in the case of CEO selection, being a current employee of the company is often a significant advantage and one that is often overlooked by the board of directors, who in this case play the role of the hiring manager.

8 Performance Appraisal and Compensation

1 For a general discussion of labor unions and the ways they impact human resource management, see Anthony, W., Kacmar, K. and Perrewe, P. (2010). *Human resource management: A strategic approach*, 6th edition. Mason OH: Cengage Learning, Chapter 16.

2 There has been a large amount of research on pay for performance and other approaches to financial incentives. For an overall view, see Dessler, G. (2011). *Human resource management*, 12th edition. Upper Saddle River NJ: Prentice Hall, Chapters 11 and 12.

3 Since the Great Recession that began in 2007 in the United States, government bodies have seen large reductions in tax revenues. This has made public employee pay and benefits a major issue of public debate. Further, less than satisfactory improvement rates for pupils in many U.S. school districts have led to widespread discussion of teacher pay and accountability. According to U.S. government figures, there were over seven million teachers in the country in 2008. Thus teacher pay is not only a subject of academic interest, but a pressing issue

in national and local debates about public employee compensation. For a sampling of academic research in this area, see Schulz, E. and Tanguay, D. (2006). Merit pay in a public higher education institution: Questions of impact and attitudes. *Public Personnel Management*, 35:1, 71–87; Dee, T. and Keys, B. (2004). Does merit pay reward good teachers? Evidence from a randomized experiment. *Journal of Policy Analysis & Management*, 23:3, 471–488; and Figlio, D. and Kenny, L. (2007). Individual teacher incentives and student performance. *Journal of Public Economics*, 91:5–6, 901–915.

4 Dessler (op. cit., p. 308) cites four reasons for conducting performance appraisals: pay and promotion decisions; reinforcement of good performance and correction where needed; career planning; and performance management.

5 Dessler, op. cit., pp. 331–333.

6 Salary increases from the organization's view are an issue of strategy. In recent years, there has been increasing emphasis on the strategic implications of human resource policies. On compensation specifically as a strategic issue, see Gerhart, B. and Rynes, S. (2003). *Compensation: Theory, evidence and strategic implications.* Thousand Oaks CA: Sage Publications; and Martocchio, J. (2011). *Strategic compensation*, 6th edition. Upper Saddle River NJ: Prentice Hall.

7 For a detailed discussion of issues and options regarding performance appraisals, see Anthony, Kacmar & Perrewe, op. cit., Chapter 10.

8 Dessler (op. cit., p. 329) suggests four main points for managers to keep in mind while conducting performance appraisal interviews. They are to: talk in terms of objective work data; avoid getting personal; encourage the person interviewed to talk; and get agreement.

9 For a detailed account of the events leading up to the bankruptcies and the emergence of GM and Chrysler from bankruptcy, written by the U.S. government's "car czar," see Rattner, S. (2010). *Overhaul: An insider's account of the Obama administration's emergency rescue of the auto industry.* New York: Houghton Mifflin Harcourt. For a longer-range perspective of the events leading up to the bankruptcies by a reporter who covered the auto industry for many years, see Ingrassia, P. (2010). *Crash course: The American automobile industry's road to bankruptcy and bailout and beyond.* New York: Random House.

10 Before wages and benefits began to be reduced as bankruptcy loomed, workers who belonged to the United Autoworkers' Union and worked in assembly plants made about $70 per hour in combined wages and fringe benefits. The jobs had neither significant education requirements nor prior skill and experience requirements. While physically demanding and extremely repetitive, the jobs were considered to be very desirable because of the compensation level.

11 During the decade between 2000 and 2010, there were several instances of so-called give-backs (employees agreeing to reduce salaries or benefits) in the airline industry in the United States.

12 During the period just before the bankruptcies of GM and Chrysler, concessions made by the United Autoworkers' Union were also extended to Ford, which did not declare bankruptcy.

13 We should note that in some other countries, notably Germany, auto workers are unionized and enjoy high wages and benefits, yet their companies have not been pushed to bankruptcy. While wages and benefits played a significant role in the failures of GM and Chrysler and the near-failure of Ford, other factors also played significant roles. The failure of American auto companies for a number of years to attain efficiencies in operation and to design cars that provided purchasers with

perceived value for their money undoubtedly contributed to the ultimate problems that confronted the industry in 2008 and 2009.

14 For a basic description of the concept of comparable worth and how it is structured into a system, see Anthony, Kacmar and Perrewe, op. cit., pp. 161–162.

15 William Heisler has analyzed the major issues involved in executive compensation. In his article, he briefly describes the various elements of executive compensation and shows the ethical implications involved in decisions about each element. See Heisler, W. (2007). Ethical choices in the design and administration of executive compensation programs. *Business Horizons*, 50:4, 277–290.

16 http://money.cnn.com/2011/04/19/news/economy/ceo.

17 There is a view of the structure of the firm, based in finance, which maintains that there is an intrinsic conflict between the interests of the owners and the interests of their agents. The classic exposition of this view is found in Jensen, M. and Meckling, W. (1976). Theory of the firm: Managerial behavior, agency costs and ownership. *Journal of Financial Economics*, 3:4; 305–360. According to this view, executive compensation is one way to align the interests of the executives with those of the stockholders. Paying executives with stock is theorized to achieve this alignment of interests.

18 http://money.cnn.com/2002/09/06/news/companies/welch_ge.

19 In a widely read book, Lucian Bebchuk, a professor at the Harvard Law School, and Jesse Fried, a law professor at the University of California, Berkeley, examine the various arguments made for high executive compensation and give reasons why they disagree with them. Rakesh Khurana has also presented an extended discussion of reasons why CEO compensation might be seen as excessive and misdirected. See Bebchuk, L. and Fried, J. (2004). *Pay without performance: The unfulfilled promise of executive compensation.* Cambridge MA: Harvard University Press; and Khurana, R. (2002). *Searching for a corporate savior: The irrational quest for charismatic CEOs.* Princeton NJ: Princeton University Press.

20 Measurement of an executive's compensation for a single year is much more complex than simply identifying salary and bonus. Large stock awards, especially in the form of options, are impossible to value accurately at the time they are granted. Some executives, such as Warren Buffett of Berkshire Hathaway and Bill Gates of Microsoft, have had their total personal wealth increase by billions of dollars in a single year because of the appreciation in value of the stock in their companies which they hold.

21 It is interesting to note that a very different standard of reasonableness for compensation is used for executives in government and public service than is used for companies. Governors and legislators in the United States normally earn $200,000 or less in salary and typically do not receive bonuses. They also do not, obviously, receive stock options. By contrast, the median pay for CEOs at 158 of the Standard and Poor's 500 Index companies for 2010 was $9 million. www.usatoday.com/money/companies/management/story/CEO-pay-2010/45634384/1.

22 Joseph Cassano, who was in charge of the London unit of AIG, was removed from his position in early 2008. His unit was principally responsible for AIG's losing many billions of dollars and requiring a government bailout that finally exceeded $150 billion. Cassano, when removed from his position, was made a consultant to the firm at a fee of $1 million per month. For a vivid description of the decision to fire Cassano and give him a consulting contract, see Sorkin, A. (2009). *Too big to fail.* New York: Penguin, pp. 160–162.

23 Khurana, R. op. cit.

9 Terminations

1 For further discussion of this important point, see Crain, M. (2010). Work matters. *Kansas Journal of Law and Public Policy*, 19:3, 365–382.

2 Payne v. Webster & Atlantic R.R. Co., 81 Tenn. 507, 519–520 (1884).

3 "The right of an employee to quit the services of the employer, for whatever reason, is the same as the right of the employer, for whatever reason, to dispense with the services of such employee." Justice Harlan in Adair v. U.S., 208 U.S. 161 (1908).

4 Halbert and Ingulli cite statistics from the U.S. Bureau of Labor Standards to the effect that, in 2009, union membership in the United States comprised 12.3 percent of the American workforce (15.3 million workers), with the membership percentage higher among government workers than in private industry. Halbert, E. and Ingulli, T. (2012). *Law and ethics in the business environment*, 7th edition. Mason OH: South-western, Cengage Learning.

5 In 2011, a number of state legislatures passed bills that modified or eliminated tenure for grammar and high-school teachers. Reduced tax revenue as a result of the Great Recession, combined with increasing concern over low performance in schools, focused attention on the difficulty of terminating inadequate teachers. Along with easier firing of teachers, there was heated discussion of merit pay for teachers. Typically, teachers in the United States belong to unions and work under contracts that do not allow merit pay. Concern for quality of teaching brought to the fore the related issues of how to measure and reward good teaching and how to improve or remove inadequate teachers.

6 An alternate approach to selecting and retaining judges is the so-called Missouri Plan. This involves having a non-partisan screening committee select a limited number of candidates and the selection by a government official (in state government, typically the governor) of one of these candidates. After a specified period of time, the judge then stands for election, but not against opposing candidates. Instead, the vote of the people is solely on the question of whether to retain the judge in office or to remove him or her. If retained, the judge then serves for a specified but extended period before facing a similar election. This plan combines elements of tenure with a review mechanism for possible removal which is less drastic than impeachment. www.britannica.com/EBchecked/topic/385765/Missouri-Plan. The selection of federal judges incorporates elements of this approach. While they are appointed by the President for life and must be confirmed by the Senate, the process of selection and confirmation usually results in a rather careful review of the candidates' qualifications.

7 For an excellent selection of classic essays on many topics that come under the rubric of organization theory, see Shafritz, J., Ott, J. and Jang, Y. (2011). *Classics of Organization Theory*, 7th edition. Boston MA: Wadsworth, Cengage Learning.

8 Montana is currently the only state in the United States to legally limit the general doctrine of employment at will. The Montana Wrongful Discharge from Employment Act (39 Montana Code Annotated Chapter 2, Part 9) is quoted in Halbert and Ingulli, op. cit., pp. 58–59.

9 In the United States, there is an increasing trend for the head of the human resources department or division to hold a law degree in addition to having advanced education in human resources.

10 A study by Paul Bernthal and Richard Wellins indicates that the cost of replacing an employee is between 29 percent and 46 percent of the employee's annual

salary. http://66.179.232.89/pdf/ddi_retainingtalentabenchmarkingstudy_es. pdf. This estimate is broadly consistent with conclusions reached by others who have studied the cost of replacing employees.

11 Dessler, G. (2011). *Human resources management*, 12th edition. Upper Saddle River NJ: Prentice Hall, p. 485.

12 Thirty years ago, in a widely read book, William Ouchi, a business professor at UCLA, suggested that one of the major reasons for the success of the Japanese business model was their version of lifetime employment. He made the point that managers and executives who knew that they would be working together at the same company for many years were much more apt to take a company-wide perspective. He emphasized that a favor done or a point yielded to another manager now might well be repaid later and both managers knew that there was time for such reciprocity to develop. See Ouchi, W. (1981). *Theory Z: How American business can meet the Japanese challenge.* New York: Perseus Books. For a variety of reasons, the Japanese business model did not succeed to the extent that was feared by Americans in the early 1980s, but Ouchi's point is worth considering.

13 Aristotle (1990). *The Nicomachean ethics* (Rackham, H., translator). Cambridge MA: Harvard University Press.

14 Some authors make distinctions between layoffs (temporary) and downsizing or reduction in force (long-term or permanent). See, for example, Dessler, op. cit., pp. 530–533; and Anthony, W., Kacmar, K. and Perrewe, P. (2010). *Human resources management: A strategic approach*, 6th edition. Mason OH: Cengage Learning, Chapter 17. For purposes of our discussion, the term "layoffs" is used to describe any situation where individuals involuntarily lose their jobs because of a management determination that staff size should be reduced.

15 Gilbert, J. (2000). Sorrow and guilt: An ethical analysis of layoffs. *SAM Advanced Management Journal*, 65:2, 4–11.

16 Different corporate strategies can lead to acquisitions. Sometimes a company acquires another company in its own or a related business in order to expand its scope and serve more customers, or to more easily cross-sell the products or services of the two companies. Such acquisitions frequently lead to layoffs in order to reduce redundant staff. Some companies acquire other companies in leveraged buyouts. In these cases, much of the purchase price is borrowed and the intent of the acquiring company is to "fix" the purchased company and then take it public by selling stock in it. Typically, firms that engage in such buyouts introduce new management and reduce staff significantly in the purchased company in order to reduce labor costs.

17 A number of studies have shown that half or more of large mergers fail to create owner value through stock price increases. See, for example, The basics of mergers and acquisitions: why they can fail. www.investopedia.com/university/ mergers/mergers5.asp.

18 Peters, T. (1997). *The circle of innovation: You can't shrink your way to greatness.* New York: Knopf Doubleday Publishing.

19 See Halbert and Ingulli, op. cit., Chapter 2.

10 Privacy: Applicants and Employees

1 For a classic work on privacy that includes an extended treatment of the value and positive benefits of privacy, see Westin, A. (1967). *Privacy and freedom.* New York: Association of the Bar of the City of New York.

2 There has been extensive discussion in management theory about the ideal or "right" number of subordinates for one supervisor. The general conclusion is that it depends on a number of factors, including the experience and professional level of workers, the nature of the work being done, the physical proximity or distance of workers from each other and the supervisor and the other tasks required of the supervisor as part of her job. A supervisor of bank tellers spends most of her day on the teller line, observing tellers, approving exceptions and doing similar work. A CEO who supervises six vice presidents is often physically separated from these subordinates, has many other required tasks besides supervision in a typical day's work and frequently knows less about the work of the vice presidents than they do.

3 As we will discuss later in the chapter, legal requirements for applicant and worker drug testing in the United States have a significant impact on managers' decisions in this area.

4 For a full discussion of alternate ways to obtain information about applicants, see Dessler, G. (2011). *Human resource management*, 12th edition. Upper Saddle River NJ: Prentice Hall, Chapter 6. Quite recently, the use of social media such as Facebook as a way for employers to gain additional information about applicants has become a topic of some controversy. For a good basic discussion of the issues involved and the advantages and disadvantages of this approach, see Davison, H., Maraist, C., Hamilton, R. and Bing, M. (2011). To screen or not to screen? Using the internet for selection decisions. *Employee Responsibilities and Rights Journal*, Online First, July 14, 2011.

5 Candidates seeking top-secret security clearances from the United States government must complete an application that is more than forty pages long. Investigators contact individuals such as former teachers, employers and neighbors to verify all information.

6 Gilbert, J., Alder, G.S. and McAllister, D. (2010). Rights and duties of employers and applicants. *Advances in Business Research*, 1:1, 73–81.

7 See Wood, J., Schmidtke, J. and Decker, D. (2007). Lying on job applications: The effects of job relevance, commission, and human resource management experience. *Journal of Business Psychology*, 22, 1–9. See also George, J. and Marett, K. (2004). The truth about lies. *HR Magazine*, 49, 87–91.

8 For a basic description of the variety and uses of personality tests, with references to academic articles in this area, see Dessler, op. cit., pages 202–205.

9 One possible way for a hiring manager to learn how a candidate has performed in the past is to check the references provided by the applicant, especially those from former employers. However, in many companies, there is a policy of releasing information only about dates of employment and last salary earned. Lawsuits charging defamation by former employees have greatly reduced the flow of potentially relevant information between past employers and prospective employers. See Cooper, M. (2001). Job reference immunity statutes: Prevalent but irrelevant. *Cornell Journal of Law and Public Policy*, 11, 1–68.

10 A discussion of test validation can be found in Anthony, W., Kacmar, K. and Perrewe, P. (2010). *Human resource management: A strategic approach*, 6th edition. Mason OH: Cengage Learning, pp. 218–225.

11 An outline of best practices for workplace drug testing can be found in Ramos, G. (2005). *Best practices for a workplace drug testing program*. www.employers-choiceonline.com/articles/drug-testing-best-practice.html.

12 Ramos, op. cit.

13 www.dol.gov/elaws/asp/drugfree/screenr.htm.

14 www.dol.gov/elaws/asp/drugfree/require.htm.

15 Ramos, op. cit.

16 Europeans and Americans tend to have different views of privacy, in the workplace and in general. See Whitman, J. (2004). The two Western cultures of privacy: Dignity v. liberty. *Yale Law Journal*, 113, 1151–1221.

17 Several legal challenges to large financial firms during the recent subprime mortgage crisis ended in very large settlements by these firms. Email evidence proved crucial in these cases and contributed substantially to company decisions to pay tens or hundreds of millions of dollars in settlements. Since email messages are stored even if the sender has deleted them, they are now standard items for discovery in litigation. What seemed at the time to be a private joke or comment can look very different to a trial jury.

18 See Dessler, op. cit., pp. 521–522 for samples of commercially available monitoring programs.

19 Personal messages sent on a company email system are legally open to management review even if company policy says that they will remain confidential and will not be used against employees as grounds for termination or reprimand. In a famous legal case, Michael A. Smyth vs. The Pillsbury Company, the court determined that Smyth, a Pillsbury regional operations manager, had no legal expectation of privacy when he sent emails to his supervisor using the company email system from home. His termination, based on the content of the emails, was upheld. It is interesting to note that, in addition to the privacy issue, the court based its decision on the fact that the plaintiff was an employee at will. Smyth v. Pillsbury Co., 914 F.supp. 97 (E.D. Penn. 1996).

20 In an interesting study, Alder *et al.* investigated whether the reactions of employees to internet monitoring at work were affected by the employee's views on the relative importance of rules and results in ethics. They also examined the attitudes of employees toward management control in general and how these attitudes affected their attitudes toward a newly introduced internet monitoring system. As one might expect, individuals react differently to the same monitoring system, and their beliefs about ethics have an impact on their reaction. Alder, G. S., Schminke, M., Noel, T. and Kuenzi, M. (2008). Employee reactions to internet monitoring: The moderating role of ethical orientation. *Journal of Business Ethics*, 80, 481–498.

11 Accounting and Financial Reporting

1 Gilbert, J. (2011). Moral duties in business and their societal impacts: The case of the subprime lending mess. *Business and Society Review*, 116:1, 87–107.

2 The business press often referred to "the eleven billion dollar WorldCom scandal" without any indication of whether this amount referred to revenues, income or some other item, or over what period the scandal occurred. The general press, in reporting on business scandals, often makes such fundamental mistakes as confusing revenues with income.

3 Duska, R. and B. Duska, (2003). *Accounting ethics*. Malden MA: Blackwell Publishing, Chapter 1 (pp. 7–23).

4 The goals or targets by which top managers (especially the CEO) are judged when their performance is appraised typically are based on financial results as measured by such accounting items as net income, return on assets and return on

equity. Stock prices, which are substantially influenced by reported financial results, directly affect the value of stock options, which in recent years have become a significant portion of top executive compensation.

5 Consider that Walmart had 2.1 million employees in 2010. A substantial percentage of these employees are sales associates who scan individual items at point-of-sale terminals.

6 This approach is consistent with the ethical views of Aristotle. He maintained that the way to determine whether an action is ethical is to consider its purpose. People, practices and institutions have goals, and actions that further those goals are ethical. The virtuous person, in Aristotle's view, is the one who has formed habits of virtue—of taking actions that properly lead to the right goals. See Sandel, M. (2009). *Justice: What's the right thing to do?* New York: Farrar, Straus and Giroux, Chapter 8.

7 Cooper, C. (2008). *Extraordinary Circumstances: The journey of a corporate whistle-blower.* Hoboken NJ: John Wiley & Sons.

8 These are contracts by which one company pays another (typically a financial institution) a fee to guarantee that, if a loan is not repaid by the borrower, the guarantor will make the lender whole.

9 Among the many books analyzing the financial crisis and its causes, and discussing derivatives and financial accounting during this period, are Lowenstein, R. (2010). *The end of Wall Street.* New York: Penguin Press; McGee, S. (2010). *Chasing Goldman Sachs.* New York: Crown Business; and Tett, G. (2009). *Fool's gold.* New York: Free Press.

10 For a brief summary of major differences between the two approaches, see Forgeas, R. (2008). Is IFRS that different from U.S. GAAP? *AICPA IFRS Resources.* www.ifrs.com/overview/General/differences.html. For a more detailed explanation of the progress to date and the problems remaining with regard to adoption by the U.S. Securities Exchange Commission of IFRS, see Securities Exchange Commission Staff Paper (2011) Work plan for the consideration of incorporating International Financial Reporting Standards into the financial reporting system for U.S. Issuers: A comparison of U.S. GAAP and IFRS. http://sec.gov/spotlight/globalaccounting-standards/ifrs-work-plan-paper-111611-gaap.pdf.

11 In the recent financial crisis, when a number of America's largest financial institutions went bankrupt, were purchased under extreme stress, or survived only through substantial government bailouts, many top executives of these companies received extremely lucrative compensation packages while their firms were failing, then received severance packages in the tens of millions of dollars when they were removed from office. See, for example, Boyd, R. (2011). *Fatal risk: A cautionary tale of AIG's corporate suicide.* Hoboken NJ: John Wiley & Sons; Farrell, G. (2010). *Crash of the titans.* New York: Crown Business; and Sorkin, A.R. (2009). *Too big to fail.* New York: Viking.

12 http://accounting.smartpros.com/x53064.xml.

13 One of the other whistle-blowers named as *Time Magazine*'s person of the year was Cynthia Cooper. She was the head of internal auditing at WorldCom during the period of their massive fraud. She and some of her staff uncovered the false entries made at the direction of senior officials over a two-year period. In her book on the events that took place, she vividly describes the conflicts of employees ordered to make false entries into the accounting systems. Two of these reluctant lower-level employees actually were convicted and imprisoned because of their actions. See Cooper, op. cit.

14 Swartz, M. with Watkins, S. (2003). *Power failure: The inside story of the collapse of Enron*. New York: Doubleday, p. 275.

15 For detailed discussion of many of the accounting methods used to hide Enron's true condition, see Eichenwald, K. (2005). *Conspiracy of fools: A true story*. New York: Broadway; and McLean, B. and Elkind, P. (2003). *The smartest guys in the room: The amazing rise and scandalous fall of Enron*. New York: Fortune.

16 For examples of the negative consequences of whistle-blowing, see Cooper, op. cit.; and Kesselheim, A., Studdert, D. and Mello, M. (2010). Whistle-blowers' experiences in fraud litigation against pharmaceutical companies. *New England Journal of Medicine*, 362, 1832–1839.

17 A classic book on these three alternatives is Hirschman, A. (1970). *Exit, voice and loyalty: Responses to declines in firms, organizations and states*. Cambridge MA: Harvard University Press.

12   Ethical Managers and Ethical Organizations

1 Aristotle (1990/1926). *The Nicomachean ethics* (Rackham, H., translator). Cambridge MA: Harvard University Press.

2 One of the central topics in the study of business strategy is the setting of overall company goals and the allocating of resources to achieve these goals. This typically involves determining a company's mission and major goals. It also involves the authority structure within a company and the determination of which individuals or groups (committees) have the right and responsibility to set and enforce company-wide policies. Almost any standard strategy textbook contains a chapter on missions, goals and values.

3 Kanter, R. (1979). Power failure in management circuits. *Harvard Business Review*, July–August.

4 For a readable history of the corporation and some of its impacts on society, see Micklethwait, J. and Wooldridge, A. (2003). *The company: A short history of a revolutionary idea*. New York: Random House. A more detailed history of the coming of the large corporation in the United States and its impact on society can be found in Chandler, A. (1993). *The visible hand: Managerial revolution in American business*. Cambridge MA: Belknap Press.

5 During much of the twentieth century, when large companies became important factors in the societies of the United States, much of Western Europe and some parts of Asia, Western philosophers were primarily occupied with logical positivism. Among the important tenets of this philosophical approach is the notion that ethical statements, since they are not verifiable, are not meaningful. Hence little development in ethics occurred during this period. Business law during this period expanded greatly (see Friedman, L. (2002). *American law in the 20th century*. New Haven CT: Yale University Press), but ethics did not keep pace.

6 The scandal at Hewlett-Packard in 2005–2006 was widely reported at the time. It involved, among other things, obtaining the personal telephone records of board members by very dubious means in an effort to determine who was leaking inside information to the press. For one version of this story, see Bianco, A. (2010). *The big lie: Spying, scandal, and ethical collapse at Hewlett-Packard*. New York: Public Affairs.

7 Morgan, G. (1997). *Images of organizations*, 2nd edition. Thousand Oaks, CA: Sage Publications.

8 Scott, W. (1998). *Organizations: Rational, natural, and open systems*, 4th edition. Upper Saddle River NJ: Prentice Hall.

9 Confirming the uncertainty of trials by jury, both Ebbers and Scrushy pleaded ignorance of the financial frauds carried on during their time as CEOs. In both trials, considerable evidence was presented that Ebbers and Scrushy were hands-on CEOs who paid considerable attention to even minor corporate expenditures. Yet, Ebbers was found guilty and received a long prison sentence while Scrushy was acquitted, although he was later found liable in a civil trial.

10 For a vivid, detailed description of this decision and its aftermath, see Farrell, G. (2010). *Crash of the titans: Greed, hubris, the fall of Merrill Lynch, and the near collapse of Bank of America.* New York: Crown Business.

11 Schein, E. (1985). *Organizational culture and leadership.* San Francisco: Jossey-Bass, p. 6.

12 For documentation of Enron's culture, see, for example, Eichenwald, K. (2005). *Conspiracy of fools: A true story.* New York: Crown Publishing; McLean, B. and Elkind, P. (2004). *The smartest guys in the room: The amazing rise and scandalous fall of Enron.* New York: Penguin; Sims, R. and Brinkmann, J. (2003). Enron ethics (Or: Culture matters more than codes). *Journal of Business Ethics*, 45, 243–256; Kulik, B. (2005). Agency theory, reasoning and culture at Enron: In search of a solution. *Journal of Business Ethics*, 59: 347–360.

13 See, for instance, Trevino, L. (1986). Ethical decision making in organizations: A person-situation interactionist model. *Academy of Management Review*, 11, 601–617; Rest, J. (1986). *Moral development: Advances in research and theory.* New York: Praeger Publishers; and Jones, T. (1991). Ethical decision making by individuals in organizations: An issue-contingent model. *Academy of Management Review*, 16, 366–395.

14 U.S. Sentencing Commission web site: www.ussc.gov.

15 Dalton, D., Metzger, M. and Hill, J. (1994). The "new" U.S. sentencing commission guidelines: A wake-up call for corporate America, in Donaldson, T., Werhane, P. and Cording, M. (eds.) (2002). *Ethical issues in business: A philosophical approach*, 7th edition. Upper Saddle River NJ: Prentice Hall, p. 318.

16 Schein, op. cit.

17 Gerstner describes his actions, and those he later took to change the IBM culture, in his highly readable book. See Gerstner, L. (2003). *Who says elephants can't dance?* New York: HarperCollins.

18 Farrell, op. cit., p. 67.

19 Gerstner, op. cit.

20 For documentation of these and numerous other stories about Cayne and the culture at Bear Stearns, see Kelly, K. (2009). *Street fighters: The last 72 hours of Bear Stearns, the toughest firm on Wall Street.* New York: Penguin.

21 Kerr, S. (1975). On the folly of rewarding A while hoping for B. *Academy of Management Journal*, 18:4, 769–783.

22 Craig, S. (2009). Merrill's $10 million men. *Wall Street Journal*, March 4, 2009.

23 For a discussion of whistle-blowing and its consequences, as well as some of the legal protections afforded to whistle-blowers, see Halbert, T. & Ingulli, E. (2011). *Law and ethics in the business environment.* Mason OH: Cengage Learning, Chapter 2.

24 For a book-length treatment of this issue, see Fishman, C. (2006). *The Walmart effect.* New York: Penguin Press. For a shorter summary, see Fishman, C. (2006).

The Walmart effect and a decent society: Who knew shopping was so important?" *Academy of Management Perspective*, 20:3, 6–25.

25 A particularly thoughtful and comprehensive collection of essays and research papers that bring together theory and research results on ethics programs can be found in Trevino, L. and Weaver, G. (2003). *Managing ethics in business organizations: A social science perspective*. Stanford CA: Stanford University Press.

Index